THE GARDEN

THE GARDEN

A History in
Landscape and Art

Filippo Pizzoni

RIZZOLI
NEW YORK

Acknowledgements
This book is the fruit of a passion, of personal research, and of the joint efforts of the many people who have been so generous with their help and support. In particular I would like to thank Emma Pizzoni for her unfailing receptiveness and invaluable assistance; Carlo Rossi, for his advice and encouragement; Gianluigi Cristiano for his unstinting patience and collaboration; Consuelo Oppenheim and Guido Tommaso, whose opinions have been invaluable; and my own family and all those friends who have stood by me throughout. Particular thanks go to my mentor, Peter Goodchild, and to Ada Segre for all they have taught me. I would also like to thank all the staff of the Editorial department and Picture Archive at Leonardo Arte, especially Lucia Impelluso and Barbara Travaglini.
F.P.

The history of the garden is a rich and complex subject, closely associated with that of architecture, the other arts, and history in general. It is a cross section – minor but significant – of the history of mankind, and of mankind's relations with nature.

Over the centuries the garden has played a series of widely differing roles, in a state of constant if gradual development: from a place set aside for horticulture and the cultivation of plants to provide food or medicinal herbs, to a space where plants were grown for purely ornamental, religious or indeed political purposes. Over time gardens, and the art of the garden, took on a range of meanings, and were embellished with any number of cultural references; the ideas and stimuli which originated in one country, or in specific historical circumstances, then frequently exercised an influence elsewhere.

A knowledge of garden history may be a source of pleasure and of cultural enlightenment, helping the visitor to understand the character of any given garden and of the architecture that finds a place within it; it also encourages us, and future generations, to learn to enjoy and preserve our natural environment with greater sensitivity. Indeed, gardens of all periods are a unique heritage making possible a dynamic exchange of ideas between past, present and future.

Hence the importance of this book which aims to present the many implications of the gardens of the West to a broader public.

Peter Goodchild

To Margherita del Nobolo Battaglia

First published in the United States of America in 1999 by
Rizzoli International Publications, Inc.
300 Park Avenue South
New York, NY 10010

Copyright © 1997 by Leonardo Arte s.r.l., Milano
        Elemond Editori Associati
English translation copyright © 1999 by Judith Landry

ISBN 0-8478-2218-4
LC 99-70587

Printed in Italy

Contents

Introduction

Recent years have seen a growing interest in green spaces, and in gardens in particular. Given impetus by a renewed awareness of nature and the environment, long dormant and confused, or perhaps equated, with the practise of gardening, a new culture of the garden is now emerging, and in recent years the cultural values inherent in the garden as a meeting place between man and nature, and nature and art, are at last being rediscovered, partly through a growing awareness of its historical and artistic past.

Closely related to other art forms like architecture and painting, theatre and stage design, and literary disciplines such as poetry and philosophy, the art of the garden has bequeathed us incomparable masterpieces. Large and small, famous and unknown, old and new, like every other artistic expression, gardens are representative of civilizations and their cultures, and in particular of every age's experience and depiction of nature.

As it developed over time — from a place for cultivation and contemplation to a symbol of power, from a space for open-air living to an area for stylistic experimentation — the garden has always offered magical opportunities for self-expression and creation.

The aim of this book is therefore to consider the history of the garden in the West, from the fourteenth century to the present day, as an art form, an expression of the taste of societies and individuals, as a project and an object of design, over various periods and cultures, focusing in particular on the key moments in its artistic development: the creations, figures and artists that most illuminate a period, a style or a country. In view of the close relationship between the garden and the other visual arts, we have also looked at changes in the methods of representing, and hence of perceiving, the garden; each chapter ends with an analysis of the various techniques used to depict it: from late-medieval illuminations to the bird's-eye view of the Baroque period, down to the use of photography in the twentieth century.

Our aim is therefore to take a fresh look at the garden as the space in which the individual can express himself and establish his own relation with the natural world; to give it back its dignity as an art form, freed at last from the limitations that reduced it to a mere adornment of the dwelling place, to a functional space, a portion of ground intended merely for exquisitely composed groups of plants and flowers. To rediscover the garden through its history, protagonists, *grands projets* and links with art, also means to rediscover its deeper values as a forgotten space still capable of offering peace, beauty and tranquillity to twenty-first century man.

The rediscovery of nature

After the fall of the Roman Empire, throughout the early Middle Ages Europe underwent a period of cultural stagnation that affected both agriculture and the art of the garden. As all trace of the gardens of the Roman era gradually disappeared the great horticultural and gardening tradition of antiquity was lost.

In central Europe, in the ninth century, above all during the reign of Charlemagne, there is evidence of a renewed interest in horticulture not just for utilitarian purposes, but also for aesthetic ones. The growing of plants and horticultural activity generally now gradually re-emerged according to the principles of classical treatises kept in monastic libraries. Indeed it was above all monks, those jealous guardians of the classical civilizations and their texts, who took an interest in plants: they tended monastery kitchen gardens and orchards, drew up programmes for the work entailed, and wrote poems inspired by country life. The practice of horticulture and gardening was still restricted to the great monasteries and those few gardeners who worked for powerful sovereigns.

Facing page: Garden of Fidelity. From the Babur-nama, *Mogul painting, 1597.*

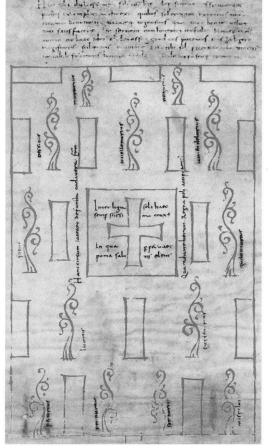

Typically medieval and Islamic in inspiration, the Benedictine cloister at Monreale has a fountain in one corner of its colonnade.

Detailed and well-annotated, the ground plan of the abbey of St Gall probably gives an idea of its ideal distribution rather than wholly accurate inform-ation. This detail shows the subdivision of an area which was both an orchard and a cemetery, with fruit trees planted beside fourteen tombs.

A detailed drawing exists of the garden of the abbey of St Gall in Switzerland, dating from the first decades of the ninth century, when it was an important Benedictine centre with a very rich library. Here too it was the monks who, on their pilgrimages and moves from one monastery to another, transmitted this newly-found knowledge of plants, particularly medicinal and aromatic ones, with exchanges of seeds, bulbs and seedlings.

Apart from convent kitchen gardens and medicinal herb gardens, as planned open spaces monastery cloisters too constituted a model which was traditionally associated with the idea of the garden. The stark space of the cloister, softened by plants, formed a unit both symbolic and typological including certain aspects which were to become typical of the late-medieval garden. It was a place for meditation in the open air, where cosmic order was given outward expression in a powerfully symbolic setting. Its geometric structure, closed in on four sides, often arranged around a central fountain and divided into sections, is redolent with paradisaical harmonies and cosmic rules.

Cloisters were intimate yet cerebral compositions expressing religious and universal concepts, translated into symbols which the monks then decoded through contemplation. The geometric rules underlying the structure of the cloister reached Christian culture as adaptations of the symbolism of the paradise-garden of Islamic tradition, which spread to Europe from the Mediterranean. The Arab presence left a deep mark on the cultures of Spain and Sicily, particularly in art and science.

Cordoba, the powerful capital of the Spanish caliphate whose court attracted enlightened artists and scientists, became an important centre for the spread of Islamic culture. From here, the rest of Europe was gradually to be brought into contact with the Arab tradition, particularly absorbing certain features of one vital aspect: the art of the garden. Perhaps even more crucially, Spain was to acquaint the whole of Europe with a number of exotic plants, imported from Syria, Africa and India to adorn the gardens of the sultans of Cordoba, Seville and Granada.

By the tenth century Arab influence, now reaching even distant and northerly countries, gave a new fillip to the European art of the garden, both in geometrical composition, and a more thorough knowledge of botany.

Over the following centuries, partly thanks to the crusades and the ever greater spread of the various monastic rules, a fruitful process of cultural interchange developed, with an increasingly active trade in plants, particularly those from the Middle East, extending the garden's potential: the various species now introduced included the pomegranate, to become the symbol of the city of Granada.

Among the oldest species known to and spread by the Arabs were the iris and the Lilium candidum *or white lily (below); the lemon (scientific name* Citrus limon) *had also been cultivated since very early times (above). Some of the very earliest plants grown are shown in the numerous Muslim texts on horticulture, often with splendid illustrations like those from Persian treatises reproduced here.*

A gift from Islam: the Arab garden

After the death of Mahomet the Arab world turned to the Mediterranean basin in its quest for new regions to spread the word of the Prophet, occupying first north Africa, then Sicily and Spain. Arab domination then spread Islamic culture throughout Mediterranean Europe.

Based on the laws of the Koran, Arab civilization had a marked bias in favour of the sciences, particularly mathematics and philosophy, though always in close partnership with religion. Significantly for our purposes, Islam also prohibited the representation of the human figure: the Arab world therefore expressed itself through a non-subjective, geometrical art, characterized by an incredible decorative richness, achieved through the abstraction and stylization of elements drawn mostly from the natural and plant world.

Throughout its vast empire, by adapting the rules of its administration to local conditions, Arab domination made possible a fusion between Islamic and local traditions, producing original and artistic phenomena largely independent of their Islamic equivalents.

One of Arab culture's most alluring gifts to European culture was the garden. The very concept is an integral part of both Islamic philosophy and religion. As with the two other monotheistic religions, Judaism and Christianity, in the culture of Islam the connection between garden and paradise is very close: the Koran itself defines paradise as a garden. But the Islamic paradise is quite different from the Christian one: it is the place where the wise alone — those who have lived according to God's rules — may go after death to partake of all earthly pleasures for eternity. It is a very concrete paradise, a garden where they may rest in cool shade, eating their fill of the fruits of its trees, enjoying the heady scent of flowers and the murmur of running, gushing water.

In the Koran, the word used for paradise and garden is one and the same: *jinna. Jinna* is all that is not desert; it is the place of delights nature offers, lush and vivified by water; it is also the seat of everlasting happiness.

The Islamic paradise is characterised by the presence of the four sacred elements: air, water, earth and fire, according to Persian tradition the source of life. It is a lush place fed by the four rivers of blessedness, symbolising redemption from

Arab art is characterized by the absence of the human figure and the richness of its more or less stylized geometrical and floral motifs, known as arabesques. Such complex and sophisticated decoration is found on the main Muslim buildings of the Mediterranean, for instance on the ceiling of the Mausoleum of Qaitbay in Cairo, which dates from the early Mameluke period and is covered with a gloriously fluent network of densely interwoven arabesques.

This Mogul painting, taken from the Va Ki'at-i Bāburi (c. 1590), representing a garden of fidelity, includes the characteristic features of the Muslim garden: enclosed by walls and filled with fruit trees and other leafy trees, it has a pool of water in the middle with four streams running from it, symbolising the four rivers of the Muslim paradise.

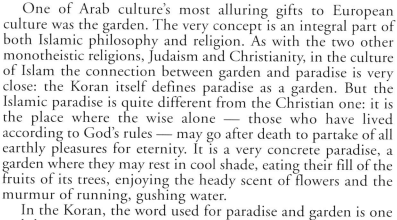

material and earthly difficulties they run with water, wine, milk and honey respectively.

At once philosophical and religious, this concept underlies the composition of the garden in Persian culture: a space divided according to geometric rules, a fertile place blessed by every bounty that nature can offer. The numerous Islamic treatises on plants and the garden all endlessly reiterate certain canonical features: rectangular flowerbeds dividing the enclosed garden into four sections symbolising the four elements; evergreen plants expressing eternity, with colour and scent provided by flowers and the shade of the trees as a reminder of life where all is desert. Above all, there is water: still or running, silent or murmurous, the supreme, all-nourishing symbol of life, water dominated the whole composition. Such gardens included a wide variety of cultivated plants, so that the symphony of their colour, the subtleties of their leaves, the mixture of their scents, and the play of light, would come together to create that world of perfect peace destined to reward the righteous and the wise.

Luxuriance and order: the Moorish gardens of Spain

Spain was under Arab domination from 712—1031, when the caliphate of Cordoba fell. Seville, however, continued to be Muslim until 1248, and Granada remained the last Islamic bastion until 1492. For over three centuries, Spanish culture was deeply marked by the Arab presence, above all artistically: the fortified citadels of the sultans were splendid palaces, sumptuously decorated and surrounded by exquisite gardens.

The Moorish gardens of Spain suggest a land of connective tissue, linking the various parts of the palaces in a close-knit interplay between internal and external spaces. Typical of these complex constructions is the patio, an intimate structure enclosed within the building, where architecture and nature merge.

In Spain, the gardens inspired by the Islamic tradition fused Arab influences with those of the various conquered countries, as well as strictly local features: other elements derived in particular from the Roman-Byzantine civilization of the Mediterranean. The gardens of Cordoba, Seville and Granada, conditioned by this conjunction, are referred to as 'Arab-Hispanic': the use of enclosed spaces — intimate and inward-looking, both fastnesses and places of delight, rigidly geometrical, with water the dominant element — is common to both cultures, whose characteristics are seamlessly brought together in the Arab-Hispanic garden. Here, some patios derive from the Islamic-Persian tradition, while others testify to the persistence of the Roman-Byzantine style. In the first case, the patios have a rectangular plan, arranged along two axes of perspective, often emphasized by strips of water or vegetation dividing the area into four quadrants. In the centre they have a fountain, sometimes shaded by a trellis, or in the form of a pavilion from which the water flows. Sometimes four small channels run out from the fountain, symbolizing the four rivers of blessedness of the Islamic paradise.

The patios in a Roman scheme, on the other hand, are even more markedly rectangular, and run along a main median axis. The surrounding walls are opened up and the interior of the building is given a sense of communication with the exterior through the filter of a portico, the classical *peristilium*, through which the axial composition can also be seen from within. The linear element often takes the form of a channel, given a sense of colour with the use of Persian-inspired majolica, but also

The basic structure of the Arab garden is its division into four quadrants, bounded by four channels flowing from a central fountain: the Moorish gardens of Spain followed this pattern, too, as we see from this patio in the Alcazar at Seville.

Regarded as the oldest of the courtyards of Seville, the Court of the Oranges stands beside the cathedral. Built in 1420 to replace an earlier Mosque, it takes it name from the orange trees planted at regular intervals in a grid pattern, irrigated by small channels fed by the central fountain.

The patios of the Alhambra were a product of the meeting between Roman and Arab tradition: the elongated form of the large basin in the centre of the Court of the Myrtles (above) is derived from the euripus, *the typical channel of the Roman garden, while the Court of the*

Lions (right) is divided up by small channels similar to those found in Muslim gardens.

deriving in part from the *euripus*, the long straight channel of the classical Roman garden. In both cases water is always present, frequently predominant, still or slightly ruffled in pools and channels, flowing or gushing in fountains and rivulets.

There are few remaining examples of Moorish gardens, but those few are among the loveliest in Europe. The Alcazar palace in Seville has the largest of all surviving Muslim gardens, with a surface area of almost sixteen hectares (forty acres). After being seriously damaged during the siege of 1248 it was recreated relatively faithfully, using Arab labour, by Pedro the Cruel, King of Castile from 1350. Despite extensions added over the following centuries, first by Charles V and then by Philip IV and V, it still retains various features typical of Muslim architecture, with a perfectly gauged balance between interior and exterior, gardens and courtyards, light and shade, still water and bubbling water. The complex consists of several porticoed patios around a central pool, and a vast area divided into eight sections framed by clipped hedges. The largest patio at the Alcazar is the *patio de las Doncellas*, overlooked by three reception rooms, and the most intimate and inward-looking is the *patio de las Munecas* (of the Dolls), with a portico of Moorish arches on slender twinned columns, decorated with coloured tiles, running round a central pool. Seville also contains what is regarded as the oldest surviving example of a Moorish garden in Spain, the *patio de los Naranjos* or Court of

the Oranges. Built during the Omayyad period (756—1031), it is a rectangular space planted with rows of orange trees, reminiscent of the rows of columns inside mosques: the water flows at pavement level in little channels between one tree and another.

Of all the Muslim gardens of Spain, those around the Alhambra and Generalife in the citadel of Granada are the most spectacular: the only examples of twelfth- to fourteenth-century gardens in Europe, though altered over time, they have retained their strongly Islamic character intact.

The Alhambra, a fortified citadel already in existence in the ninth century, was converted into a royal residence between 1333 and 1391, with the accession of the Nazarite dynasty and above all with the building of palaces for Yusuf I and Mahomed II. The complex consists of a series of interlinked buildings and gardens forming an elaborate composition that towers over the town. Here the gardens form the main link between the various buildings which were added, extended and altered at various times.

In the gardens and patios of the Alhambra the vistas and vanishing points are always marked by some architectural element: a fountain, a pool or pavilion.

In accordance with Islamic tradition, in these gardens water, the symbol of life, is omnipresent, in various forms, whether bubbling or silent, flowing or gushing. In the middle of the *Cuarto dorado*, in the eastern part of the complex, the water first wells up from a fountain in the centre of an octagonal basin, then flows all around it in a channel. The *patio de los Arraynes* or Court of the Myrtles, on the other hand, built towards the middle of the fourteenth century, is a sun-drenched space, 37 metres (121 ft.) long and 24 metres (79 ft.) wide, taking its name from the clipped myrtle hedges added relatively recently that flank either side of a long pool, seven metres (23 ft.) wide and running the whole length of the patio. Here the water is almost still, its surface, a little below the level of the paving, barely ruffled by the gentle flow from two small circular fountains at each end. The main lie of the patio looks towards the three-light window in the adjacent *torre de Comares* overlooking the countryside, adding depth to a space which already has a distinctly elongated feel.

To the south-east is the more private part of the Alhambra, with the famous *patio de los Leones*, begun in 1377 and so-called after the central basin supported by twelve lions. This patio is surrounded by an open gallery whose two short sides broaden to form two pavilions. Water flows along channels in the paving, dividing the large rectangle into four sections. A vein of water thus runs through the whole space, welling up from four small basins on ground level, inside the two pavilions and two other rooms, making up four spaces, each corresponding to one of the four cardinal points. Water, the linking element, flows from inside the covered spaces towards the exterior, to surround the fountain, but at the same time leading the eye outwards from the centre towards the surrounding areas. To the north, the vein seems to move towards the *patio de la Lindaraja*, or House of the Sultana, which, like the adjoining *patio de la Rejna*, is of a later date. The former has a Renaissance layout, with geometrical compartments bordered with box hedges and planted with cypresses and orange trees, though the Arab tradition can also be sensed in its richly-scented, shady atmosphere. The *patio de la Rejna* is characterised by its splendid paving of black and white pebbles around a circular fountain surrounded by four cypress trees.

Unlike the Alhambra, where the sophisticated decorative architecture has a predominant role, in the Generalife the built elements take second place to the gardens, which are the dominant feature in a complex based on an even closer

A symbol of life and wealth, with its cool, refreshing sound, water is the dominant feature in the Moorish gardens of Granada. At the Alhambra even the smallest patios have fountains, surrounded by the shade of tall cypress trees as in the patio de la Lindaraja *(left), or set in cobbled patterns as in the* patio de la Rejna *(bottom right); at the Generalife water is used more imaginatively, sometimes forming little streams running down grooves in the parapets of the stairways (above right).*

One of the most alluring courts in Granada is the patio de la Acequia, *or Court of the Long Pond: the central canal, with high spouts falling into it from each side, the lavish marble cladding of its sides and the profusion of plants and flowers — myrtles and cypresses, roses and orange trees scenting the air — makes this court the real jewel of the Generalife. With its rigid structure exquisitely balanced by its exuberant vegetation, and its long central canal offset by the verticality of its fountains, it is an utterly perfect blend of calm and movement.*

relationship between pavilions and gardens.

This garden, whose name derives from the Arabic *Jinna-el-Arif*, 'the Most Noble of Gardens', or the 'Garden of the Architect', was created a few years earlier than the Alhambra, between 1315 and 1325. The oldest part is the *patio de la Acequia*, or Court of the Long Pool. Its elongated rectangular form is emphasized by a long channel with marble-clad sides, running along the centre of the patio. This elongated perspective, and the general lie of the composition, are further intensified by the play of the fountains situated along its edges, falling back into the middle of the channel; by the narrow lateral beds densely planted with flowering shrubs, and by the two porticoes on the short sides. Here the classical quotation of the arcades and the long channel, reminiscent of the Roman peristyle and *euripus*, and the traditional Islamic feeling for colour and decoration,

are twinned to produce an inspired 'picturesque' result. Water is used in different ways, sometimes to mesmerising effect, as with the veil of flowing water that covers the steps of the staircase linking the garden to the nearby *patio de la Lindaraja*. Here the Moorish character is more in evidence than in the previous patio: the *Lindaraja* is square and the water flows in an unusual U-shaped channel around three sides of a platform, to give the idea of an island planted with oleanders, cypresses and roses, with a square basin and a fountain at its centre.

The upper garden is divided into terraces densely planted with shrubs and connected by a rustic flight of steps, decorated with basins with a central jet and a sort of handrail of water running down a groove scooped out of its side parapets. The *Mirador*, a tower in the belvedere, looks down on to the two patios below.

The Arabs' traditional expertise in the use of water made the parks of Norman Palermo true exemplars of the earthly paradise. In this painting, dating from 1922, Rocco Lentini reconstructed the interior of the Pavilion of la Zisa and its elaborate system for circulating water: visible on the ceiling in the background are the stalactites from which the water came down, and the channels cut into the floor into which it flowed before running out into the pool outside.

This reconstruction of the exterior of la Zisa gives an idea of the close relationship between building, water and garden in the park of la Favara (Palermo). A smaller building stood in the large basin, like an island surrounded by water, with dense vegetation all around; at the time of Roger II this consisted mainly of pines, palms, lemon trees, orange trees and lime trees.

All that remains of the great Norman gardens of Palermo is their pavilions: la Cuba, once at the centre of a large pool in the middle of the Genoard, now stands on a stretch of banked-up earth, stifled by the city and its traffic.

ARAB INFLUENCE ON ITALIAN GARDENS

Arab rule in Sicily lasted almost two centuries, from the destruction of Syracuse in 878 to the landing of Roger I of Hauteville in 1061; during this period Islamic traditions made a deep impression on Sicilian culture. The style and compositional features of Islamic art became thoroughly embedded in Sicily, and continued to characterize its art, and that of the Tyrrhenian coasts, even after the Norman conquest. The Norman sovereigns themselves were heirs to the Arab artistic legacy, particularly in architecture and the art of the garden.

Between the eleventh and thirteenth centuries the Arabs had introduced hitherto unknown trees to the island which subsequently became part of the heritage of the entire Mediterranean. Alongside the various citrus plants, they also imported almond trees, peach trees, apricots, pomegranates and date and banana palms.

Following Islamic tradition, the royal gardens of the Norman period were conceived as so many paradises: la Favara, Roger II's park in Palermo, entirely enclosed and stocked with freely roaming animals, was planted with orange, lemon and lime trees, and water was an all-pervading presence. All that remains of this vast park is the Pavilion of the Zisa, a building in the Moorish style decorated with exquisite mosaics and stuccoes. Narrow channels and small basins sunk into the paving of the entrance bear witness to the internal presence of water, stressing its importance as the symbol of life par excellence: beneath a ceiling decorated by stalactites, the water flows down from small cascades to gather in little rills, and then reappear in the basins outside. The Arabs' hydraulic techniques were so advanced that the *padiglione della Cuba*, probably originally situated in the centre of the other great park in Palermo, the Genoard, created by William II,

Typically Moorish in taste, the arcades of the courtyard at villa Rufolo, at Ravello near Salerno, are evidence of this medieval building's long history. In May 1880 this magically evocative garden was Richard Wagner's inspiration for the mythical garden of Klingsor that was to figure in the second act of Parsifal.

Overlooking the sea, the garden of villa Rufolo was given a new lease of life in the second half of the nineteenth century by the Scotsman Francis Neville Reid, who added magnificent trees that were exotic at the time but which are more widely found today: cycads and dwarf fan palms, bergenia, dracaena and yuccas stand alongside ancient pines and cypresses.

stood foursquare in the middle of a large pool. Sicilian and Campanian culture was gradually adapting the elements of Muslim tradition to its own needs through independent aesthetic and stylistic experimentation. If on the one hand the mosaics of la Zisa also included representations of the human figure, on the other various compositional principles deriving from Islam were used in religious architecture: the main features and typical atmosphere of the Muslim garden recur in the cloisters of the cathedral at Monreale, and in those of San Giovanni degli Eremiti in Palermo and the Cathedral at Amalfi.

Similarly, the Arab mood is still present in the splendid garden of Villa Rufolo at Ravello, on the coast near Amalfi. A complex of various buildings dating from the middle of the fourteenth century, Villa Rufolo stands on steeply sloping terraced ground overlooking the sea. An avenue leads from the lookout Tower to an arcaded courtyard with typical Moorish arches of which only three sides remain. Inland are the *palazzo* itself, built in the thirteenth century, and the upper garden, with traces of a pergola reminiscent of descriptions of Roman villas. Further down, the lower garden is one vast terrace, rising vertiginously out of the sea, with flowerbeds and splendid specimens of Mediterranean

flora. In 1851 Villa Rufolo was acquired by Francis Neville Reid, a great connoisseur of plants. He restored the palazzo and more particularly the gardens, to which he gave a strongly romantic atmosphere with the introduction of many ornamental species. Despite the numerous alterations made to the garden even during this century, Rufolo still retains the feel of a Moorish garden: the plethora of Mediterranean plants originally introduced by the Arabs, the Arab-style decorations of the buildings, together with the appeal of its long history and the spectacular view from the terrace, make this garden a small but glowing jewel on the Mediterranean.

The medieval garden: all heaven in a grain of sand

After the year 1000, the spread of knowledge, and cultural exchanges in general, were intensified partly as a result of the crusaders' contacts with the east, but above all through the founding of convents and monasteries throughout Europe.

With the import and exchange of plants, particularly from the East and South, and the growth in botanical knowledge they implied, this period saw the start of a lively interest in the classical texts on agriculture and horticulture which were preserved and transcribed in monastery libraries.

The monks now began to reinstate traditional practices for the growing and processing of medicinal plants. Though these were mainly cultivated for utilitarian purposes, their aesthetic and decorative aspects were now increasingly appreciated. Convent kitchen gardens and small simples gardens — of medicinal herbs — were now enriched by a wide variety of plants: an increasing number of aromatic and medicinal herbs was joined by flowers, now being grown to decorate altars during religious rites as ancient pagan floral traditions were

reclaimed for the Christian religion.

For Europe, the thirteenth century was a period of recovery: improvements in social and economic conditions, demographic growth and a greater sense of security and stability, fostered renewed confidence in the countryside, projecting interest outwards from the cities and fortified abbeys.

Gardens became increasingly complex structures, with an ever-greater variety of plants, laden with symbolic meaning as a result of the renewed religious fervour which swept Europe between the twelfth and fourteenth centuries.

The hortus conclusus

At the root of the medieval concept of the garden lay the idea of the 'paradise-garden': medieval man recreated the perfection of the lost and promised Eden in an enclosed space, in a safe, idealised world. The medieval garden was a *hortus conclusus*, lovingly enclasped and walled in, where the original beauty of creation was restored, and supernal harmony revived. However, in the medieval garden religious undertones were also associated with those of a more worldly, down-to-earth inspiration.

Towards the end of the Middle Ages, the rediscovery of the old horticultural treatises also led to the rediscovery of the garden: the tilling of the earth acquired a new significance. Nature was cultivated in a small space, as shown in this woodcut depicting the delicate process of pruning, taken from a 1496 Paris edition of De Ruralium Commodorum.

Interest in plants led to the publication of botanical texts such as the Tacuinum Sanitatis, *which gave information concerning the various species of medicinal plants, their household uses and medicinal powers. This illustration, from the Codex Casanatensis, shows the tending of marjoram, one of the many plants found in simples gardens.*

Besides their utilitarian role, as time went by plants were also grown for purely aesthetic reasons, and the Tacuinum Sanitatis also reproduced flowers grown for their ornamental beauty: roses, in particular, were used for the decoration of altars and the weaving of garlands.

Queen among flowers, in the thirteenth century the rose inspired the gallant French poem Le roman de la Rose, *in which the protagonist falls in love with a rose, the symbol of beauty, courtesy and youth. Implicit in the idea of the garden and its depiction was the contemplation of nature's bounty in an enclosed and protected space where man nurtured all the beauties of the created world.*

In the fictitious universe of many medieval epic poems, such as the *Roman de la Rose*, the garden was a place of pleasure, the *hortus deliciarum*, the seat not only of the delights of fruit and flowers and all the other marvels of nature, but also of the pleasures of love, '*l'amour courtois*'.

No medieval gardens have survived intact, but we can reconstruct their main lines from images perpetuated in illuminations and through literary and religious allusions and the fantastical descriptions in chivalric poems.

The garden was a place apart, where nature enabled man to commune with God, and where all the joys of creation were gathered together. The emphasis was on scents, colours and gentle murmurings: plants soft to the touch, scented herbs and coloured flowers, pergolas and fruit trees, everything was selected and arranged to delight the five senses. In its every aspect, the garden recalled the wonders of an earthly paradise, proffering an idyllic vision prefiguring the great age of the garden in the era of Humanism and the Renaissance.

The term for the garden that recurs most frequently in medieval Latin is that of *herbarium*. The *herbarium* was a place for the growing of herbs and flowers; an enclosed space, drawing on the literary paradigm of the *hortus conclusus*, to be

enjoyed from the windows of the dwelling-place, and dallied in for recreation and entertainment. Usually square or rectangular, surrounded by walls or trellises, the *hortus* was essentially a flower-filled meadow. Along the sides were flowerbeds, often raised, their borders planted with lilies, roses, irises, peonies and other bulbiferous plants, and over time with ever-more flowering plants. Climbing roses, honeysuckle, ivy and vines were trained over the trellises. Built elements consisted mainly of a central pool — whose typology assumed increasingly complex forms — with a fountain, surrounded by flowerbeds, seats, or sometimes just a lawn. The pergolas along the sides, simple or arched, were almost always made of wood and covered with climbing plants. The chequerboard layout typical of the medieval garden is found in numerous illustrations: the interwoven canes on which the roses climbed might have a chequerboard pattern, as might the alternating flower-filled and grassy sections, or the two-coloured paving.

At first, the raised beds along the edges contained rows of plants of a single species; but as the number of known plants grew, and the influence of the Arab garden made itself felt, so different types of plants and shrubs were placed side by side, sometimes in pots. Arches of clipped evergreens, laurel, box

and yew made an appearance, as did hedges clipped *à l'estrade*, where the plant was clipped so that strips of foliage alternated with strips of bare trunk.

Larger gardens usually also had an area known as the *viridarium*, that is, planted with various species, where fruit-trees mingled with other trees, in a pleasing mixture of flowers and fruits, providing a shady area for walks and relaxation. Often these wooded parts, particularly in the great royal gardens, were also used for hunting.

Since they often represented plants, flowers and horticultural labours, tapestries such as the one shown here are among the most useful sources for the medieval idea of the garden. In this late- *fifteenth-century example Narcissus contemplates his image in a typical hexagonal fountain in a meadow filled with herbs and flowers, the medieval* herbarium, *dotted with lively little animals.*

Opposite, left: During this period the garden took on distinctly symbolic connotations, as a hortus conclusus, *a private and hallowed space containing every virtue. The door to this walled garden, from an illustration to a manuscript written for François I of France, bears the word Nature: this is the only way to enter and join the goddesses of Olympus — Minerva, or Wisdom; Venus, or Love; and Juno, or Virtue — in their flower-filled bower.*

Opposite, right: As the repository of all the beauties of the created world, the garden was also a sacred space for the contemplation of divine harmony. Virgins were frequently painted in rose gardens or reclining on flower-filled meadows, like this resplendent Virgin of the Rose garden, *now in the Museo di Castelvecchio at Verona. The inspiration for this picture was probably one of the numerous Persian miniatures that depicted gardens, which reached Europe via the Arabs.*

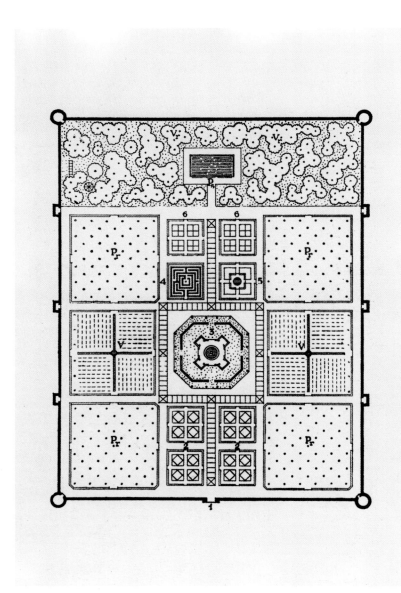

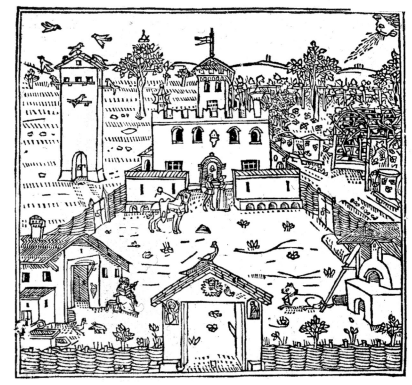

This reconstruction of the largest garden described by de Crescenzi shows the exact distribution of its spaces, each with its own productive or aesthetic role. Opposite the entrance (1) are the flowerbeds (2) and a fountain beneath a pavilion (3). Four other compartments contain a maze (4), a pavilion with a pool (5) and two beds for medicinal herbs (6). The large side sections were for orchards (Pr) and kitchen-gardens (V). The wooded area, the viridarium (Vr), has a fishpond (Ps.) in the middle.

The link between agriculture and garden was still very close, as we see from this frontispiece to a 1495 Venetian edition of the work, which is essentially a treatise on agriculture. The garden runs to the right-hand side of the courtyard in front of the fortified villa, bounded by a typical fence of woven wicker, and the several features we can see characteristically span the utilitarian and the aesthetic: beside the beehives and fruit trees stands a pergola covered with climbing plants.

A BASIC TEXT: THE *DE RURALIUM COMMODORUM*

Pietro de Crescenzi wrote the treatise *De Ruralium Commodorum*, a compendium of the art of agriculture and horticulture, between 1299 and 1305.

The sources used by de Crescenzi, a jurist who lived at the Angevin court of Naples, included writings from the Arabic tradition and the classical treatises on horticulture, but also the works of numerous other thirteenth-century writers from northern Europe, like the well-known Albertus Magus. As it was circulated far more widely than any of these, the *De Ruralium Commodorum* was for a long time the best-known work of reference throughout Europe.

The eighth of its twelve books, which were dedicated to Charles III of Anjou, deals specifically with the art of gardens and sets out a picture of the more mature form of the medieval garden. It starts with the proposition that the garden is a universal necessity for all men, regardless of class: thus descriptions and advice concerning the layout of three types of garden are provided, their sizes varying according to the owners' means. The first is a small garden, square in shape; its layout includes all the typical elements of the medieval *herbarium* consisting mainly of a lawn bordered by beds of scented herbs — rue, marjoram, sage, basil and mint — brightened by multi-coloured flowers like lilies, roses and violets. Shady corners for relaxation are provided by a pergola, while in the centre the clear waters of a fountain give a cooling touch.

The medium-sized garden, for the better-off, might encompass as much as two and a half acres This garden is bounded by moats and hedges and, should the owner wish to plant rows of trees, de Crescenzi suggests pomegranates for southern regions and hazel

The woodcuts in the printed editions of de Crescenzi's text give us a clearer, sharper picture of the garden, less detailed than those shown in illuminations but with a more incisive line: the regular flowerbeds under the pergola, the low walls that can be used as seats and as supports for pots, the trellises around the garden, the man playing an instrument, the rabbit, symbol of fertility, and the welcoming-looking woman not only allude to the religious theme of Eden, but also indicate the convivial mood permeating the humanist garden.

In this illumination, where the model of the hortus conclusus is emphasized by the high surrounding wall, the plants are represented more naturally and exuberantly, and are arranged as suggested by the author. Fruit trees stand along the edges in a sheltered position, while the squared flowerbeds, criss-crossed by paths, are filled with flowers, and vines and jasmine clamber over the walls.

or quince for cooler climates. Here too one part is left as grass and for flowers, with vines, also in rows, climbing over a pergola.

The garden suggested as being fitting for kings and noblemen is more complex. Within some five hectares (twelve acres), it is entirely surrounded by creeper-covered walls, with four small towers at the corners. To the north is a large area to be used as a *viridarium*, a dense copse of different kinds of trees, with wild animals to hunt and a pond for rearing fish. The rest of the garden is divided up into regular sections by broad parallel right-angled paths; in the centre of the resulting grid is a basin with a fountain, whose jets are gathered in small channels to irrigate the garden. The fountain might be shaded by a pergola or pavilion, beneath which chairs and tables beckon invitingly. The regular divisions create areas variously laid out and cultivated as an orchard, a flower garden, a herb garden and a maze.

The description of these three types of garden, especially the last, contains all the typical features of the cultures brought together here: the Roman tradition of the *viridarium* and *pomarium*, or orchard, with trees arranged in a quincunx or chequerboard pattern; the monastic tradition of the simples garden, and the Persian and Islamic tradition of the regular division into sections, with water present as part of an elaborate irrigation system.

Because of the clarity and simplicity of its descriptions, *De Ruralium Commodorum* had considerable success, as we see from its numerous translations and editions. After the first translation into French, commissioned by Charles V in 1373, many other manuscript versions circulated around the courts of Europe, with several printed editions appearing towards the end of the fifteenth century: in Latin in 1471, in Italian in 1478, in French in 1486 and in German in 1493. Although it was never translated into English, we know that in 1473 Edward IV of England owned a superbly illustrated French edition.

An ideal place to contemplate beauty

Midway through the fourteenth century Giovanni Boccaccio expounded upon the typically humanist ideals of conviviality in his *Decameron*. A group of Florentine noblemen and woman flee the plague-ridden city and take refuge in a villa up in the hills; here, in a pleasant garden replete with every delight, they tell each other stories to while away the days in voluntary seclusion.

The garden described by Boccaccio is that earthly paradise, a garden of love and pleasure, where men and women enjoy one another's company singing *canzoni*, weaving garlands, succumbing to the sheer loveliness of the place amidst birdsong and murmuring fountains. It is a garden where play and spirituality combine, an ideal setting for a long untroubled feast, for reading poetry and speaking of love.

With humanism, man becomes the centre and fulcrum of all things, and the garden a wondrous receptacle to gather and set forth the beauties of creation for his pleasure.

Europe's cultural reawakening brought a new concept of the individual, and a renewed faith in his capacity and potential stimulated study of the cultural and artistic legacy of antiquity. In a spirit of passionate antiquarian enquiry the Italian humanists re-established the classical principles of Greek and Roman civilization as ideals of absolute perfection.

In particular, the study of classical texts prompted a redis-covery of the natural environment's more agreeable aspects and the rejection of the distrust of nature typical of previous centuries. Together with a more benign view of rural life, this encouraged the establishment of places of peace and enjoyment where *otium* and *negotium* might alternate — that is, action but also contemplation.

From the end of the fourteenth century the fortified castles found throughout the peninsula were transformed into more comfortable dwellings and, little by little, new ones were built around the cities. Towards the middle of the fifteenth century the typology of the *villa suburbana*, complete with garden, became established, along the lines suggested in the treatises of the Roman period.

Humanist gardens: the return to the classical texts

The humanist garden, unlike the medieval one, was an indispensable feature of the villa, with which it tended to form a single organism, in conformity with a specific ethical and aesthetic concept, no longer purely utilitarian. Cultivation of the land became synonymous with cultivation of the soul, and rules governing the composition of the villa and surrounding land reflected the values of beauty and harmony expressed in the classical treatises, and now reformulated in contemporary equivalents.

In the ten books of his treatise on architecture, *De Re Aedificatoria*, Leon Battista Alberti expounded anew the basic

With the coming of Humanism, people gathered in the garden for philosophical discussion, to sing canzoni, *pick flowers and weave garlands, as we see in this woodcut from the* Dream of Poliphilus,

the text that was to be the great source of inspiration for the humanist and Renaissance garden.

The splendid pergola at Trebbio, the fortified

villa belonging to Cosimo the Elder de' Medici — also depicted in contemporary illustrations — is supported by columns of rounded pianelle, *the traditional brickwork also used around flowerbeds.*

canons of classical architecture. Completed in 1452 and printed in 1485, Alberti's treatise, which harked back to such classical texts as those of Vitruvius and Pliny the Younger, was to be a fundamental point of reference for artistic developments in the Renaissance. As far as the history of the garden is concerned, the ideals of harmony and unity of the parts expounded by Alberti were to inform the humanist and Renaissance garden, particularly those of the Medici and their court in Florence in the second half of the fifteenth century. In Alberti's view, absolute priority was to be given to the correct choice of site for the villa, following classical Roman criteria: hilly sites were to be preferred, with views over the countryside, broadly exposed to the sun and health-giving winds. For the garden, topiary was particularly advocated, that is, the classical practice of mercilessly clipping plants into geometric shapes.

On the basis of Alberti's architectural criteria, the compact and inward-looking nature of medieval volumes was now superseded by the introduction of loggias, stairways and terraces, and the garden now required specific planning in accordance with the rules of architectural design. The choice of site, with an eye to the panorama and the views of the countryside from it, had one particular implication: now that boundary walls had vanished, the eye could wander freely over the landscape. The characteristic lie of the predominantly rolling Tuscan countryside meant that terracing — a typical

agricultural feature — would now also follow aesthetic guidelines. The use of descending terraces overlooking the countryside, variously treated and interpreted, was to be an enduring feature of the classical Italian garden over subsequent centuries. The patronage of the Medici court, a meeting-place for philosophers, men of letters and artists — convinced as they were of the benefits of a return to the countryside as an alternative to city life, in accordance with the traditions of the classical world — also made Florence the epicentre of the European art of the garden.

The architectural ideas of Leon Battista Alberti, and neoplatonist philosophy, found a passionate supporter in Cosimo de' Medici. Wishing to encourage scholars and men of letters to gather round him and to add lustre to his government, Cosimo embarked on a series of projects, first converting fortresses into country dwellings, then building completely new ones.

With the help of Michelozzo Michelozzi, around 1451 Cosimo began work on the castle of Trebbio and the small fortress of Cafaggiolo. Here, once work had been completed, the gardens — though still retaining their powerful boundary walls — were large enough to be regarded as an outward extension of the dwelling. If at Cafaggiolo the building still had something of the enclosed character of a fortress, at Trebbio Michelozzi lightened the structure by adding a loggia, and covered passages on the bastions and tower, overlooking the

In the fifteenth century Ca' Marcello at Monselice, in the province of Padua, was transformed, like the fortresses of Cosimo the Elder around Florence, from a castle into a residence opening on to the outside world. Small terraced gardens were added to the loggia overlooking the inner courtyard, linked by flights of steps, following the criteria of the classical villa adopted by the humanist treatises.

surrounding countryside. Beyond a small wood to its rear, a modest rectangular garden was laid out at Trebbio, divided into eight sections for flowers and herbs, with vine-covered pergolas along the longer sides. One of these is still in existence, supported by columns made of *pianelle*, rounded superimposed bricks, with stone capitals and bases.

Michelozzo was also commissioned to modernize the fortress of Careggi (1457) and to build the villa at Fiesole (1458—61). If the former expressed Alberti's ideal of fidelity to the models of classical Rome, the latter took a decisive step in the direction the Renaissance villa was increasingly to take. With the abandoning of the medieval scheme, at Careggi the architectural structures opened outwards with an airy double

loggia overlooking the small garden; in the villa at Fiesole, where a sense of outward projection was emphasized by the use of terraces, the garden became a filter between architecture and landscape. Two broad surfaces cut into the hillside, supported by strong walls and linked by flights of steps and ramps, overlook the Arno valley, in accordance with Alberti's recommendations concerning the siting of villas. The layout of the terraces, with a pergola of vines midway up the slope, has remained more or less unchanged over time, the exception being the conversion of the kitchen-garden on the lower terrace into a garden with a regular geometric plan. The section to the west — the *giardino segreto* — a more intimate space, for reflection and reverie — has remained unchanged.

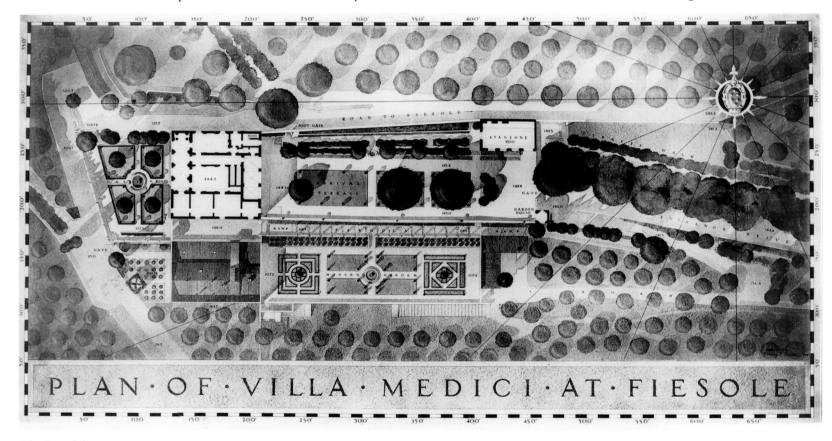

PLAN · OF · VILLA · MEDICI · AT · FIESOLE

The first of the new villas built according to the canons formulated by Leon Battista Alberti, the Medici villa at Fiesole was surrounded by terraced gardens on several levels. To the rear of the villa, another small terrace was built on the side opposite the two main ones: divided into four sections around a central fountain, this now became the 'secret garden', a private space deriving from the medieval model of the hortus conclusus.

Villa Medici, Fiesole. This interesting period photograph makes it clear that the villa was designed according to Alberti's advice on the choice of site: overlooking Florence and the Arno valley, it had the advantage not just of a glorious view, but also a particularly salubrious position, windswept and sunny.

This drawing gives an idea of how the hanging garden in the Ducal Palace in Urbino must have looked in the fifteenth century. A truly secret garden, it was concealed from outside view by windows in a wall overlooking the countryside, and was accessible only from the palace. Like the garden at palazzo Piccolomini at Pienza, the hanging garden marks the transition between the enclosed garden within the dwelling, and the traditional Italian terrace.

Built at the end of the garden proper, the secret garden at palazzo Te in Mantua, laid out by Federico II Gonzaga for his mistress Isabella Boschetti, has something of the rapturous silence of the gardens of love typical of the romance tradition. The enchanted atmosphere is heightened by the cleverly designed grotto, reached from the secret garden and decorated with shells, stuccoes and coloured stones.

GIARDINI SEGRETI

The implications of the *giardino segreto*, the secret garden, vary according to historical circumstances, and not all can be seen as deriving from a single model. The term was born of the recognition of an ideological or philosophical component inherent in the Renaissance garden, an element of the medieval tradition which had endured.

The term *giardino segreto* is a recent coinage embracing an older concept. The late nineteenth-century rediscovery, by the English-speaking world, of the powerfully structured Tuscan and Florentine Renaissance garden made up of 'rooms', highlighted the idea of secrecy typical of late-medieval tradition. This same concept is at the core of the *hortus conclusus*, the enclosed garden of medieval religious tradition. As it developed into the secular garden of courtly love, it became charged with erotic undertones and added secrecy. Gardens of love are always secret gardens, and vice versa. Representations of the myth of the fountain of youth, found throughout medieval culture, were set in walled gardens: here too the secrecy of the consummated rite is inherent in the rite itself.

A secret space, secluded, intimate and private, is often found in Italian gardens. In the fifteenth century it was still a restatement of a medieval structure, a cultivated space surrounded by walls, a sort of openair 'room'. In this sense the hanging gardens of palazzo Piccolomini at Pienza and the palace of Montefeltro at Urbino may be considered 'secret gardens'. During the Renaissance the secret garden was given additional architectural elements like nymphaea and water theatres, which gradually became an integral part of first the Mannerist garden, then of the Baroque. The concept of the enclosed and private garden is still visible in the water theatres at

Standing behind the sixteenth-century Villa Barbaro, designed by Andrea Palladio at Maser, in the province of Treviso, this enchanting nymphaeum is cut out of a small space with direct access to the more private rooms of the villa; here Mannerist decoration is combined with the concept of the secret garden, conceived as a private space reserved for the owner, Marcantonio Barbaro, who probably also designed the sculptures.

The secret garden at castello Ruspoli di Vignanello, in the province of Viterbo, is both a flower garden and a garden of love. Situated at a lower level than the main garden, it can be seen from above and appears to be inaccessible. The route leading to the delightful geometrical box-edged flowerbeds is also secret, or at least concealed.

Secret and secluded, the garden of the Casino at Caprarola, deep in the woods, at some distance from the palazzo, is surrounded by a low retaining wall supporting a series of herms placed at regular intervals: the herm was an ancient symbol conveying a sense of boundary and enclosure.

Villa Piccolomini Lancellotti at Frascati, with its tall hedges serving as walls, and at the nymphaeum at Villa Barbaro at Maser, an area with strong connotations of privacy and intimacy, cut into a small area behind the villa and in close contact with its rooms.

From the end of the sixteenth century the enclosed garden also became the place to indulge the nascent passion for collecting and growing valuable flowers.

The concept persisted in late-Renaissance and Mannerist gardens, though its uses changed. The secret garden now became larger: the space around the Casino in the wood behind Palazzo Farnese at Caprarola is a secret garden. Intended for the Cardinal's leisure use, far from the pomp and circumstance of the palazzo, the garden here became a more elaborate and complex composition, with refined decoration: the herms placed above the small boundary walls symbolize the limits of the garden, emphasizing its secrecy.

In the late seventeenth century the idea of the private garden spread and took on great importance in sumptuous royal creations such as Versailles, where any kind of boundary disappeared, and a sense of separateness was given by distance. This is the case with the Trianon, built in the park of Versailles as a secluded private residence by Louis XIV. At the Trianon, furthermore, the Sun King cultivated a wide variety of flowers, his personal passion. Thus the concept persisted, though the strictly architectural aspect was lost: these gardens were no longer walled, merely separate, removed from the main action but no longer secret in a strictly structural sense.

The secret garden now became the private garden, intimate and personal, and as such we find it in the 'green rooms' of twentieth-century Anglo-Saxon gardens like Sissinghurst, in Kent, belonging to the writer Vita Sackville-West.

The illumination, or miniature, a distinctive art form known since the time of Byzantium, went through a fascinating period of development, to reach its apogee in the fourteenth and fifteenth centuries. Its name derives from the word *minium*, the cinnabar or red lead with which amanuenses decorated the capital letters of their manuscripts. From the earliest geometrical and floral motifs used to ornament their pages, over time illuminations developed into specific illustrations appended to texts. With the perfection of draughtsmanship abstract motifs were joined by figurative and naturalistic ones, so that the scenes represented become increasingly complex, including buildings and landscapes framing the text. Analysis of illuminations depicting green spaces and natural settings enables us to reconstruct the image of the gardens of the past. In keeping with the profound cultural changes of the thirteenth and fourteenth centuries, the first ideal and thoroughly symbolic images developed into realistic, objective and vivid representations of real life, peopled with figures and objects.

In illuminations, the move away from the medieval conception of nature as disturbing, amorphous and alien increasingly represented life in the open air, reflecting man's growing enjoyment of the beauties of creation. An ever greater number of worldly, everyday scenes began to appear alongside symbolic depictions of religious themes. Traditional representations of the months as successive phases of work in field and garden were now replaced by more detailed depictions of the green spaces where such work took place, and religious images were partly superseded by scenes of life in the garden, inspired by the chivalric poems.

Illuminations, with their minute details, are highly informative about the elements of the late-medieval garden, its architectural ornament, the flowers grown there, and above all the life lived there.

THE REPRESENTATION OF THE GARDEN: ILLUMINATIONS

1. In older illuminations, the representation is always highly symbolic in character, with single subjects shown in a schematic and idealized manner. Here, the illumination of the mythical plant known as Balm is set in a fortified castle, surrounded by walls to emphasize its precious nature, and confirming the idea of the garden as a space apart, protected from the outside world. Balm is a species of impatiens *which, according to legend, had been brought from India by the Queen of Sheba as a gift for King Solomon.*

1

2. When men began to feel less distrustful of nature, they began to view work on the land, and the rites connected with it, in a more confident fashion; there are many illustrations of such work in the fields, and of the pastimes involved, as we see in this Lombard illumination. Scenes of country life were often depicted, like sowing, harvesting and the grape harvest, marking the succession of months in calendars, or in cycles of tapestries of the seasons.

2

3

5

4

4. *Maugis and la belle Oriande, the protagonists of the Roman de Renaud de Montauban, c. 1475, seated in the blissful peace of an elaborate medieval garden.*

Although it has sturdy walls, the garden is surrounded by a trellis, to set it apart from what lies around it. The fountain is of the 'basin' type, with a hexagonal base; the low brick wall

provides a sort of grassy seat, the lawn is still wild and dotted with flowers and herbs; the refinement of courtly emotion is expressed in the elegant pots containing a carnation and a

shrub which has been vigorously subjected to the ars topiaria.

3. *The greatest of all illuminated manuscripts is the book of hours of the duc de Berry, Les très riches heures, illustrated by the De Limbourg brothers at the beginning of the fifteenth century, from which this illumination of the month of April is taken. Medieval symbolism now seems to have been set aside: depictions became more detailed, more indicative of men's habits and attitudes. The concept of hortus conclusus has lost its religious symbolism to take on a distinctively worldly character, anticipating the coming of the secret garden. Nature, woods and crags are no longer alarming, and knights and noblewomen venture out of the enclosed garden to enjoy the approach of summer.*

5. *The* Fountain of Youth, *from the treatise* De Sphaera. *The mythical rite of bathing in the fountain that gives eternal youth takes place in a typical garden whose walls separate it from the city. By now the garden has become the place where courtly life unfolds: protection from the outside world is no longer for the benefit of the plants, nor does it safeguard the hallowed nature of the space; rather, it underlines the seclusion proper to the rarefied pleasures the garden makes it possible to enjoy. The various elements are represented with great precision: the high surrounding wall; the climbers and trees, whether clipped or otherwise; the lawn with little herbs and flowers, including cyclamen; and the figures in their midst, bathing, playing instruments, singing, eating, drinking and making love.*

The sixteenth
century

From the classical to the wonderful

In the Renaissance, the numerous illustrations to the Dream of Poliphilus, *inspired by antiquity and the classical myths, amounted to a virtual catalogue of garden design. The small structures found in medieval tradition, like the pergola with a hexagonal basin, were now joined by innumerable quotations from classical art, such as the inscriptions and bas-reliefs that decorate the base of the fountain in this illustration.*

The Fountain of Parnassus at villa Lante at Bagnaia.

The deep religious schism caused by the Protestant reformation, the process of reunification and the piecing-together of feudal and territorial fragments — in train since the end of the fifteenth century — made the sixteenth century a period of cultural and political renewal for Europe as a whole. This was the century of the Renaissance, if the term is used to mean the 'rebirth' of classical art and architecture.

For the first two decades of the century especially, Rome was the fulcrum of European art and architecture, radiating a new language based on the reinstatement of the classical architectural orders, and the taste for complex forms of spatial organization centred on axes of symmetry. With its general reworking of the typological models of Greek and Roman antiquity, this new vision of art had already begun to spread from Italy around the end of the fifteenth century, when foreign sovereigns and noblemen, bestriding the peninsula with their armies, had come into contact with the sophisticated cultures of the humanist courts. Utterly won over, on their return they took with them not just a memory, and a desire for emulation, but also a number of architects, painters and sculptors. Throughout the sixteenth century Italian artists were to be called upon to work at foreign courts, and Italian art became a universal touchstone, particularly in France. With the arrival of Primaticcio and Rosso Fiorentino at the court of François I, the School of Fontainebleau was born — the first stirrings of the Renaissance in France.

Of all the art forms, it was the art of the garden that displayed the greatest uniformity throughout Europe. Italian gardens dominated the European scene: the great patrons, enamoured equally of art and the countryside, summoned architects and men of letters and vied with each other creating their own paradise to mirror their power, culture and wealth. This led to the construction of those incredible architectural complexes where villa and garden form a seamless whole, the fullest and most assured expressions of the Renaissance ideals.

The invention of printing, too, played its part in the spread of the Italian model. The wide circulation of knowledge and fertile interchange of ideas characteristic of the Renaissance soon set in train a process which — based on the humanist ideal of a contemplative life and the return to a mythical Golden Age, linked to the classical *topos* of the countryside in contrast to the hurly-burly of the city — made the villa and garden a *sine qua non* for every self-respecting prince and potentate.

Thanks to its many illustrations and wide circulation, the *Hypnerotomachia*, or *Dream of Poliphilus*, was the main source of inspiration for the Renaissance and Mannerist garden. Traditionally attributed to the Dominican friar Francesco Colonna, and printed in Venice in 1499 fifty years after it was written, the *Hypnerotomachia* is an allegorical narrative of the dream of the love between Poliphilus and Polia in the garden of Cythera, the mythical island sacred to Aphrodite. With the help of Will and Reason the two lovers, borne on a wonderful boat, manage to negotiate the labyrinth and reach the island and its garden. The garden of Cythera is inaccessible, both physically and symbolically, to those who cannot grasp the rational laws which govern it. A miracle of harmony and perfection, the island is laid out so as to lead its visitors on a journey of initiation, following a complicated architectural route linking the various parts into a unitary whole. Composed of circular, concentric and superimposed terraces, it forms a pyramid: the layout is absolutely regular, punctuated by geometrical forms where architecture and nature meet and merge. Its structure, and decoration, is made up of balustrades and statues, fountains and pergolas, topiaried trees and cypresses, flowers and climbing plants, geometrical flowerbeds with elaborate designs, ancient ruins and classical inscriptions. The text is illustrated with no fewer than 147 woodcuts, almost all depicting features of the garden: each one teems with statues and fountains, loggias and stairways, clipped hedges and flowers, and together they make up an ideal model that was to influence the concept and composition of many sixteenth-century gardens. Indeed, the *Dream of Poliphilus* contains all the characteristics of the Renaissance garden: the architecture takes the limelight, laden with symbols and allegorical messages, adorned with classically-inspired inscriptions, in a work that aimed to give expression to the newly discovered and revivified ideals of classical civilization; but also a sense of universal harmony restored, the measure and embodiment of the greatness and prowess of the reigning lord.

With the succession of ever more spectacular creations, the Italian garden had become a model throughout Europe, giving rise to a style more recently known as the 'giardino all'italiana', which continued to be widely revived well beyond the sixteenth and seventeenth centuries.

Only in the eighteenth century did the English landscape revolution, and the coming of the 'informal' style, dictate an absolutely new and alternative direction for the garden.

Architectural structures derived from antiquity played a key role in the garden of Cythera described in the Dream of Poliphilus. *Conceived as a series of superimposed circular terraces, its layout also included assorted highly elaborate constructions. Apart from wooden pergolas, masonry structures such as loggias, balustrades, temples and aedicules now became* de rigueur *in Renaissance gardens.*

Villa d'Este, Tivoli. Vieing with one another as to who could create the most sumptuous and spectacular palaces and gardens, princes and prelates at the splendid sixteenth-century Italian courts produced absolute masterpieces, giving rise to a style imitated throughout Europe. One of the most important gardens was that commissioned by Ippolito d'Este at Tivoli, which attained unprecedented fame and prestige: illustrated by Etienne du Perac in 1573 and described at length by Michel de Montaigne in 1581, Tivoli became the very embodiment of the art of the garden.

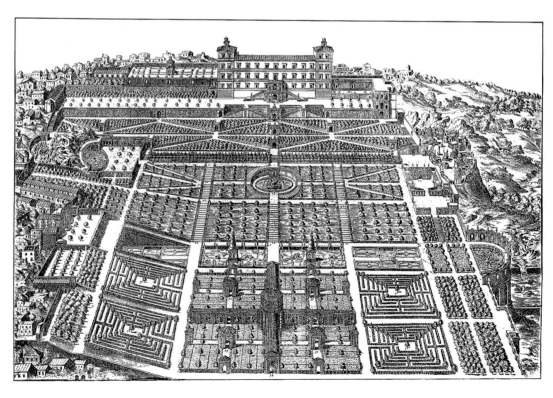

Villa Pia, Città del
Vaticano. In Rome and
Latium the newly resur-
rected canons of classical
architecture made a
great impression on
garden design during
the sixteenth century:
identifying themselves
with the glorious and
powerful emperors of
ancient Rome, the popes
used the architectural
styles and orders of
antiquity to proclaim
their own power and
prestige. The Vatican
City and its gardens
became the place par
excellence for this rein-
statement of the classical
grandeur that was
Rome. Built for Pius IV
in 1566, villa Pia,
together with the
nymphaeum and stone
ornaments — urns,
statues and obelisks —
of its garden, is one of
the most elegant exam-
ples of this trend.

Interest in the classical
world, and the desire to
reinstate its basic
values, stimulated an
interest in ruins; they
now played an impor-
tant role in bringing
antiquity to life again,
as we see from this
woodcut from the
Dream of Poliphilus.

Opposite: Hadrian's villa, Tivoli. The hemicycle of the Canopus was built by the emperor Hadrian in the second century as an adornment for his vast villa on the plain of Tivoli, in memory of the temple and channel of the same name at the mouth of the Nile. Hadrian's villa and the temple at Palestrina were among the ruins that provided the main inspiration for the Italian gardens of the Renaissance.

The Italian Renaissance garden: nature and architecture at one

In the first years of the sixteenth century, the Renaissance principles that had already found concrete expression in the Tuscan villas and gardens of the second half of the fifteenth century acquired a new authority at the papal court in Rome. Encouraged by its ancient ruins, the rediscovery of its classical sculptures and the study of the architectural orders of antiquity, the policy of buttressing the Papal State identified the popes with the old Roman emperors.

The Renaissance restoration of the canons of classical art, in the form of splendid complexes of villas and gardens, amounted to more than mere imitation of ancient models. Rather, it was the perpetuation — according to the Ciceronian concept of *cultus*, the thorough-going cultivation of the land and of the mind — of classical principles in the living present. The garden therefore became the ideal place for the celebration of the ancient world: the purpose was not to recreate the past, but to reinstate the values of a gloriously refined civilization in order to give lustre to the present. It was an offshoot of humanist thinking that expressed man's power as an active being, and emphasised his control over nature.

Villa and garden now became the venue for supreme self-aggrandisement: architects and decorators designed great sumptuous spaces, men of letters and 'antiquarians' devised elaborate encomiastic iconographies, every nerve strained to proclaim the prestige of their patrons. Even more than the villa, the garden became the emblem of the creative and controlling powers of its owner; it was here, through the making of vistas and panoramas, that man's new-found capacity for observing the world and nature was made manifest. Compositions no longer turned on a single focal point: now the eye travelled along various axes, and interior and exterior were unified in a single project. The greatest architects of the time, working on both buildings and gardens, produced powerfully structured

The loggia of villa Giulia in Rome, and indeed the whole elaborate layout of its open spaces, are reminiscent of the architectural complexes of the Roman villas of the imperial age, which consisted of a complex succession of spaces and structures set in green spaces. At villa Giulia the sequence of spaces between building and garden is achieved through a gradual movement between interior and exterior, with the architectural composition reigning supreme.

and coherent organisms in which the garden, obeying the geometrical rules of architecture, became a rigorous and measured composition, unfolding at the foot of the building like a drawing, its ideal exterior projection.

The gardens so designed were divided into symmetrical sections containing flowerbeds, slender rectangular compartments bordered by low, square, evergreen hedges. Conceived as two-dimensional drawings, the third, the vertical, was provided by the various minor buildings and sculptures scattered throughout, as well as by potted plants and topiary work, though always placed so as not to distract from an immediate reading of whole design. The architectural element, the underlying structure that was at the same time its ornamentation — the symbol of man's ability to mould nature to his will — was superimposed upon the garden of the senses that had characterised the previous period. Elaborate complexes of terraces, stairways, ramps, fountains, temples, loggias, pergolas, nymphaea and sculpted groups now carried the day.

Each element was a quotation, bore a message or an inscription, constituted a pause or stage in the complicated symbolic routes that made the garden an allegory of life itself. Botanically,

evergreens predominated, often in the form of aromatic plants, with a marked preference for those with dense and compact foliage as better suited to forming geometrical hedges and borders.

Trees — mainly ilex, pine and oak — assumed great importance in the Renaissance garden. Now that the looming perimeter walls had disappeared, the bays of clipped hedges lost their medieval sense of protection from the outside world, and merged with groups of trees. In some cases squared hedges were directly incorporated into the wooded mass of the 'barco', the area for hunting, clearly demonstrating the superiority of rational design over wild, disorderly nature. Even though all that has survived of them is their architectural structures and hedges, this does not mean that the Italian Renaissance garden was lacking in colourful, scented flowers. During the sixteenth century, thanks to geographical discovery and the frequency of exchanges and contacts, a vast number of new species were introduced into Europe. Citrus fruit, particularly lemons, now reigned supreme: inspired by the golden apples grown in the garden of the Hesperides, the conquest of which was the eleventh labour of Hercules (a myth to be emulated and, if possible, outshone),

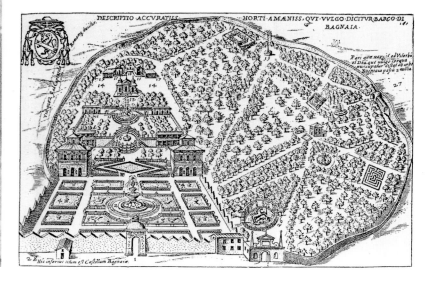

Plans of flowerbeds from an engraving from the four books of the treatise by Sebastiano Serlio, Tutte l'opere d'architettura, *of 1537. In the sixteenth century interest in garden design shifted definitively from treatises on agriculture to those on architecture, as already with the work of Alberti at the end of the previous century. Achitects became increasingly interested in the subject, even creating complicated designs for flowerbeds, with their geometric subdivisions typical of the Italian Renaissance garden.*

Villa Lante, Bagnaia. Designed as a rigidly geometrical structure, the Italian garden achieved the harmony and rationality striven for by Renaissance art by means of its division into regular compartments. Conceived as a place for celebrating man's ability to impose order upon the natural world, villa Lante is one of the most successful examples of such gardens, particularly in its level section, whose square shape is subdivided into further squares around the famous fontana del Quadrato (Fountain of the Square).

The garden at Villa Buonaccorsi, Potenza Picena, Marche. Flowers were omnipresent in the Renaissance garden, in Italy as in the rest of Europe; such gardens were structured around severe evergreen hedges, but flowering plants also played a part. This photograph gives an idea of how the garden must have looked in the sixteenth century, despite the later layout and flowers other than the original tulips and anemones.

lemons became the emblem of the garden par excellence. In the second half of the sixteenth century citrus fruit became a positive rage, particularly in Florence, where Francesco I (1574—87) brought together a huge collection of trees with innumerable varieties of lemons, oranges, limes, bitter oranges and bergamots.

But the most spectacular and best-known of Italian gardens were those created around Rome in the second half of the century: the gardens of palazzo Farnese at Caprarola, of Villa Lante at Bagnaia and of Villa d'Este at Tivoli. These masterpieces of architecture and the art of the garden, visited, admired and described by generations of artists and writers, were to confirm the greatness of the Italian model throughout Europe.

Rome and the passion for antiquities

The great age of the Roman Renaissance began in 1503 with the ascent of Julius II della Rovere to the papal throne. The study of classical antiquity was stimulating an interest in archaeology, and vitally important excavations and surveys were being carried out: Nero's *Domus Aurea*, Hadrian's villa at Tivoli and the temple of *Fortuna virilis* at Praeneste, the present-day Palestrina. Ruins, more or less omnipresent, rediscovered statues and sculptural groups, like the *Laocoön* on the Esquiline — so many physical confirmations of literary knowledge — gave new impetus to the passion for all things classical, and popes and cardinals began to collect ancient statues and sculpture.

No sooner had he been made pope than Julius II commissioned Donato Bramante to lay out a large sloping area between the medieval Vatican buildings and the villa of Innocent VIII, known as the Villa Belvedere. Bramante's project produced to the famous courtyard of the Belvedere, an architectural masterpiece and an important turning-point in the history of the Italian garden. Though not really a garden as such, the courtyard of the Belvedere retained certain features: it was a vast open space — for strolling in, and for the exhibition of a huge collection of statues — whose design reflected the architectural canons. Bounded by two side walls punctuated by three architectural orders and further divided into three superimposed terraces — probably inspired by the ancient temple at Palestrina — viewed as a whole the courtyard was complementary, if not fundamental, to the entire Vatican complex.

References to the classical age were not limited to architectural quotation: the statues from Julius II's antiquarian collection were placed here in a highly evocative setting. Among the many masterpieces of ancient sculpture laid out on the upper terrace, both the famous Apollo — known as the 'Apollo of the Belvedere' — and the imposing group of the *Laocoön*, look out from niches against backdrops painted with leafy trees, flowers and birds.

After the removal of the statues during the pontificate of Pius V, and several later alterations, the courtyard was definitively divided into two with the building of the large library commissioned by Sixtus V across the main axis, but Bramante's layout, documented in numerous sketches and paintings, left an enduring mark on the sixteenth-century development of the Italian garden.

The garden was now assuming primary importance as the perfect setting for eye-catching displays of antiquities. Country villas — or 'vigne' (literally vineyards), as such retreats were then known — became very fashionable among popes and

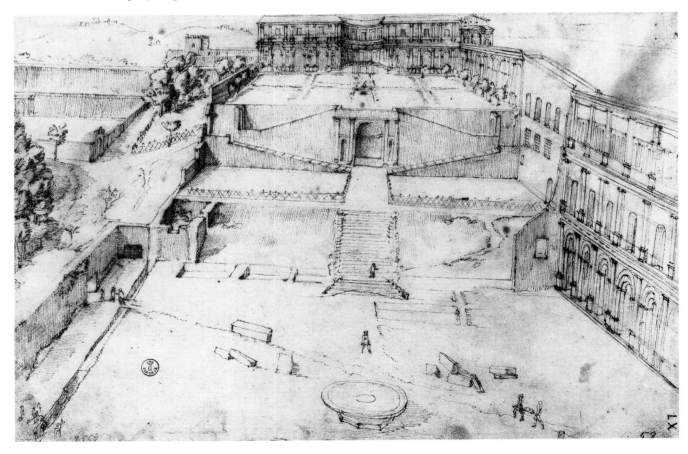

This drawing, showing the building of the courtyard of the Belvedere, in the Vatican — a vast open space designed by Bramante using the compositional criteria of classical architecture — does ample justice to the feeling it conveys of being an architectural project. The subsequent fame of the Belvedere was to be of fundamental importance for the development of the art of the sixteenth-century garden.

cardinals, while the building of elaborate architectural complexes was an ideal opportunity for rich aristocratic families to proclaim their status and power. The statues themselves — together with sculpted fragments salvaged and restored — were not just curiosities to be admired and collected, but, like ghosts from a glorious past, spoke cogently of the classical atmosphere in these garden settings, turning them into gymnasia and academies, into caverns of the Muses and *sacri boschi* (sacred groves).

All Italy's most powerful families were present in Rome during these years; their members, almost always cardinals, fired by a positive fervour for art and building, were inspired patrons. The Medici were among the most active, leaving their mark on the art of humanism and the Renaissance, not only in their native Tuscany, but also in Rome.

If the house of Medici had already given ample proof of an interest in gardens in the fifteenth-century villas of Cosimo the Elder and Lorenzo de' Medici, in Rome this interest was even more closely associated with the rediscovery of the classical models, particularly in the first half of the century when two Medici, Leo X (1513—21) and Clement VII (1523—34) virtually succeeded one another on the papal throne.

The building of Villa Madama and its gardens, begun in 1519 for Cardinal Giuliano de' Medici, Pope Clement VII, was based largely on a project by Raphael. It too was inspired by classical antiquity, filtered through Alberti's treatise and the recent example of Bramante's Belvedere. But the building of Villa Madama was far from straightforward, interrupted on several occasions and never completely finished; nor, more to the point, were its gardens. Begun under the guidance of Raphael it was taken over on his death, by Antonio da Sangallo, with the assistance of Giulio Romano. After a further pause in 1523, work ceased for good with the sack of Rome in 1527.

Several autograph drawings of Raphael's project for the garden have survived, as well as various descriptions, including one by Vasari, which make it possible to reconstruct its original layout. The villa, which was to be entered from the side through a circular courtyard probably inspired by a visit Raphael made to Hadrian's villa at Tivoli stands on the slopes of Monte Mario, its main facade overlooking the Tiber. The incomplete circular courtyard ended as an exedra; the project for a further extension of the garden was never executed either. The surviving drawings show an extremely complex layout revealing the influence of the terracing of Bramante's Belvedere, as well as the gardens and hippodrome of Pliny the Younger's villa at Tusculum near present-day Frascati, described in his *Letters*. The gardens were to have been laid out to the side of the villa, divided into three terraces going down towards the Tiber, the first square, the second circular and the third elliptical, linked by flights of steps. Today the villa has two terraced side gardens, one with trees and fountains and the *Piazzale delle Fontane*, with a large pool.

The passion for antiquities implied by Raphael's complex design for Villa Madama, was more thoroughly formulated at Villa Medici, on the Pincio. Built by Annibale Lippi in 1540 for Cardinal Ricci, the villa was acquired by Cardinal Ferdinando de' Medici, later duke of Tuscany. Here Ferdinando created the first garden based on a unitary project, intended

The presence of ruins all over Rome and its outskirts, and frequent finds of classical statues, further stimulating the passion for classical art and antiquarian collecting, made gardens a favourite place for re-creating the atmosphere of the mythical and glorious past. The statues themselves, arranged in such gardens, evoked the splendours of the ancient Graeco-Roman civilization, as in this drawing (c. 1530), showing one of the terraces of villa Medici in Rome.

mainly for the exhibition of his large and renowned collection of Greek and Roman statues.

The design of the garden used the characteristic layout, divided up by flowerbeds, of the Florentine Quattrocento, which lent itself to a rational presentation of the sculptures salvaged from archaeological excavations; the only stylistic innovation was the appearance of a small artificial mound. An allusion to Mount Parnassus, sacred to the Muses, it served to exhibit works of art laid out along the path that wound up around it.

The compositional rigour of the Villa Medici was a case apart in the panorama of the Roman villas and gardens of the second half of the sixteenth century. Those built by the great families after the long hiatus caused by the sack of Rome had now abandoned for good the more intimate and severe character of the early Renaissance in favour of more 'mannerist' creations based on quite different criteria, albeit similar in outward expression.

Medici gardens in Tuscany

The sack of Rome saw the departure of many artists from the city, either to settle abroad — as did Leonardo da Vinci, who went to the court of François I in France — or elsewhere in Italy. Many went to Florence which for a time once again became the centre of garden culture.

After the short interlude of the republic, in 1531 the Medici had returned from exile, establishing the *de facto* Signoria. In 1537, when Cosimo I the Great became Duke of Florence, the second great age of Medici patronage began. But the late fifteenth-century model was still very much alive in Florence, and gardens continued to be created as places for private enjoyment, reserved for their lord and his close circle of intimates.

This was the case with the villa at Castello, above Florence, commissioned by Duke Cosimo from Nicolò Tribolo in 1538. On three terraces cut into the gentle slope of the hill, the garden at Castello, while retaining the ordered simplicity typical of the sixteenth century, broke with traditional schemes by taking a first step in the direction of a 'Mannerist' art. The layout is entirely based on a central axis, the co-ordinating backbone of the composition, along which basins and sculptures succeed one another according to a specific iconographic programme celebrating the greatness of Cosimo, and of Florence. The medium for its message is water: the symbolic reconstruction, within the garden, of the river system of the Florentine region, with its orderly sequence of basins, grottoes and fountains, is an allegory of the good governance of Duke Cosimo. In the centre of the terraced surface in front of the villa stands the fountain of Hercules and Antaeus by Bartolomeo Ammannati, representing the rivers Arno and Mugnone. Surrounded by a grove of cypresses, further along the axis, originally stood Giambologna's Fountain of Venus emerging from the waters, an allegory of the city of Florence. In the eighteenth century the lower terrace was

Setting collections of ancient statues in gardens became a positive passion, and indeed at villa Medici (Rome) the garden was actually conceived in terms of the sculptures belonging to cardinal Giulio de' Medici; this engraving shows how they were to be distributed, and each statue has its own reference number. To the left is a mound with a path winding up to the summit, along which some of the statues were arranged.

Opposite: Modelled on the Belvedere, the gardens of Villa Medici in Rome, designed by Raphael, were structured as terraces cut out of the slope of the hill. Only the two Giants, by Baccio Bandinelli remain to guard the 'secret garden', sole remnants of the elaborate system of statues for which Villa Medici was famous.

given a new and simpler layout by the Lorraine family: the cypress grove disappeared and the Venus was moved to the Medici villa of Petraia; the entire vast sloping area was divided up by regular flowerbeds bordered by box and decorated with pots that still contain the famous collection of old citrus plants, with several hundred varieties of orange, lime, bergamot and lemon.

From here the visitor goes down onto the middle terrace, known as the Terrace of the Lemon Trees, with the famous *Grotta degli animali* (Grotto of the Animals) opening up in the middle of the retaining wall supporting the upper terrace. Here three large niches hold marble basins with groups of bronze and marble animals rising above them. Framed by rich wall decoration with masks and friezes of coloured stones and shells, these splendid polychrome sculptures by followers of Giambologna create a magical and fantastical atmosphere: animals like the unicorn and the giraffe, the bear and the lion, but also the dog

and the goat, together with the *giochi d'acqua* which surprise the unwary visitor, are a first example of the extravagance that was to characterize later Mannerist creations.

Above the grotto, in the centre of a huge rectangular pool surrounded by oaks and ilexes, towers Ammannati's bronze statue of a chilled-looking old man symbolising the month of January, and also the Apennine. Together with the grotto, this statue — whose waters feed the various fountains in the garden — is an allusion to the hills and springs where the rivers that flow through Florence and its plain originate, and it thus completes the celebratory allegory formed by the cycle of water.

Behind the Apennine was a wooded area for hunting, the *selvatico*, intersected by the small straight paths of the *ragnaia*, the typical plantation of trees and shrubs for bird-catching.

The Boboli gardens, conceived as a more public and celebratory setting for palazzo Pitti, a city residence, are completely

This and previous two pages: Although the box compartments were remodelled in the sixteenth century, the villa at Castello (above Florence) still retains much of the appeal it had at the time of Cosimo de' Medici (1537—1569). Laid out on a gentle slope, it consists of several terraces running from the top of the hill down towards the façade of the building. The most interesting aspect of the

garden at Castello is the complex iconographical programme devised as a status symbol for the figure of Cosimo: a sophisticated system of statues and fountains, for instance of Hercules and Antaeus (below), an allegorical reference to the rivers running through the Florentine plain, and the famous Grotta degli animali (left), symbolising the duke's good governance over both the waters and the city.

different. Also begun by Tribolo, Boboli and Pitti were no longer the inspiration of a single figure seeking outward expression of his prestige, as had always previously been the case with *ville suburbane*; they were a symbol of the Medici dynasty as a whole. At Boboli, the whole space was devised to flaunt Medici splendours: the palazzo overlooked a large natural amphitheatre, a green hollow, serving a double purpose. Here practical and aesthetic functions merged: the amphitheatre was at once a vast celebratory stage-set, and an ideal place for court festivities and entertainments. Tribolo's original layout, subsequently partly altered by Bernardo Buontalenti and Ammannati, made use of a single central axis: from the *fontana del Carciofo*, near the palazzo, notionally crossing the ampitheatre, this axis guides the eye towards the top of the hill, to the fish-pool of Neptune and the upper terraces, and further westwards right up to the walls of the fortress of the Belvedere. Like Castello, Boboli too has its own

magical grotto. Begun to a design by Vasari as a setting for Michelangelo's unfinished *Prigioni* (Slaves), it was subsequently completed by Buontalenti: three successive spaces house sculptural masterpieces, pastoral and mythological scenes, spectacular decorations in mosaic and fake sponge, creating an atmosphere where the imagination distinctly lords it over reason. The sense of order so apparent in the Renaissance garden is here displaced by a taste for the bizarre and fantastical, though certain intellectual and learned superstructures also continue to proclaim the ruling ascendancy.

The present-day Boboli gardens have retained little of their original appearance: additions and alterations succeeded one another throughout the sixteenth and seventeenth centuries; the great green amphitheatre was transformed into a permanent architectural structure by flights of stone steps along its sides, giving it a distinctly 'built' appearance. The garden was also

Two great artists who worked on the Medici gardens were Bartolomeo Ammannati and Giambologna. Under the guidance of Bernardo Buontalenti, Ammannati made the gigantic sculpture personifying the Apennine, which projects into the large pool at Pratolino (left); Giambologna made the statue of the chilled-looking old man at Castello, symbolizing both the month of January and the Apennine (right).

extended towards Porta Romana to the east, with a second axis at right angles to the previous one, in the form of a long sloping avenue known as the 'Viottolone'. Giulio and Alfonso Parigi laid out two adjacent areas as *bosquets* and mazes, and created the garden of the Isolotto at the end of the vista. A large space was opened up in a clearing, with an elliptical basin surrounded by a marble balustrade, an *Isolotto* (small island) at its centre, approached by two small bridges on which stood the Fountain of the Ocean by Giambologna, with the statue of Neptune rising above three figures symbolizing the great rivers of antiquity, the Ganges, the Euphrates and the Nile. This new layout already had something of the theatrical and the spectacular which was to become so prevalent in the gardens of the mature Baroque.

In the nineteenth century the Boboli gardens were once again remodelled according to English landscape taste, and the *bosquets* around the Viottolone were given the more natural appearance typical of the romantic era. Other Medici gardens were similarly transformed, but the most serious loss was the destruction of the sixteenth-century gardens at Pratolino, created between 1568 and 1581. One of the most glowing examples of the garden of marvels, Pratolino was the fruit of the genius of Buontalenti, and here the rigid Renaissance rules were supplanted by prodigiously elaborate and fantastical Mannerist devices. Commissioned by Francesco I for his mistress Bianca Capello, the garden of Pratolino was a piece of complex hydraulic machinery famous throughout Europe for its wonderful *giochi* and *scherzi d'acqua*. Among its trees, flowers and freely roaming animals water was the garden's protagonist, omnipresent in a thousand forms. Basins and pools, fountains, waterfalls and rivulets, all fed by the pool with the towering statue of the Apennine attributed to Giambologna, conspired to create an incredible spectacle, arousing the utmost stupefaction in guests and visitors. But the Mannerist love of contrivance that reached its apogee at Pratolino, failed to ensure its survival: the garden was destroyed in 1819 and redesigned *all'inglese*. All that remains of the original is the lonely Apennine.

Pratolino, seen here in a lunette from the well-known cycle of the Medici villas painted by the Fleming Giusto Utens in 1600: a truly spectac-ular garden with count-less fountains, giochi d'aqua *and* automata.

Opposite: The seveteenth-century, garden of the Isolotto at Boboli, with Giambologna's Fountain of the Ocean in the centre, offers a foretaste of Baroque theatricality.

The Sala d'Ercole in the palazzo Farnese at Caprarola. The nymphaeum was one of the most frequent motifs derived from ancient models. Before becoming the sine qua non *of any garden, it served as a learned and sophisticated decoration for the interior of a great house.*

Giochi d'acqua *were another noteworthy feature in the gardens of the time. A symbol of the owner's mastery over nature, the coercing of water into elaborate fountains ensured spectacular effects, as in the countless examples at Villa d'Este in Tivoli; the Fountain of the Dragons sent out powerful intermittent jets of water rising upwards and outwards so as to form a sort of 'water wheel'.*

FONTANA DE DRAGHI DETTA LA GIRANDOLA SOTTO IL VIALONE DELLE FONTANELLE

NYMPHAEA, GROTTOES AND GIOCHI D'ACQUA

Of the many classical features reinstated during the sixteenth century, one of the most widely used in the Renaissance garden was the nymphaeum. Sacred to nymphs and river gods, in ancient Rome the nymphaeum was essentially a vaulted room characterised by the presence of water: monumental fountains and triumphal arches were built in large niches and apses, from which streamlets flowed and fountains gushed, a welcome source of coolness on hot summer days.

In the Renaissance, the first building conceived essentially as a nymphaeum in relation to a garden was the casino Colonna at Gennazzano, near Rome. Reliably attributed to Donato Bramante and now in ruins, it was a pavilion of several rooms set against the slopes of a small valley. Here — not far from palazzo Colonna in the centre of the town — a large nymphaeum, with a portico overlooking a small stream, served as the destination for leisurely strolls and open air entertainments.

Built around 1550 for Pope Julius II, the nymphaeum at Villa Giulia in Rome was also closely related to a building. Situated between the villa and the garden, it opens up beneath a semicircular balustrade: here, at the feet of four caryatids arranged in a semicircle as supports for the balustrade, the water runs around a mosaic pavement, also of classical inspiration.

A recurrent motif in Renaissance thought, the notion of art as both imitation of and improvement on nature, meant that the nymphaeum, as a place sacred to river gods, tended to have more naturalistic implications, to the detriment of architectural design. The serene classicism of the early sixteenth century was transformed into an interest in natural curiosities and eccentricities. Exotic plants and animals, rare minerals and 'monstrosities' were removed from *studioli* and *wunderkammern*, into the magical and fantastical spaces of grottoes. Niches

became larger and more numerous, with whimsical rustic decorations in pumice, artificial sponge and other encrustations. The host of petrified animals in the grotto at Castello was widely imitated, for instance in the Fountain of the Elephant in the castle of Catajo in the province of Padua. Human figures were created out of strange materials, taking on weird attitudes like those of the sculptures and grotesques in the grotto at Boboli and the nymphaeum at Villa Barbaro at Maser. Wall decorations, which in the early sixteenth century had taken the form of grotesques, in imitation of the decor discovered during the excavation of underground rooms of classical buildings, developed into picturesque three-dimensional compositions made from coloured stones and pebbles, shells and stalactites.

The incredible versatility of water and the passion for the rare and the spectacular, also led to the rediscovery of automata, mobile figures worked by hydraulic mechanisms in antiquity and described in the classical treatises. Now positive gardens of wonders were created, dotted with *giochi d'acqua*. The fountains, cascades and 'water-wheels' at Villa d'Este at Tivoli were famous throughout Europe, but Pratolino was the garden most admired and copied. Set into the base of the villa, a series of grottoes sparkled, their walls encrusted with minerals and crystals, and in the garden ingenious hydraulic mechanisms activated all manner of marvels: gods playing instruments, singing birds, branches of coral from which real water gushed, impertinent and unexpected jets of water falling upon the unwary guests, multi-coloured basins and fountains. The passion for automata, grottoes and *giochi d'acqua* spread first among the French, but became a feature of the gardens all over Europe during of the eighteenth century. The Arcadian, more 'natural' feel of the landscape garden was to transform these compositions into something wilder and more rustic: stalactites and artificial encrustations gave way to more faithful imitations of nature, and grottoes became ghostly life-like caverns.

From Renaissance to Mannerism

The sack of Rome in 1527, with the devastation of the Eternal City by German mercenaries under the orders of Charles V, suddenly shattered humanism's deep faith in the close relationship between celestial order and earthly harmony. fomenting a mood of intellectual and cultural disquiet which, over the course of several decades, led to a deep change in artistic awareness. The faith that had viewed man's capabilities as an expression of the divine now faltered, and a new certainty took hold, in man no longer as God's creature, but as an individual.

From the middle of the century, Italian gardens were increasingly predicated on the celebration of the individual lord; as it lost its depth and originality, so symbolism now became a 'feature', to support a growing obsession with artifice and eccentricity. Like other forms of artistic expression, the garden became 'Mannerist'; the aim was no longer to recreate a sense of measure, like nature herself, but rather to configure ever vaster spaces dictated by an unbridled imagination.

The image of the turbulent city was countered by the ideal of a salubrious countryside, fertile and serene, and the garden once more became a retreat from urban turmoil and disorder; but, as we have already seen in the complex allegory of Castello, it now had a clear-cut celebratory purpose. In a world shaken by the fall of the mythically invulnerable Eternal City, and also of the Church, the garden was no longer an expression of perfection and cosmic harmony, but of personal power.

The pursuit of the strange, of the offbeat effect, the tendency towards exaggeration and over-emphasis typical of many Mannerist gardens, was now transferred to the plants themselves, which were frequently trained into the most outlandish or heraldic shapes, as we see from this illustration to the herbal I cinque libri di piante *by Pietro Antonio Michiel.*

Giardino del Bosco at Fonte Lucente near Florence. The term 'Mannerist' is used to describe the gardens created around the middle of the century that renounced typically renaissance rigour: they tended to be more extensive, and scattered with decorative features; their allegorical messages, too, became more complex. Flowerbeds took on novel shapes and greater attention was paid to the lie of the land.

Increasingly elaborate, the allegorical component now sometimes also became obscure, aimed solely at the initiate, replacing the symbolic systems once dear to the humanists with abstruse and cerebral excesses. A harsher and harder state of affairs inspired a different way of understanding nature, with an eye to her weirder, more bizarre and monstrous manifestations. The architectural composition of space thus became more sweeping and more complex; the layout of the garden, while still dominated by a single axis, was now diversified, with orthogonal schemes which gradually acquired their own importance. Decorative elements proliferated, with any number of stairways, balustrades, fountains, belvederes and seats arranged among hedges and clearings.

Such elements became a challenge, inspiring the most dazzling creations. The rules of geometry continued to reign supreme, but each structure now had its own autonomy, albeit as part of a unitary design with its raison d'être in elaborate eulogistic iconographies for personal aggrandisement. As gardens grew in size, their relations with such structures changed accordingly; with the opening-up of preferred views over the countryside, the boundaries of the garden gradually became less rigid and noticeable, and the various geographical features were exploited, to create compositions of incredible intricacy. The garden itself not only adapted to the site, but was sensitive to its prominent features, angling them so as to demonstrate the owner's creative powers. Water chains and *giochi d'acqua*, automata, large-scale sculptures, grottoes and other fantastical elements left the visitor dazed with admiration.

Another feature of Mannerism was the complex articulation of inner and outer spaces: at Palazzo Te, in Mantua, house and garden are indissolubly interlinked in one unitary programme. Though already foreseen in the original plan by

Giulio Romano, the exedra which closes in the view at the end of the courtyard-garden was added later.

One of the first examples of Mannerism in architecture was Palazzo Te at Mantua, where the genius of Giulio Romano forged architecture, decoration and garden into one seamless whole. Here the canons of classical antiquity lost their severe nobility to become the instruments of a whimsical and image-laden style, sometimes verging on the grotesque.

The building has an open plan and the interior decorations themselves suggest wide space and views outwards. The transition from interior to exterior is mediated first by a loggia, then by a small masonry bridge over two large rectangular pools, and into the vast garden formerly complete with elaborate bays of clipped hedges. Palazzo Te has a small *giardino segreto* too, but one already distinguished by a typically Mannerist sense of whimsy: one side has a grotto with a rustic portal encrusted with imitation sponges, reminiscent of the entrance to a real cave. Inside, the wall decoration of painted stuccoes and shells is suggestive of a space both natural and magical, a pointer to the typical Mannerist taste for the odd and the bizarre that makes a passionate study of the virtues and characteristics of peculiar materials.

Masterpieces of Roman Mannerism

The gardens which princes and cardinals began to create in the Roman countryside from the second half of the century, outdoing one another in splendour and grandeur, are typically Mannerist in conception.

The same period, between *c.* 1550 and 1570, saw the creation, a few dozen miles apart, of three gardens that were the acme of the sixteenth-century art of the Italian garden: those of Alessandro Farnese at Caprarola, of Cardinal Gambara at Bagnaia and of Ippolito d'Este at Tivoli.

The grandiose works required to convert the fortress of Caprarola into a sumptuous palazzo, begun several decades earlier by Baldassare Peruzzi and continued by Antonio da Sangallo the Younger, were specifically conceived to proclaim the prestige of Alessandro and the Farnese family. An imposing pentagonal construction on four floors, it was built on the solid walls of the old fortress that towered dramatically over the modest houses of the little town.

Vignola was put in charge of the overall project, while the elaborate iconographical programme was devised by Annibale Caro, who lavished the greatest care on the building and its decoration. The palazzo at Caprarola thus became an intricate pictorial poem culminating in the marvellous cycle of frescoes in the Sala dei Fasti Farnesiani. The layout of the gardens adjacent to the palazzo, however, does not have the lavish celebratory character of the interior. The two small spaces laid out by Vignola are mainly traditional in approach: the two rectangular enclosures aligned behind the pentagonal building, below the Summer and Winter apartments, are divided up into four sections, subdivided in their turn into four regular flowerbeds, in an orderly and harmonious composition to be viewed from the windows of the building.

The garden of the Casino, on the other hand, created some years later on the hill behind the palazzo, is completely different in character, and profoundly innovative. Set well away from it, at the end of a long avenue, a clearing opens up in a dense wood of ilex, cypress and oak, a genuine 'green room'. with a pavilion to which the Cardinal could retreat in his leisure. Around it, on a slight slope, Vignola arranged an orderly sequence of staggered levels centred on a single axis, the back-

The nymphaeum at Villa d'Este on Lake Como, built for the powerful Cardinal Tolomeo Gallio around 1568, is a typical example of the most sophisticated Mannerist taste. Here the nymphaeum becomes the vehicle for a passion for highly original natural materials: two side-scenes in the form of wide exedras, decorated with herms, niches and pinnacles, are entirely clad with mosaic decoration in coloured pebbles, refracting the light reflected from the waters of the lake.

bone of the composition, with the Casino at its centre.

The visitor approaches from below, where a square clearing with a circular pool in its centre, a sort of entrance hall, leads to a splendid water chain; framed by two pavilions decorated with grotesques and cut into the retaining walls, in the centre of a ramp running up the slope, a cascade of water flows along elegant stone scrolls carved with small basins and dolphins.

Proceeding in the opposite direction from that of the flow of the water, at the top of the ramp we enter a sort of oval room with the Fountain of the Rivers, enclasped by two circular staircases leading to the upper level. Here, in a kind of secret garden, with bays of yew hedges and bounded on three sides by balustrades with statues, we find the Casino with its double loggia.

At each side of the building two flights of stairs lead to an upper level, that of the entrance to the second floor of the Casino, to the rear. The balustrades feature water flowing through small basins and stone dolphins. A wide *piazzale*, decorated with splendid pebble mosaic paving and the *fontana del Giglio* (of the Lily), the emblem of the Farnese, continues as a slight grassy slope of small terraces with shallow flights of steps decorated with grotesques, and ends in the theatrical exedra of the Nymphs, the focal point of the perspective, against the backdrop of a wood.

But the great leap forward for the Mannerist development of the sixteenth-century garden was Villa Lante at Bagnaia, some dozen miles away. Unlike at Caprarola, at Bagnaia the villa takes second place: broken up into twin *casini*, built at different periods but undoubtedly anticipated in the original

At Caprarola the absolutely regular layout is given a sense of movement by changes in level, and by the plasticity of its ornamental structures. Designed along a single axis, the garden unfolds along a route punctuated by various remarkable decorative features, such as the spectacular water chain centering on the Casino. The spaces succeed one another as elements in a composition with an increasingly private and intimate character, cradled in dense surrounding woodland.

project; it is quite simply a complement to the garden. Placed symmetrically either side of the central axis along which the entire composition unfolds, the two pavilions appear part of the decoration of the garden, like side-scenes juxtaposed to frame the perspective and emphasize the garden's axial lie.

The garden was based on a pre-existing *barco* for hunting, created at the beginning of the sixteenth century for Cardinal Gambara of Brescia: on becoming Bishop of Viterbo in 1566 he became the owner of Bagnaia, one of the city's episcopal possessions. The many features common to this garden and that of the casino at Caprarola, and the close relations between Gambara and the Farnese Cardinal, have led to Bagnaia being traditionally attributed to Vignola, though no reliable documentation exists apart from some letters between the two Cardinals. But the dates — Vignola died in 1573 — leave room for doubt: certainly the presence in Bagnaia of Iacopo Del Duca, who had been active at Caprarola, might corroborate an original plan by Vignola that Del Duca himself completed. At all events, the close relationship between the two gardens is evident not just from their layout — in both cases the garden follows a central course laid out over the slope of a hill — but above all in the repetition, at Bagnaia, of elements like the water chain and the Fountain of the Rivers also found at Caprarola. Although the overall area is of relatively modest dimensions, Villa Lante embodies the Renaissance ideal of a unity of elements within a harmonious geometric whole: an area of four hectares is covered with five superimposed terraces made up of modules of rectangular enclosed areas, extending up over a gradient of some fifteen metres. A symmetrical series of alternating squares and rectangles, subdivided into further bays, emphasizes the axis of perspective; water is also a dominant presence, running straight along the central axis, punctu-

ated by circular fountains and vertical jets. Ideally, the route to be followed through the garden runs uphill; as at Caprarola, from the entrance level the visitor proceeds in an inverse direction to the flow of the water, in a movement faintly reminiscent of the typical gait of the crayfish — the Cardinal's emblem, repeated at various points throughout the garden — which moves forwards over land and backwards in water.

The water cycle follows a complex symbolic system alluding to the history of the world, from the mythical Age of Gold to the Cardinal's own epoch, in a narrative where water, assuming a variety of different forms, combines with sculpted stone to create superbly decorative compositions. Above, the water rises as a shower of rain in the Fountain of the Flood, an apparently natural cave overlooking a pool, set between two small classical pavilions dedicated to the Muses: they symbolize the two peaks of Parnassus emerging from the waters of the Flood, and mark the end of the Age of Gold from which everything subsequent develops. Water reappears further down in the Fountain of the Dolphins, in an enclosed area with an octagonal basin representing the ocean, bordered by low box hedges; the fountain, which originally stood beneath a temple covered by greenery and imitation coral, takes its name from the sixteen pairs of dolphins which decorate it. A few steps lead down to the sloping terrace from whose centre the famous 'chain' begins. Here the water, gushing from the claws of a crayfish, runs downwards along an exquisitely decorated stone channel, at the end of which it is collected and then propelled upwards to feed the Fountain of the Giants. This is a monumental sculptural group consisting of a semicircular basin and two reclining river gods set against the retaining wall of the terrace. Water appears again, as if by magic, in the centre of a curious long stone table, where it runs in a channel originally used for

(Left) Caprarola. The motif of the water chain formed of small richly decorated basins is repeated on the parapet of the staircases to the *sides of the Casino; these link the terrace, subdivided by box hedges, to the upper terrace to the rear of the building.* *(Right) Standing on its exquisite pavement of cobbles and mosaic, the Fountain of the Lily is framed by the exedra of the Nymphs.*

Situated at the entrance to the garden at Bagnaia, the Fountain of Parnassus, with Pegasus and the nine Muses, introduces the visitor into an all-pervasive and complex symbolism.

The ground plan of Villa Lante at Bagnaia is very similar to that of nearby Caprarola. Here too the garden follows a linear course which is the backbone of the whole design. The real innovation at Bagnaia is that the garden utterly dominates the villa, which takes the form of twin pavilions.

cooling wine, to disappear again to feed the Fountain of the Lights. A typical Mannerist creation, this fountain is an elaborate circular composition on six superimposed levels: half cut out of the retaining wall and half projecting outwards from the lower terrace, its design is reminiscent of the double concave-convex staircase in Bramante's exedra in the courtyard of the Belvedere. It takes its name from the sixty jets which spout up from it, and which 'look like so many silver candles in their candlesticks', according to a description dating from the time of Gregory XIII's visit in 1578. From here two stairways set up against the Casino lead down to the elaborate composition of basins on the lower level, its flawless geometry symbolizing man's gradual mastery over the world, and nature, through his cultivation of reason and knowledge. Extremely complex in design, this level is subdivided into sixteen sections, with the four central ones forming the monumental fountain of the Square. In the centre of four square basins surrounded by balustrades, each complete with its own small fountain-boat, is a circular fountain with three superimposed basins. Once overlooked by a circular pyramid sending out innumerable jets, as we learn from Michel de Montaigne in his *Diary of a Voyage to Italy* in 1581, it was remodelled after 1590 by Cardinal Alessandro Peretti Montalto, the nephew of Sixtus V, who replaced the pyramid with a sculpted group of four figures supporting the Montalto coat-of-arms. Here, by reducing nature to its own serene if rigorous ends, architectural artifice testifies to man's newly acquired mastery of his surroundings.

The bays of flowerbeds which originally surrounded the fountain were replaced, probably around the end of the seventeenth and the beginning of the eighteenth centuries, by the more subtly flowing lines of a *parterre à la francaise*.

In 1656 the villa at Bagnaia passed into the hands of the Lante della Rovere, who lived in it for almost three centuries. Today it belongs to the state, which maintains the garden perfectly, ensuring a balanced dialogue between tranquillity and fast-flowing water, between the light-filled splendour of the fountains and the shade of the woods which surround them.

The Mannerist passion for artifice and invention reached its peak in the Villa d'Este at Tivoli: here the powerful Cardinal Ippolito d'Este, the son of Lucrezia Borgia and Alfonso I Duke of Ferrara, had ambitions to eclipse the splendours of Caprarola belonging to his great rival, Alessandro Farnese. If at Caprarola the building dominated the garden, and at Bagnaia the opposite occurred, at Tivoli the composition is perfectly balanced, and the celebratory iconographical apparatus is in evidence in both the rooms of the villa and the numerous decorative features of the garden. As a fitting complement to the great villa, this is naturally larger in size, to maximize the effect of its astounding architectural and hydraulic marvels, and to assert the power and greatness of its owner.

Pirro Ligorio began work in 1560, when Ippolito d'Este, now governor of Tivoli, came into possession of a house there built on the site of an old convent. Though the main structures were finished by 1575, further additions and embellishments were added over a further fifteen years. The laying out of the garden required extensive excavations to level the steep gradient, which had a double incline: the wide expanse of natural terracing below the villa sloped down towards the north-west, while to the east it was bounded by a sheer wall of rock. 'Together, the art of men, and the power of the Cardinal of Ferrara, coerced and shattered the nature of the place...' according to a contemporary account, written in 1576 to give

Villa Lante, Bagnaia. Here too there is a water chain, but dophins are replaced by two crayfish (gamberi), a reminder that the garden's creator was Cardinal Gambara, Bishop of Viterbo.

Villa Lante. Water and fountains were the mainstay of the late sixteenth-century garden. Until the wonderful giochi d'acqua at Tivoli revolutionised garden design, the models were still canonical: the pairs of dolphins decorating this fountain symbolize the ocean, while its hexagonal form looks back to the typology of the medieval basin.

an idea of the scope of the work required to create the five terraces, linked by ramps and stairways to the villa above, looking out over the valley of the Aniene. Once again, in all probability, the model was the temple of Fortune at Palestrina, which Ligorio had studied in detail during those same years.

The double incline, however, inspired Ligorio to create a completely novel work: once a main axis centred on the villa had been put in place, he flanked it with a series of terraced avenues at right-angles, creating numerous lines of direction alternative to the main one. The result was a varied and intricate scheme, suggesting no clearly defined, *a priori* approach; each of the numerous architectural features that composed it — sculpted groups and fountains placed as backdrops to the avenues — was independent of the others, though linked to them by relations of perspective and allegorical allusions. The last of the five terraces, running over a wide plain, was regularly and symmetrically punctuated by pools and bays either side of the central axis, closed in to the east by a series of elaborate fountains built into the hillside and with a sweeping view to the west over the valley below.

Monumental fountains and fabulous *giochi d'acqua* were the main attraction: the fountain-makers at the Villa d'Este used the most advanced hydraulic techniques of the day to obtain the maximum number and variety of spectacular effects: soaring water-spouts, water bubbling along the balustrades as in a hot spring, cascades and 'water-wheels', veils of water falling fanwise from the edges of the basins, organs with sound-making automata, were all activated by sophisticated hydraulic bellows fed by water from the Aniene, which they channelled upwards and then drove downwards again.

One particularly original feature was the Avenue of the Hundred Fountains, the axis parallel to the front of the villa

Villa Lante. The so-called group of the 'Four Moors' in the centre of the Fountain of the Square gets its name not from the fact that the carved figures represent so-many Moors, but from the particular dark patina assumed over time by the peperino from which they are carved.

Villa Lante. As often happened in historic gardens, not all the sections date from the same period: additions, replacements and simplifications, together with the transient nature of the vegetation itself, brought about considerable modifications to the original design. Apart from the anachronism of the hydrangeas planted throughout, the very lovely box decorations of the flowerbeds are clearly in the French style and were put in place by the Lante family in the eighteenth century, replacing previous ones now regarded as outmoded.

As we see from the ground plan of the garden at Villa d'Este, the spaces were now articulated in a more complex manner than in earlier layouts. There was no longer a single main axis, but rather a variety of elements interlinked by numerous avenues. If one main orientation centred on the villa did persist, the possible routes to be taken were now more numerous, and forms had become freer. At Tivoli the visitor, dazed by such grandeur, could actually lose his way.

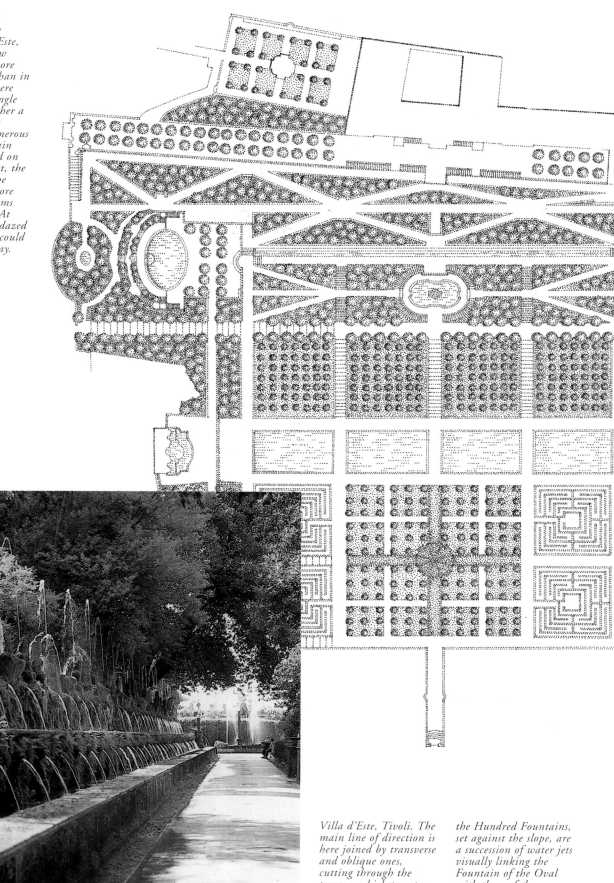

Villa d'Este, Tivoli. The main line of direction is here joined by transverse and oblique ones, cutting through the terraces which punctuated the garden; along the so-called Pathway of the Hundred Fountains, set against the slope, are a succession of water jets visually linking the Fountain of the Oval with those of the 'Rometta' which can be seen in the background.

which links the *fontana dell'Ovato* (Fountain of the Oval) to the sculptural group of the 'Rometta'. The water overflows from the tall central basin of the Fountain of the Oval, producing a veil-like effect, with the water falling into the oval basin below. The fountain represents the town of Tivoli; the three statues set into the rock are the three local rivers, the water which gushes from above alludes to its famous fountains and the grottoes opening up in the exedra behind the basin stand for the *monti Tiburtini* (Tiburtine hills). The water which collects in the basin of the Ovato feeds the series of 25 small fountains — in the shape of boats, the fleur de lys and the Este eagle — which run along the avenue of the Hundred Fountains, built against the retaining wall and sending their high jets into a small channel. At the end of the avenue is the so-called 'Rometta', a peculiar structure portraying the Seven Hills of Rome of which little remains, conceived as a complex of sculptures it also functioned as a highly original fountain with innumerable jets.

The other remarkable hydraulic creation at Tivoli is the Fountain of the Organ: a monumental composition beneath a grandiose architectural façade, a foretaste of Baroque developments to come, in its centre was an aedicule originally containing an organ activated by water. The same device is found again in the *fontana della Civetta* (Owl Fountain), where a hydraulic machine activated a little owl and a group of birds, causing them to emit pleasant if unexpected sounds.

The iconographic programme of the garden was based on the repeated theme of virtue triumphing over vice, also found in the rooms of the villa: the Grotto with the beautiful Venus contrasted with that of the virtuous Diana, thus allowing the visitor to choose whether to take the easy route leading to the former, or the more arduous one leading to the latter. The Cardinal's celebrated virtue, victorious over vice, was repeatedly alluded to by the myth of Hercules, the symbol of strength and the Este's protector, and by the myth of the Greek Hippolytus, the chaste priest of Minerva. The symbolic references to Hercules made allusion to the splendid gardens of the Hesperides more obvious, outshone as they now were in the Cardinal's gardens by opulence and beauty: pots of citrus plants were lavishly scattered throughout, while several varieties of espaliered limes bordered the lower avenue and the square mazes of the vast terrace, long since vanished.

The abundant water of its pools and fountains, its endlessly varied sculptures and architecture, made Villa d'Este one of the most famous gardens in the world, and indeed many pleasure gardens and places of entertainment have been named after Tivoli, best-known being the public garden in Copenhagen.

At the same time as these fantastic and monumental gardens, many less exalted gardens of more modest dimensions were coming into being, places of delight where more specifically Renaissance elements still lingered, as in the very beautiful garden of Castello Ruspoli at Vignanello. Set on a terrace supported by sturdy ramparts and linked to the castle by a drawbridge, it is a meticulously geometric composition of twelve bays of clipped hedges forming patterns and coats-of-arms, visible

Villa d'Este. The Fountain of the Oval is so-called because of the oval form of the receptacle from which the water spills out like a veil, but the subject of the whole composition is an allegory of Tivoli, its hills and fountains. When they were made, the fountains at Villa d'Este struck contemporaries as a veritable miracle of hydraulic expertise; equally astounding was the outpouring of money expended upon channelling the waters of the Aniene.

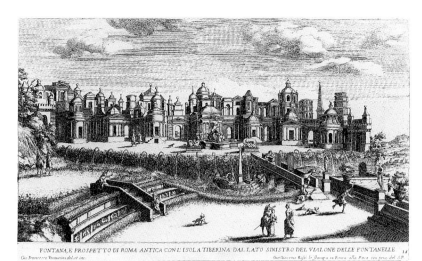

FONTANA, E PROSPETTO DI ROMA ANTICA CON L'ISOLA TIBERINA DAL LATO SINISTRO DEL VIALONE DELLE FONTANELLE

Villa d'Este. Originally, another feature of the complex programme of symbols and allegories had been the bizarre structure of the Rometta, a miniaturized version of ancient Rome and its buildings, from which jets of water issued in various forms to constitute one large fountain.

from the windows of the castle in all its regimented glory. We do not know exactly when it was laid out, but tradition, and the heraldic designs in the flowerbeds, would seem to point to Ottavia Orsini — the daughter of the more famous Vicino Orsini, the creator of the Sacro Bosco at Bomarzo — as its initiator in 1601, though the markedly traditional character of the whole composition would seem to imply an earlier date. With its enchanting *giardino segreto*, or *d'amore* (love garden), placed up against the ramparts below the main garden, Vignanello is a true masterpiece of the Renaissance art of the garden.

The development of the Italian garden: on hill and plain

If, during the sixteenth century, building activity was most intensive in the areas around Rome and Florence, many other villas and gardens were also created elsewhere in Italy. When commissioned by clients of more modest standing, gardens were usually more homely and less monumental, following purely Renaissance canons, devoid of whimsical Mannerist devices.

In the second half of the century, with the coming of the Genoese Republic and the rule of Andrea Doria, Genoa went through a period of great prosperity. The city's opulence became tangible with the construction of a number of villas set in very lovely gardens, almost all of which, unfortunately, have since disappeared. The hilly Ligurian countryside, overlooking the sea, or with sweeping views inland, was particularly auspicious for the art of the garden.

In 1543 Andrea Doria himself had commissioned Giovanni Antonio Montorsoli to design the gardens for Palazzo Doria. Laid out on a slight slope overlooking the sea, the gardens took the form of various superimposed terraces, both in front of the palazzo and behind. They ran along a central axis with a succession of fountains, pergolas and flowerbeds divided up by

The great fountain of the Rometta, now very incomplete, is in a state of serious disrepair.

Villa d'Este, Tivoli. The most theatrical of its fountains, the Fountain of the Organ, takes its name from the hydraulic organ in whose water pipes produced sounds similar to those of the instrument itself. The baroque aedicule above it, by Lorenzo Bernini, was added later.

(Below) Originally designed as a fortress by Sangallo, the villa of Ruspoli at Vignanello has one of the loveliest renaissance gardens in all Italy, which has survived intact. The hedges, made up of a variety of plants in the custom of the time, form intricate designs, most notably the initials of its creators.

(Above) Vignanello. From the castle windows the secret garden can be seen in all its glory; while certain gardens were yielding to the lure of Mannerism, in others the tradition of the renaissance garden persisted, conceived as one immense pattern to be viewed from above.

Villa Cambiaso, Genoa. Alessi's villas served as models for much aristocratic Genoese architecture: overlooking both sea and hills with wide loggias, they stand foursquare in the middle of their typically terraced gardens.

hedges. The large marble group with Neptune on his chariot — put there in 1599 to replace an earlier statue, also of Neptune, that stood in the centre of the long central axis — still survives, although part of the gardens was destroyed during the city's nineteenth-century extension.

The use of descending terraces was highly appropriate for the steep gradient, and indeed became standard, appearing within the city itself, where such little space as was available in the dense and compact medieval fabric had to be exploited to the full. The Strada Nuova too, the present-day Via Garibaldi, was being built during those years: an unbroken curtain of palazzi celebrating the prosperity of the merchant city, it was a novelty not just as a unitary piece of town-planning, but also for its typological solutions that were to become typical of Genoese building. The palazzi stood half-way up the hillside, against rocky escarpments, and the restricted external spaces originally created by excavation and embankments afforded the perfect site for wonderfully dramatic hanging gardens. Loggias, terraces and stairways combined to form little gardens like great open-air drawing-rooms, offering shade and coolness on hot summer evenings.

The cramped spaces of the city obliged Genoese noblemen and wealthy merchants to migrate to the surrounding hills, and a number of new villas were built there between 1550 and 1590, mostly designed by Galeazzo Alessi of Perugia.

The *villa suburbana*, with more space at its disposal, developed as a compact and eye-catching structure, with loggias on the ground floor overlooking the sea, and ones overlooking the

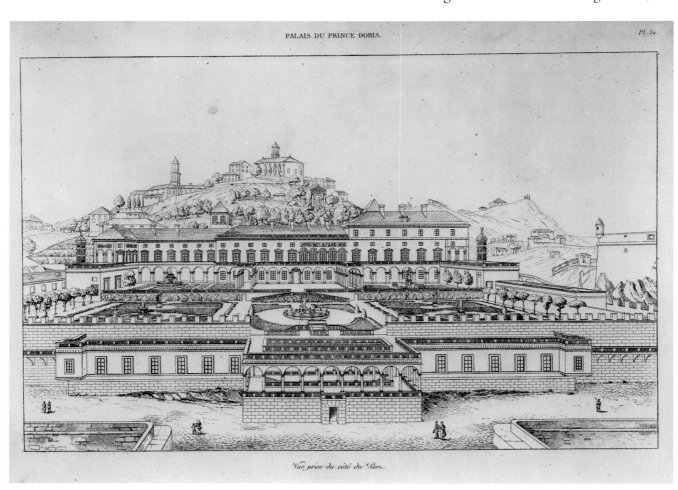

PALAIS DU PRINCE DORIA.

Pl. 52.

Vue prise du côté du Port.

The hilly terrain in and around Genoa favoured the development of terraced gardens sloping down towards the sea: the garden of the palazzo built for Andrea Doria, for instance, to a design by Montorsoli, overlooked the water with a loggia placed on an axis with the building. Much of this garden disappeared as the city expanded.

Although it has been remodelled several times, the Giardino Giusti, at Verona, still has its original sixteenth-century atmosphere. If the layout of the flowerbeds is clearly relatively recent, the young cypresses — evidence of the care with which it is maintained — put the visitor in mind of the splendid rows of such trees to be seen in the gardens when they were first created.

hills on the *piano nobile*, surrounded by gardens oriented in a north-south direction. As part of a richer, more complex composition, the gardens were highly dramatic spaces, perfectly suited to the coastal landscape. The layout of the descending terraces, arranged axially to the villa, was starkly geometrical, accentuating the verticality of the building.

In contrast to that of Liguria, the mainly flat and agricultural countryside of the Veneto gave rise to gardens of quite another kind. Over the sixteenth century, as the terra firma was relentlessly and ever more intensively exploited, the Venetian nobility were obliged to build themselves permanent dwellings in the main centres of agricultural production. One of the greatest architectural achievements of all, the many villas designed by Andrea Palladio, were incorporated into the landscape in a spirit of symbiosis with the surrounding land; they were conceived as working agricultural centres, which left little space for the creation of gardens.

The Giardino Giusti in Verona, a masterpiece of sixteenth-century Veneto architecture, was another matter. A Florentine family exiled from the city around the middle of the century, the Giusti built themselves a palazzo and a garden closer, in fact, to the Tuscan cultural tradition. But here the entire layout was a reversal of the typical Renaissance composition, with the villa on the hill and the garden extending in front of it, overlooking the valley; the building overlooks a broad plain,

which then rises suddenly to form a steep slope. The flat part is divided into regular sections edged with small box hedges flanking a central avenue of cypresses. From the end of the avenue a route lined with all the typical elements of the sixteenth-century garden winds up the steep incline slope: ancient statues and marbles, grotesques and grottoes seem to point to a symbolic itinerary clearly inspired by the ancient world. After a series of reconstructions and alterations, the garden was restored to its original state this century.

Among the few sixteenth-century gardens of northern Italy to have survived in a perfect state of preservation are those of Villa Cicogna Mozzoni at Bisuschio, in Lombardy: together with the building itself, these modestly-sized gardens are a perfect example of the sixteenth-century manorial residence. Despite several later additions and alterations, the peaceful walled space, overlooked by the ground-floor loggia of the villa, still retains its original character. Closed in by tall hedges, the garden consists of two rectangular basins bordered by a stone balustrade, with two beds of box surrounding two typically Renaissance fountains. Numerous jets of water rise from the basins with enchanting sound effects: while not part of any carefully designed system of *giochi d'acqua*, jets, basins and fountains give the garden a sense of freshness, as does the long water chain running down from the hill in the middle of a staircase.

The water chain in the garden of Villa Cicogna Mozzoni in the province of Varese is proof that the taste for elaborate architectural compositions permeated even the regions furthest from Rome and the countryside of Latium. Although never as grandiose as those of the great courts, smaller gardens too could boast all the typical components of the art of the garden.

Overlooked by the courtyard of Villa Cicogna Mozzoni, the garden appears as a perfectly proportioned, secluded space, which retains traces of the tradition of the medieval enclosed garden. Surrounding walls, basins, fountains and box hedges harmonize flawlessly with the façade of the building.

Brightly painted at the time, though only a few traces of colour now remain, the monstrous, gigantic sculptures of the Sacro Bosco must have aroused immense wonder and disquiet. As Vicino Orsini himself wrote in 1575, he had 'already added colour to several statues in the wood'.

ALLEGORY AND CAPRICE: THE SACRO BOSCO AT BOMARZO

In contrast with the rigid geometry of earlier gardens, the incorporation of the natural element at its freest and most unregimented, already found in the wooded settings around Caprarola and Bagnaia, became the central inspiration for the Sacro Bosco at Bomarzo near Viterbo.

At the foot of the small fortified town with the towering palazzo of the Orsini, in a dense thicket of oak and pine, enormous carved figures loom into view as if by magic: an apparently random horde of monsters, giants, sirens and demigods evokes a wild and wonderful world of nature. With a typically Mannerist love of weirdness and distortion, the Sacro Bosco seems to symbolize man's liberation from the abstract, geometrical symmetry of the Renaissance to rediscover an unknown, unpredictable yet natural universe, a foretaste of the realm of the possible which was to be the hallmark of the Baroque vision in the seventeenth century.

The brainchild of the luxuriant and fervid imagination of Prince Vicino Orsini (1532—85), this 'caprice' was created between 1552 and 1583, exploiting the erratic masses of peperino which had fallen from the hills to the bottom of a small shady valley. Pierfrancesco 'Vicino' Orsini was a noted eccentric: passionately interested in weaponry, literature, the fantastical and the esoteric, he shared his outlandish literary tastes with a wide circle of friends. Drawing inspiration from an astounding variety of sources, Orsini produced a highly original composition which he himself defined as 'a sacred wood which resembles itself alone, and like unto no other'.

Apart from a few pieces of evidence from literary sources, including the short description by Annibale Caro of 1564, little is known about this garden: originally coloured — as

Bomarzo is strewn with inscriptions, often obscure in meaning, indicating some sort of route to the visitor, who now embarks on a fantastical adventure. 'For your heart's ease, alone' seems to be the motto underlying Orsini's creation.

Particularly mesmerising is the figure of the dragon attacked by hounds, and here the Mannerist love of artifice is at its height: the dragon, an imaginary creature, is depicted defending itself so forcefully from its assailants that it becomes almost realistic.

'All you who wander through this world in search of awesome wonders, come hither, where you will find horrendous faces, elephants, lions, bears, ogres and dragons.' With this invitation, their creator beckoned the visitor into a magical world where rule and symmetry give way to the apparently haphazard, in a garden devoid of straight avenues or vistas, whose entire composition appears as a random succession of forms.

Orsini's own writings tell — and played upon by jets and fountains that have long fallen into disuse, the sculptural allusions were both specific and obscure and, despite the inscriptions carved into the monument, have still not been deciphered with any certainty.

The arcane symbolism, the dreamlike, weird and wonderful mood which characterised the Sacro Bosco, has been variously interpreted over time. It has been suggested that they imply a journey of initiation, towards some spiritual process of growth that gradually separated man from the beast within himself, or possibly one of release, as reflected in the inscription that seems to underlie the whole

composition: 'For your heart's ease, alone'.

The references in the garden are too various and disparate for us to be at all certain as to the intentions of this eccentric aristocrat. Incidents inspired by the *Dream of Poliphilus* and *Orlando Furioso* are found alongside references to styles like the Etruscan tomb and classically-inspired grotesque, and images taken from oriental fairy tales and Greek and Roman mythology. On one terrace, two sculptures symbolizing day and night might allude to the passage of time, while a statue with the attributes of Ceres, the goddess of agriculture, succeeded by the figures of a dragon, a sphinx, an elephant and a gigantic head with open

jaws, suggest the constant dangers threatening man. Guarding the staircase marking the end of the route through the Wood, and the small temple to Giulia Farnese, the prince's wife, are the dog Cerberus and the Sirens, both symbols of transition and change.

Today, just as much as when it was first created, the visitor is unsettled by this phantasmagoria of heroic images and exotic innuendoes, this dream with its cast of ghosts and monsters. Unsurprisingly, when Salvador Dali first visited the Sacro Bosco in 1949, he instantly succumbed to the surreal and magical aura emanating from this astounding intellectual caprice.

A model for all Europe

Although throughout the sixteenth century the Italian principalities suffered general political instability fomented by foreign territorial claims, Italian art and artists nonetheless dominated the European scene. The Italian garden, in particular, was broadly influential throughout Europe, and its underlying principles were gradually adopted as models for gardens beyond the Alps. Although each country and culture naturally tempered the characteristic elements to their local situation, nonetheless gardens conformed to the symmetrical layout, punctuated by geometrical sections and superimposed terraces. Sculptural and architectural features became frequent, and elaborate compositions making use of water became a *sine qua non*.

In England, where the end of the Wars of the Roses and the reign of the Tudors ushered in a period of regeneration, the stylistic features of the Italian garden were absorbed through the intermediary of French art, since many French gardeners had gone into exile in England for political or religious reasons. While they retained many typically English aspects, decorative motifs from France mingled with those of the Italian model in English gardens of this period.

Henry VIII's gardens at Hampton Court, at Whitehall and above all at Nonsuch were inspired by his ambition to outshine those of his great rival, François I of France.

One of the typical elements of this period was the mount garden: this traditional local feature was an artificial mount, or mound, with mistletoe, sacred to the Druids, growing on its summit. At Hampton Court this was replaced by a pavilion deriving from the Italian tradition. Another popular feature was the presence of heraldic symbols and beasts, like the lion and the unicorn, carved in wood or stone, brightly painted or gilded all over. Coats-of-arms and heraldic festoons were also used for the decoration of 'knot gardens', the term knot referring to the elaborate designs of the bays and flowerbeds of such gardens. Related to the *parterres* of the French garden, knots were narrow borders of low evergreen hedges, often of aromatic plants, inside which flowers, or, more rarely, white or grey-blue pebbles, formed backgrounds of a single colour. Flowers already played an important part in the English garden, reflecting the Anglo-Saxon love of colour under skies so often grey.

Towards the end of the century the Italian influence became more pronounced. Larger gardens began to conform to the Mannerist taste, with the introduction of one feature which was to become very popular in the English garden, the grotto, which made a first appearance at Nonsuch. In Holland, where the architectural canons of Alberti had been a key influence on garden development, references to the Italian garden were even more frequent. Often enclosed and compact, typically urban, these green spaces were made up of geometrical flowerbeds, and structures such as pergolas, pavilions and

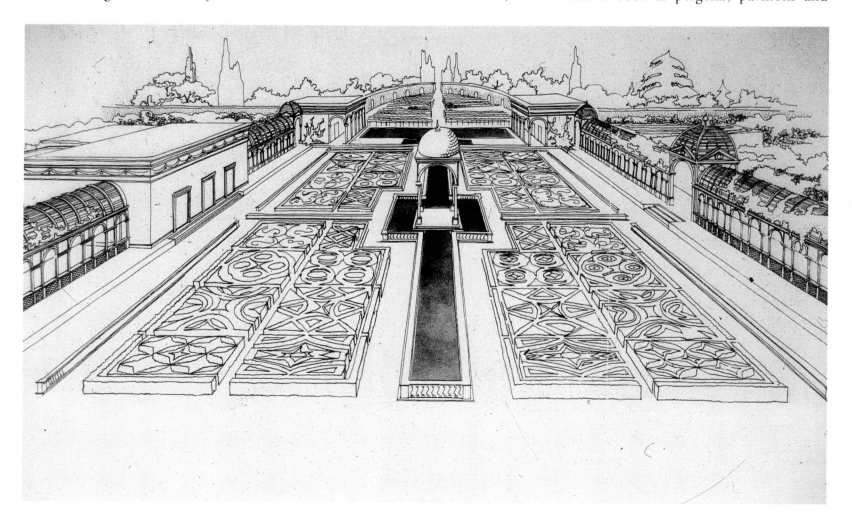

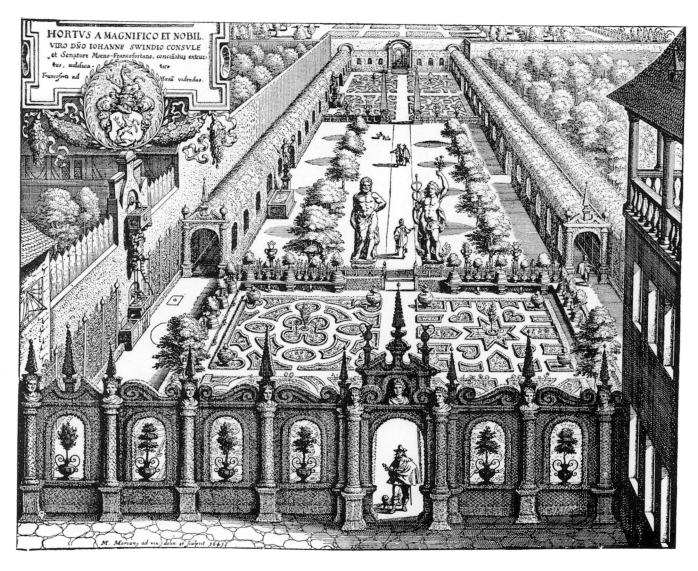

HORTVS A MAGNIFICO ET NOBIL. VIRO DÑO IOHANNE SWINDIO CONSVLE et Senatore Moeno-Francofortano, concinatus extructus, aedificatus Francoforti ad Moeni videndus.

M. Merian, ad viv. delin. et sculpsit 1641

Gardens throughout Europe, including those of the northern countries, were deeply influenced by the Italian Renaissance model, and Germany in particular continued to be influenced by them until the late seventeenth century. This engraving, dated 1641, of the garden of the burgomaster of Frankfurt, shows how closely garden and architecture were related; the decoration of the entrance seems to derive from the arcading shown in the woodcut from the Dream of Poliphilus reproduced on page 36.

The most important German garden in the renaissance style was the Hortus Palatinus at Heidelberg, created around 1620. The traditional river fountain makes an appearance here too with the very lovely Fountain of the Rhine, though the demigod in this version of the classical model is far less patrician, with more down-to-earth and human features.

(Opposite) A reconstruction of the gardens at Poggio Reale in Naples. The magnificent gardens of the Angevin court were the first model to be exported across the Alps: admired by Charles VIII of France, they formed a point of reference for the first sixteenth-century French gardens, for instance those of Amboise, Gaillon and Blois.

loggias. Topiary was particularly popular in Dutch gardens; the borders of the flowerbeds were frequently decorated with pots of clipped evergreens alternating with pots of flowers. The Dutch passion for flowers emerged as early as the sixteenth century, though the real vogue for botanical collecting did not sweep the country until the next century.

In Germany, on the other hand, the Italian influence made itself felt in the creation of botanical gardens following the model of those built in the main Italian cities during the sixteenth century. The first large garden influenced by the Italian style was the *Hortus Palatinus*, created at Heidelberg some time after 1620 by Salomon de Caus, a French Huguenot who had travelled in Italy before settling in Germany, and who had laid out various gardens on the Italian model in England at the court of the Stuarts.

It was in France, where the arrival of Italian artists in the train of Charles VIII had brought a rapid spread of the Italian style, that the rules of the Italian garden were first and most rigorously applied. Drawing directly on the early Italian Renaissance garden, the French adopted its principles in both layout and features, for example division into rectangular flowerbeds, marble fountains, pergolas and pavilions. This set the tone for the incredible artistic flowering of the French garden, that peaked in the masterpieces of the seventeenth century.

The French Renaissance

Throughout the fifteenth century French gardens were medieval in style — basically small kitchen gardens, enclosed and separated from the château by deep moats, where trees and fruit were grown for domestic consumption or recreation.

Charles VIII was captivated by his first contact with Italian taste and culture, in 1494, in particular by the gardens of the Aragonese court at Naples. He returned home taking twenty-two Italian artists with him. Among them was a Dominican friar, Pacello da Mercoliano, who had worked on the Neapolitan garden of Poggio Reale; it is he who is traditionally credited with introducing the Italian garden into France. Rigid compartmentalization into geometrical sections, planted alternately with flowers and fruit trees, adorned with heraldic insignia and topiary figures in box or rosemary hedges, now invaded spaces still characterized by the typical medieval layout. The utilitarian gave way to newly fashionable aesthetic ideals, and greater attention was paid to the garden's architectural

The nineteenth-century restoration of the garden at Chenonceaux, while it did not reproduce the original subdivision into squares planted with fruit trees and greenery surrounded by roses and pansies, still has something of the sixteenth-century mood of the time of Catherine de' Medici: the flowing lines created by slight hedges of lavender, together with the topiary spheres, anticipated the designs of the first French parterres *as they moved away from the geometrical stiffness of the garden* all'italiana; the small hibiscus trees, too, serve as a reminder that they were introduced in the sixteenth century.

(Opposite) Alessandro Francini, the brother of Tommaso, the creator of the great fountains at Pratolino, produced a series of engravings of the gardens of St-Germain-en-Laye and Fontainebleau at the time of Henri IV. This engraving (1614) shows the Grotto of Orpheus at St-Germain-en-Laye, one of the countless and spectacular giochi d'acqua *found throughout the garden.*

structures: pergolas, pavilions and fountains became more important than plants, with rickety wooden constructions gradually transformed into masonry. Increasingly sophisticated irrigation networks prompted research into a whole range of effects that could be obtained from water, and basins and fountains became prominent features in new gardens. Works of sculpture too took on growing importance in overall design.

The developing interest in ornament sometimes led to the import of items directly from Italy, as with the fountains in the gardens at Gaillon, created by Pacello for the Cardinal of Amboise, and the classical structures moved to Fontainebleau between 1540 and 1543 by Primaticcio and Vignola for the complex sculptural commissions of François I.

In the following years, with the extension of the gardens at Fontainebleau and Chenonceaux embarked on around 1560 by Catherine de' Medici, the wife of Henri II of France, Italian influence took a firm hold. Almost all the sixteenth-century gardens in France have now vanished, having been abandoned or remodelled in the seventeenth century. If, as at Fontainebleau, altered in the seventeenth century, the Renaissance layout is barely discernible, at Chenonceaux, unusually, the appearance of the garden has remained relatively unchanged.

Cÿ est La Grotte dOrphée qui est au Chau de S. Germain en Laye laquelle n'est que la façade ou sont les Mouuemens estant en la Seconde Gallerie au lieu Marqué F. aud portrait de S. Germain

The gardens lie either side of the wide courtyard in front of the château, which is built as a bridge with great piers spanning the river Cher. The eastern terrace, still separated from the courtyard by a canal, was built by Diane de Poitiers between 1551—55; today it has a Renaissance layout based on a late nineteenth-century restoration, with topiaried box, little flowering hedges of aromatic plants, flowers and small hibiscus trees. Catherine's garden, on the other bank of the river, has completely disappeared, as has the large circular *rocaille* fountain surrounded by trellises, which she had laid out on the terrace to the west of the courtyard.

During the last decades of the century, once the Italian model had been assimilated, the composition of the French garden became more structured and harmonious: Italian elements were no longer mere disjointed quotations. The project for the royal garden of St-Germain-en-Laye near Paris, clearly Italian in inspiration, was the first French garden to be conceived as a whole, as a harmonious fusion of its parts. At St-Germain the Italian influence was further reinforced by the presence of Tommaso Francini, who had worked with Buontalenti at Pratolino, called upon to supervise the construction of astounding hydraulic automata in imitation of those in the garden of Pratolino that were already famous throughout Europe.

The immense expanses of land available in the French countryside also made larger gardens feasible. At first this led simply to the creation of long tree-lined avenues culminating in great *cours d'honneur* leading to the château — as in the gardens at Anet, built between 1546 and 1552, also by Diane de Poitiers. Later it led to highly ambitious compositions like the projects for the gardens of Charleval and Verneuil-sur-Oise attributed to Jacques Androuet du Cerceau. These two gardens were never actually realized, but the designs for their intended layout already show how far they had moved from the limited confines of the Italian models, towards a greater complexity and openness to the countryside that were typical of the following century's mighty creations.

Undoubtedly the most important innovation introduced into the Italian garden during the sixteenth century was that of the *parterre*. In the second half of the century the strict geometrical squaring of the flowerbeds took on ever more complicated forms, to the point of creating whorls, scrolls and elaborate minglings of aromatic herbs, like hyssop and thyme, and other woody trees suitable for hedges. The first examples of this kind of *parterre* were created soon after 1580 in the garden at Anet, replacing the previous layout by Claude Mollet, founder of a veritable dynasty of gardeners who served the kings of France until the eighteenth century.

This particular design, reminiscent of the elaborate curlicues found in embroidery, was subsequently named *parterre de broderie*. Developed and refined in the following decades by Claude's sons, designs *à broderie* were to become one of the basic — and possibly best-known — components of the seventeenth-century French garden.

The reconstruction of a sixteenth-century layout in the gardens of Villandry by a Spaniard, Dr Joachim Carvallo, dates from the beginning of this century. Basing his designs on drawings and reconstructions, he used a series of box hedges around flower-filled beds for the making ab initio *of an ornamental garden, a* jardin d'amour *and a* jardin potager.

The elaborate design of the hedges recalled the symbolism dear to the sixteenth-century Romantic and courtly tradition, but the motifs of dagger blades, hearts, butterflies and masks bespeak the romantic reworking of the past typical of the early twentieth century.

VILLANDRY: THE RECREATION OF A DISTANT PAST

After 1870 a passionate nationalism spread through France, together with a desire to celebrate the artistic heritage of the past. In a widespread rediscovery of the seventeenth century, the *Grand Siècle*, the country was swept by an urge to reinstate the classical garden. Ambitious restorations that were in fact out-and-out reconstructions, followed one after the other in rapid succession right up to the First World War, thanks in particular to the work of two great landscape gardeners, Henry and Achille Duchêne. The gardens of the château of Villandry, in the Loire valley, were conceived in this mood of inspired and passionate historicism. In 1906 the château was acquired by the Spaniard Joachim Carvallo, who decided to recreate its gardens in the French Renaissance style. On the eighteenth-century terraces at the side of the manoir, built in 1536 for Jean Le Breton, Carvallo laid out the various characteristic components of the sixteenth-century French garden. On an axis aligned with the entrance avenue and *cours d'honneur*, an enchanting *jardin d'ornément* was laid out. Around a classical mixtilinear basin with water-jets, four-square flowerbeds with elaborately clipped box hedges represented the four kinds of love: hearts, flames and masks for *l'amour tendre*, butterflies and fans for *l'amour volage*, a maze of hearts for *l'amour folie*, and swords and dagger blades for *l'amour tragique*.

In spring, white carnations and tulips flower among the hedges amidst the blue of forget-me-nots, replaced in summer by dwarf pink and yellow dahlias. Just as these flowers reveal a twentieth-century taste, so too, typical sixteenth-century compositions would never have included box, introduced only after 1582, to divide up the flowerbeds: other plants were preferred, their differing shades of green

Sections in box, a species actually introduced only in the seventeenth century, form the figures of the crosses of Malta, Languedoc and the Basque Country. The forget-me-nots that give a touch of colour to the flowerbeds are clear evidence of twentieth-century taste. The series of restorations and reconstructions carried out over the nineteenth century and until the late twentieth further helped to confuse ideas of the plants traditionally grown in early gardens.

combining to great effect. Other ornamental designs close in the terrace towards the south; beyond an avenue of limes is a water garden, with a large basin linked to the château's moat by a canal.

The most interesting reconstruction is on the west side of the château: an area of approximately two and a half acres is occupied by nine large bays, each of a different geometrical design, forming a very lovely kitchen garden inspired by the traditional *jardin potager*. In the sixteenth century the château of Villandry was famous for its kitchen gardens, as we learn from a letter dated 1570 in which the Cardinal of Aragon, describing his visit to the pope, says that he had seen salads even more luxuriant than in Rome.

Inspired by the engravings of Jacques Androuet du Cerceau, collected in two volumes with the title *Les plus excellents bastiments de la France* (1576—79), the main documentary source for sixteenth-century French châteaux and gardens, Carvallo's nine elaborate dovetailed sections were surrounded by rows of fruit trees, with arches of climbing roses where the paths crossed. The result was a garden of herbs, vegetables and fruit whose colours turn magically from season to season: predominantly blue-green in spring; red, orange and pink in summer; and gold, yellow and green-bronze in autumn.

Joachim Carvallo's descendants maintain this exquisite garden with no less care and devotion than inspired its creator: in the same spirit, they have recently planted a garden of medicinal herbs, scrupulously applying the methods and techniques of Renaissance tradition.

The humanist passion for the reworking of the antique, characterizing the art of the sixteenth century, also reintroduced the classical tradition of decorating interiors with frescoed landscapes. Alongside epic and celebratory representations of the glories of the master and his ancestors, internal walls were adorned with idyllic and Arcadian landscape views, like so many windows opening on to the countryside. Further paeans to the power and prestige of the lord — already flaunted in the house and garden — these landscape scenes depicted the properties — farms, villages, castles and palaces — over which his power extended.

A manifest of one's possessions, a decorative feature that was also a display of wealth became an extremely popular, if secondary, artistic genre often practised by specialist painters in the same laudatory spirit as a more esteemed and elevated genre, portraiture.

In its earliest examples, the great houses were merely elements in a landscape or classical quotations, but this now-fashionable genre took on the precise detail of the portrait. The garden in particular, at first merely sketched in as an annex to the property and part of a general landscape, now gradually became an indispensable part of the villa, a sumptuous and vital conclusion to it, the protagonist of the painting, minutely represented in ground plan and ornament. The garden was no longer an ideal place where man garnered and marshalled the beauties of creation, but an elaborate vehicle for the celebration of the power of its lord, clearly recognizable to the visitor at a single glance.

THE REPRESENTATION OF THE GARDEN: PROPERTY DEPICTED AS A DISPLAY OF POWER

1

2

2. Caprarola, Viterbo. Painted by Federico Zuccari between 1566 and 1569, this view, showing the palace and town of Caprarola, completely excludes the garden: the aim was undoubtedly simply to decorate the walls of the room in which it stood, following the classical custom of frescoing idyllic landscapes in the interiors of dwellings as though they were a sort of opening on to the outside world. Here the reference to antiquity is highlighted by the grotesques which frame the work. The walls of another room in the villa also have a fresco of the property of Caprarola, together with others belonging to Cardinal Farnese, but again the garden is barely visible.

1. The Courtyard of the Belvedere, Vatican City. This fresco by Perin del Vaga depicts an aquatic battle taking place in the unfinished court- yard, which has been flooded for the occasion; such a spectacle aimed at emulating the festivi- ties and public enter- tainments of ancient Rome, and the pictorial technique itself seems to derive from the mural paintings in ancient villas.

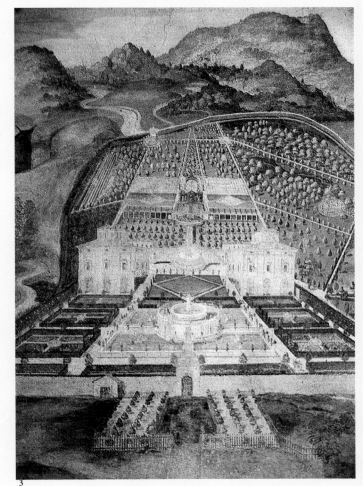

4. La Petraia, Florence. This is one of the seven- teen paintings commis- sioned from the Fleming Giusto Utens by the Grand Duke Ferdinando I of Tuscany to represent all his vari- ous estates. These were now positive 'portraits', show- ing each property in minute detail. The subject is neither villa nor garden, but the two together, considered as a single organism.

3. Villa Lante, Bagnaia (Viterbo). The real transition from a mere representation of a property, still shown in a generic fashion, to a detailed 'portrait' of the garden, attributed to Raffaellino da Reggio, occurs on the walls of Gambara's pavilion. Significantly, the tech- nique is that of the classical perspective taken from a very high hypothetical vantage- point, which makes it possible to take in the structure of the garden in all its complexity. The adjacent walls also have reproductions of other glorious villas around Viterbo.

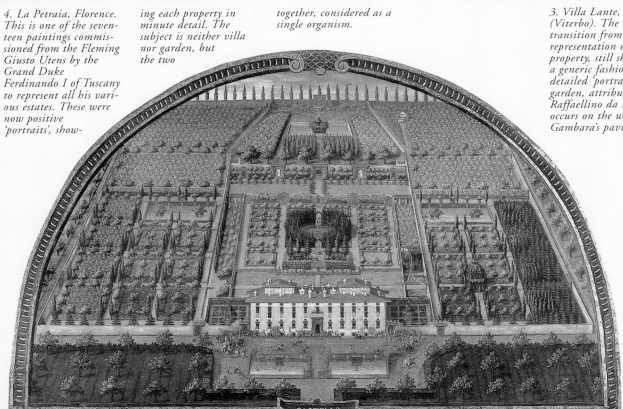

CASTELLO

The theatre of nature

The first half of the seventeenth century was a period of crisis throughout Europe. The wars of religion and separatist pressures and uprisings in the first decade culminated in the Thirty Years War in which all countries were embroiled from 1618 to 1648. The problems of war itself were compounded by a serious economic crisis and aggravated by plague, famine and a marked decline in population.

The Peace of Westphalia, which saw France established as a European power, introduced a period of greater stability. Advances in scientific knowledge and a dawning sense of objectivity led artists to interpret and represent nature more subtly and elaborately. On the other hand, absolutism, by dictating the rules of thought and action, affected every aspect of society and culture, with art no longer in the service of God, but rather of the sovereign. Thus was born the concept of official art: closely bound up with power, but also an instrument of consensus, Baroque art became the mouthpiece for an all-inclusive model of behaviour.

If the Baroque of papal Rome, with its Counter-Reformation values, found expression above all in religious and urban architecture, in the rest of Europe it proved to be an art more closely linked to the sovereign and the glorification of his power.

It was Paris, in the secular, worldly and absolutist France of the Sun King, that was to assert itself as the capital of art and culture in the second half of the century. The French Baroque broke away from strongly confessional patterns to become a true court art with highly original characteristics. Evolving from the principles and symbolic systems of the classical aesthetic, its magnificent and grandiose creations glorified earthly vanities, and were the emblems of release from all the conflicts and anxieties of the first half of the century.

Developing from Renaissance schemes, houses and palaces became elaborate organisms, consisting of the residence proper, the various service buildings, the garden and park, forming a unitary and indivisible

Arithmetic by Laurent de la Hyre, 1650. The design of the garden was added to the painting — an example of the interest in the natural sciences which matured over the course of the seventeenth century — at a later date, to emphasize the close ties between the structure of the garden and the rigours and beauties of calculus.

The theatricality and grandeur of nature as controlled by man are the hallmark of the seventeenth-century garden. Water, the versatile element par excellence, becomes the protagonist in the most intricate and dazzling compositions, such as this exquisite cascade at Chatsworth, Derbyshire.

(Opposite) Sceaux. The cascades.

(Opposite) The nymphaeum at villa Gamberaia at Settignano. The baroque idea of space was completely unlike its renaissance precursor, and in the garden too the landscape and setting acquired a particular importance by virtue of their relationship with the various architectural structures.

Bassin des Cerfs *(of the stags) at Sceaux. The great sheets of water are particularly magical in autumn when they reflect the flaming colours of the autumn trees.*

whole. In such complexes the garden played a vital role: a venue for spectacle and entertainment *par excellence,* in the seventeenth century it developed as a statement of power expressing itself precisely through radical transformations of the natural environment. Offering opportunities for a display of monumentality and magnificence, drama and spectacle, from being places for hunting and entertainment gardens became indispensable adjuncts to every prince's palace worthy of the name.

Such self-aggrandising aims transformed garden design. More flowing, less rigidly geometric and schematic forms began to predominate, with the unremittingly straight lines of the Renaissance garden now joined by the circular, elliptical and diagonal, opening up new vistas and introducing varied and less obvious perspectives. Dramatic and picturesque effects were

The central axis which formed the backbone of the garden favoured the lengthy vistas and panoramic swoops across the landscape typical of the seventeenth-century gardens in the Grande Manière, *of which Vaux-le-Vicomte was the first great example. Engraving by Aveline.*

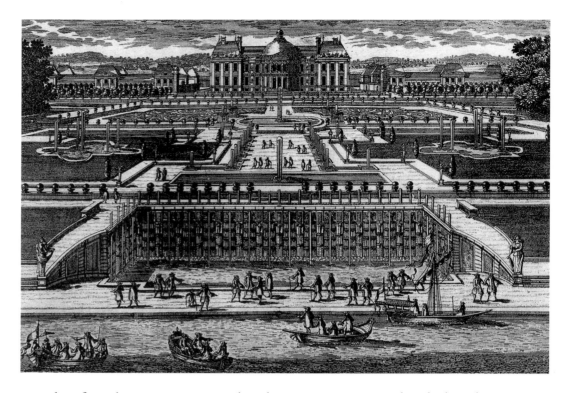

sought after, drawing nature and architecture into a single whole. The Baroque idea of space, in fact, envisioned the entire complex of house and gardens from the point of view of both vista and landscape. Part of the surrounding countryside became incorporated into the garden and remodelled, extending its dimensions and lengthening the views it offered. Landscape features with the most dramatic potential were exploited to the full: panoramic views determined the main lines of direction, gradients and sudden changes in height — particularly in smaller gardens — were turned to account for particular optical and panoramic effects. The presence of woods, hills and water courses became of primary importance in determining the layout.

This drawing-in of the countryside implied a new awareness of the natural elements: elaborate 'naturalistic' compositions, already experimented with in the Mannerist period, played a vital role in the grandiose creations of the Baroque. Artificial caves, cliffs and rocks appeared, fountains and nymphaea assumed larger dimensions; cascades and water chains were now the backbone of the composition, adding their own welcome touch of complexity and theatricality. Vegetation, previously rigidly dragooned, now acquired depth and volume through greater stress on the vertical; the symmetry of large clumps of trees was valued for their natural chiaroscuro.

These general characteristics, common to all Baroque gardens, were inevitably given an individual slant in each country. In Germany garden development was inevitably hampered by war. Detachment from Mannerist canons was slower in Italy and in the rest of Europe the principles of the Italian garden were gradually reworked to the point of producing works completely independent of their original model. In France after 1660 the power of Louis XIV and the genius of his garden designer André Le Nôtre were to impose a new model throughout Europe, above all with Versailles. Copied and emulated, ultimately it ousted the Italian model once and for all.

The *Grand Siècle* of the French garden

During the first half of the century France was engaged in the lengthy process — begun by Henri IV and continued by Richelieu and Mazarin — of bolstering royal power and settling internal conflict, that was to lay the foundations for the glorious reign of the Sun King.

As an official instrument, art was now the affair of the Academies, arbiters of aesthetic ideals and guardians of the country's cultural life. Absolutism and academicism went hand in hand with a resolute nationalism: under Henri IV (1589—1610) commissions for the great works of town-planning and royal gardens had already been given to French architects and engineers. If Italians still figured as designers of the Tuileries and St-Germain-en-Laye during the first decades of the century, from around 1650 French artists and technicians began to exercise a positive monopoly. Only painting and the decorative arts retained any links with Italian culture.

The long regency preceding Louis XIV's reign had seen the aristocracy become increasingly wealthy, with country residences, palaces and gardens springing up throughout the land. Though still conceived as an important complement to the house, the garden had already acquired a character of its own. Spaces became larger, clear boundaries vanished, compositions became more elaborate. But it was not just the structure of the garden that was changing: new features and forms were also being introduced.

The royal gardens in particular were places for experimentation and innovation. From the end of the sixteenth century, the French monarchy's passionate interest in and generous patronage of the arts had created extremely favourable conditions for all manner of fruitful collaboration between artists, and dynasties of gardeners developed new ideas as father gave way to son. From the end of the sixteenth century, families such as those of Mollet, du Cerceau and Le Nôtre worked for the royal court, assisted by the Francini, hydraulic engineers from Florence called Francine by the French, who were responsible for the fountains at Versailles. The innovative preeminence of these artists is reflected in the number of French expressions coined at this time and subsequently adopted in the international terminology of the garden.

The softer, more flowing lines that had replaced the rigid Italian division into compartments were gradually reworked as part of more complicated schemes; architectural structures were overlaid with vegetation, and water became a dominant element.

New designs were created, and new types of decoration experimented with for the *parterres*: dwarf box, introduced from Italy where in fact it was not much used and popular in France for its sweet-smelling leaves, began to take precedence over other species as a plant for borders. Architectural structures, which continued to be in wood or masonry throughout the sixteenth century, were now covered with clipped shrubs: the hornbeam, which was very easy to shape, was used in any number of geometrical forms — *charmilles*, from *charme*, the

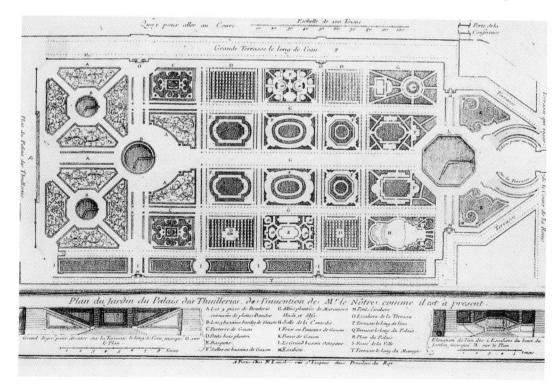

Engraving by Jacques Perelle of André Le Nôtre's plan for the gardens of the Tuileries. The stiff renaissance designs within the various sections, Italian in origin, were now replaced by more varied and supple compositions which were to become the paradigm throughout Europe.

Detail of a fountain at Versailles. Le grand gout, *the patrician taste predominant in seventeenth-century France, laid down the rules of art and decoration, which now served to glorify the sovereign's greatness. Ornaments became all-important and groups of sculpture and fountains became more frequent.*

French word for hornbeam, were hedges pruned to form green walls, also known as *palissades*. Green 'rooms', or *cabinets de verdure*, were created, sometimes with arcades; expertly clipped hedges formed full-blown architectural structures, complete with their own details and decoration. Expanses of water grew larger; alongside the traditional fountains and water staircases, vast pools and artificial canals were dug out to create wonderfully effective set pieces.

If architectural design had been predominant in the Italian garden, the French garden of the *Grand Siècle* was forged into an accomplished architecture of greenery, where sheer size was valued for the vistas it made possible. As in architecture and town-planning, in the composition of gardens, too, the lines of symmetry became all important in relation to the concept of centrality. Centre, focus and convergence of axes became the rule, speaking the language of officialdom, indicating and reinforcing the sovereign's striving for co-ordination. The more rigid classical dictates of architectural composition were redoubled for a new sense of unity. Each element was related to the other, creating dramatic and highly consistent compositions.

It was to this foundation, in the second half of the century, that the art of André Le Nôtre was grafted, to make one of the supreme expressions of cultural wealth and power in the France of the Sun King.

(Above) The cabinet de verdure, *reproduced here from the treatise by Dezallier d'Argenville, was a typical component of Le Nôtre's garden design.*

(Below) The Grand canal *at Sceaux. Expanses of water and endless canals were present on a grand scale in the French classical garden.*

(Opposite) Frontispiece from the treatise Théâtre des plans et jardinage, *1652, with the portrait of the author, Claude Mollet.*

In 1661, Louis XIV finally took up the reins of government and completed the work of reorganization undertaken by his predecessors. Centralizing mercilessly, he asserted the figure of the sovereign as the sole source of power, confirming the divine right of kings. Art was a crucial instrument: with the setting up of the Royal Manufactures art, under the sovereign's iron control, became both symbol and inspiration of the *Grand Siècle*, and was proffered to the court and the people as the representation and celebration of the monarchy.

The Academies correspondingly struck an increasingly intransigent note in asserting France's intellectual and artistic supremacy. Wealth was concentrated in the hands of the king and a few dignitaries, who courted popular acclaim and reverence by flaunting their incredibly grand and sumptuous houses. With the long reign of Louis XIV, a golden age now dawned for the art of the garden. Many new ones were created and many older ones adapted to the new taste. Most of them were by André Le Nôtre, whose projects, Versailles first and foremost, marked the apogee of the French classical garden.

The building of Versailles was a blatantly political act: on the one hand the new palace drew the powerful aristocratic families into the king's sphere of influence, on the other, lavishing of resources on palaces and gardens created a grand stage set, enduring proof of royal absolutism. The sheer size of

Versailles, the immense vistas extending *à perte de vue*, the complete remodelling of the landscape, were tangible symbols of the Sun King's infinite power.

Even if, in the projects of Le Nôtre, the building was the focus and dominant element, nonetheless the park was no longer a mere extension of the palace; it was a vital component of the whole. The gardens covered an enormous area, organized on orthogonal lines of sight, or as tridents or star-shaped configurations, cut out from vast wooded areas, and ornamented with numerous architectural and sculptural elements which, as focal points in the immensity of green, gave the sequence of spaces a sense of rhythm. These elements succeeded one another along a central axis, from the palace towards the countryside and the infinitely distant horizon. Broad terraces, with their horizontal *parterres à broderie*, were followed by avenues and strips of water, the surrounding wooded areas serving to cut off the view, vertically as well as horizontally, as far as the eye could see. Trees lost their individuality to become mighty masses of green, with a sense of depth firmly emphasized. Stretches of water, basins and canals, served to expand surfaces with reflections of sky, creating an aerial perspective by exploiting the effects of evaporation, which blurred and softened everything into one boundless vastness. To the sides of the main avenue, enclosed by dense woodland, the stroller would suddenly come upon a *bosquet*, an ornamental grove surrounded by geometrical hedges and containing fountains, sculptures and topiaried greenery.

Le Nôtre's immense gardens were designed to be peopled by human figures, to be viewed from the palace but also walked through. The king's ritual daily stroll, or sumptuous court receptions, would give sudden life to a stage on which, as in some huge theatre, surprise scenes would be enacted and symbolic messages conveyed.

If the French garden attained its apogee with Le Nôtre, its rules and characteristics had been theorized about and codified for some time. Claude Mollet's first designs for *parterres* appeared in Olivier de Serre's treatise *Théâtre d'agriculture*, printed in 1600, though his views on the practice of gardening were collected only in the posthumous *Théâtre des plan et jardinage* of 1652. A year earlier this had been preceded by his son André's *Le jardin de plaisir*, which set the definitive seal of approval on the compositional principles of the classical French garden.

Disengagement from the Italian model

Although French gardens had started to stray from the Italian model for some time, nonetheless during the first half of the seventeenth century the Italian garden remained their main point of reference. As Catherine de Medici, the wife of Henri II, had brought Italian culture to the gardens at Fontainebleau, Chenonceaux and the Tuileries in the sixteenth century, so Marie de Medici, the wife of Henri IV, built the palace and gardens of the Luxembourg (1615—35), in memory of the Pitti palace and the Boboli gardens. But in Paris, although the general layout was reminiscent of Boboli, with its broad amphitheatre-like space running along the internal facade of the palace, the details bore the mark of Jacques Boyceau de la Barauderie, subsequently codified in the *Traité du jardinage selon les raisons de la nature et de l'art* of 1638. Boyceau was the

Design for a parterre de broderie *by Jacques Boyceau. The intricate decoration typical of the Baroque era radically altered the design of the hedges in the flowerbeds: these now imitated the intertwining scrolls and curlicues of the rarefied embroidery of the time.*

The Luxembourg gardens in Paris, designed by Boyceau for Marie de Medici, demonstrate how, in the first half of the century, the Italian model was still present in the plan but no longer in the choice of decoration, which was acquiring greater freedom and variety.

first writer to concern himself specifically with gardens and their ornaments — thereby uncoupling gardens from agriculture — and to expound the basic principles underlying the development of the French garden. Great importance was attached to variety in design: compositions were to consist not only of straight lines but of curved ones too, and asymmetrical elements now featured to the sides of the central axis of symmetry. But variety was desirable above all in vertical elements and prominent features, with the creation of *berceaux, bosquets* and *salles* or *cabinets de verdure* — architectural structures where vegetation predominated — and by exploiting and emphasising the natural slopes and gradients of the terrain.

To this end, the *parterre* in front of the Palais du Luxembourg was slightly lower than the building itself, and surrounded by a high stone border, a pedestal decorated with pots and statues. Among other complex arabesques, the design of the *parterre* also included Marie's monogram. The fountains and *jeux d'eau* were made by the Francini and a nymphaeum, the *Grotte de Luxembourg*, with the armorial bearings of the Medici and the statues of the Rhône and Seine, formed a backdrop beyond an *allée* of elms.

The Luxembourg gardens, now a public park, have been extensively altered over the centuries: in the second half of the nineteenth, the great works of town-planning reaching their height with the construction of the rue de Medicis, the nymphaeum was moved further north, to stand at the end of a canal.

Of the dynasties of royal master-gardeners most important were the Mollets. Claude was originally responsible for designing the *parterres* — subsequently elaborated *en broderie* — created in 1582 during the modernization of the gardens of the château at Anet, built for Diane de Poitiers between 1546 and

1552, where the head gardener was Claude's father Jacques. Claude himself became head gardener to Henri II, and worked on various royal gardens from 1595—1610. He built the *Jardin de l'étang* (of the Pool) at Fontainebleau, an island garden, now destroyed, rising out of the lake opposite the *cour de la Fontaine*, which he decorated with *parterres de broderie* using box for the first time. In the gardens of the Tuileries he created new *parterres* around which he laid out *allées* of white mulberry trees, and *palissades* of Judas trees trained into arches. But it was Claude's sons who were to rework the *parterre de broderie* into ever more sophisticated motifs: their lines became increasingly sinuous, reminiscent of the real embroidery from which they later took their name. With Claude, the use of dwarf box became *de rigueur*, as did borders of grassy strips and coloured stones as backgrounds for the embroidery, contrasting with the green of the box and grass.

Boyceau's principle of variety in line and level, the emphasis given to the central axis with asymmetrical elements to the sides, formulated by André Mollet in his treatise of 1652, and in the large-scale works begun in 1628 by Cardinal Richelieu for his residence in Poitou — where a canal intersected the main right-angled axis — were among the components used by Le Nôtre in building the masterpieces of first Vaux-le-Vicomte, and then Versailles.

Le Nôtre in the service of the Sun King

The work of André Le Nôtre, who was the king's gardener from 1637 until he died in 1770, dominated the entire second half of the century. He worked on all the existing royal gardens and created new ones, not only for the Sun King but also for many court dignitaries.

Son of Jean, who made several designs for the *parterres* and hedges of the Tuileries, he showed an early interest in painting, but when he succeeded his father in 1637 as head of the Tuileries gardens he discovered his natural talent in the art of gardening. After first working on the gardens of the Tuileries and Luxembourg, in 1645 he designed the *Jardin de l'Orangerie* at Fontainebleau.

Well versed in the main artistic disciplines, Le Nôtre successfully assimilated the classical tradition of the Italian garden, and more recent French creations, while simultaneously reworking them according to a unitary model that was completely autonomous. His originality lay in adapting the sixteenth-century concept of the well-ordered garden, subject to architectural rules, to the peculiarities of the local setting, achieving a result that was entirely new.

The principles of his gardens were perfectly adapted to the simplicity and clarity of Cartesian thought: nature once more acquired precedence over man's intervention, and was now remodelled rather than positively forced. Brutally squared terraces were replaced by lighter reshaping of the terrain. The result was gentle grassy slopes and changes in level marked by short wide stairways, nymphaea and other architectural elements. The great masses of trees typical of the forests of the Ile de France outweighed stone constructions, though they were cunningly set away from the main building to frame broad vistas and act as a backdrop to the architecture.

Water, available in large quantities, fed fountains and *jeux d'eaux*, but also large pool and canals — great stretches of water reflecting the constantly changing sky of the Ile de France — extending over hitherto unthinkable distances. The resulting composition was simple in its general layout, majestic in size and gloriously varied in ornamental detail. The centrepieces of such designs were still the *parterres de broderie*, which formed

Plan of Fontainebleau by Alessandro Francini (1614). This is how the gardens at Fontainebleau looked at the beginning of the century, before Le Nôtre remodelled them, doing away with the late-Renaissance design and in particular with the large parterre *seen in this illustration.*

This statue of André Le Nôtre, one of the Olympian figures active during the Grand Siècle, *is in the garden at Chantilly, which he designed for the Prince de Condé.*

(Following page) The Grand canal at Fontainebleau — 39 metres (128 ft.) wide and almost a mile long — strides away into the landscape flanked by rows of elms.

(Page 91) The chateau of Vaux-le-Vicomte, commissioned by the minister Fouquet, retained the traditional sixteenth-century moat. No longer serving any defensive purpose, it now became another extremely effective ornament introducing the theme of water, which recurs in the form of pools, fountains and canals.

impressive adornments to the broad treeless terraces situated, at a slightly higher level than the rest, in front of the main body of the château. Seen from the windows the garden became one vast panorama extending to the horizon, along vistas carved out of clumps of trees and small woods.

Le Nôtre's first great opportunity to put his ideas on the art of the garden into practice, encouraging Louis XIV to appoint him head of the gardens of Versailles, was the gardens at Vaux-le-Vicomte. In 1656, the *surintendant des finances*, Nicolas Fouquet, commissioned the architect Le Vaux and the painter Le Brun, who had studied painting together with Le Nôtre, to build and decorate the château of Vaux, with Le Nôtre to design the gardens. Their collaboration produced a deeply impressive work, on which previously unheard-of means were lavished. The natural conditions were exploited to the full: a double slope, the water of the river Anqueil and extensive areas of woodland. A sensitive restoration, begun in the nineteenth century by its last owners, together with scrupulous maintenance, have kept the gardens true to their original design.

From the château, which stands on an artificial rise and is entirely surrounded by a broad moat, a wide axis of perspective closely follows the slope: from the first terrace, decorated with *parterres de broderie*, it proceeds to another slightly sunken level with two large grassy *parterres* around two circular basins. Beyond a large square pool are the *Grandes Cascades*, an elegant architectural composition with the waters of the Anqueil gushing from it, the first surprise for the stroller because, being at a lower level than the garden, they are invisible from the château. Beyond the *Cascades*, perpendicular to the main axis, runs the *Grand Canal*, with the so-called *Grotte* as a backdrop, a large retaining wall with seven *rocaille* niches. The masonry of the *Grotte* supports a terrace with a balustrade from which the visitor has an unexpected view: an inverse vista, running back towards the cascades and the château. From the terrace rises a long meadow, flanked by the trees of the wood and surmounted by a colossal statue, a copy of the Farnese Hercules.

The history of the gardens of Vaux-le-Vicomte is as well-known as it is extravagant. They were inaugurated with a great reception given by Fouquet in honour of the very young Louis XIV, the extravagance of which so enraged the king that Fouquet was arrested five days later. Louis saw the flaunting of such opulence as a challenge, and Le Nôtre and Le Brun were summoned to Versailles to work on a new residence worthy of his magnificence.

The first of Le Nôtre's masterly creations, Vaux lay along the characteristic central axis, with symmetrical parterres de broderie *incorporated into it, and a vista which finally merges with the wood in the background.*

The dimensions are vast, but a well-judged distribution of the parts directs the gaze effortlessly from the top of the hill back towards the château.

(Opposite) A shady avenue of ancient trees leads to the gigantic copy of the Farnese Hercules, the embodiment of the classically-oriented French Baroque of the age of Louis XIV, and the focal point of the entire composition.

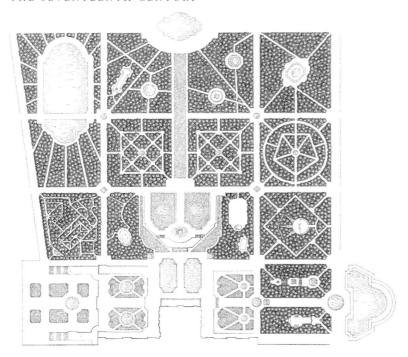

Plan of the Petit Parc, *Versailles. Elaborated and extended, the layout follows the earlier one for Vaux. The* Grand Parc *runs all around it, an immense wood criss-crossed by avenues disappearing into the landscape.*

Versailles, the Rhône: the spectacular parterre d'eau *is bordered by statues of the rivers of France, symbolising the range of the Sun King's ubiquitous power.*

Still new to power, recently humiliated by the revolts of the *frondeurs* noblemen and impressed by the display of splendour put on by his minister, Louis XIV was only twenty-three when he began work on the palace of Versailles. Where the hunting-lodge belonging to his father had once stood, he decided to build a palace proclaiming the role of the monarchy, and serving as the centre of political and administrative life. The sun was the symbol he chose: the brightest body in the heavens, illuminating and dominating everything.

Versailles was also an exercise in power: the site itself, utterly unsuited to such an ambitious project, was completely reshaped, and the landscape was thoroughly changed. Hills were levelled, rivers and streams diverted, thickets rose where previously there had been none, and vast expanses of water filled enormous, specially-excavated basins. Spectacular gardens were created around the immense palace, with views extending as far as the eye could see towards an infinite horizon: stage sets to celebrate the myth of Apollo, the sun god and lord of time, symbol of light and beauty, an explicit reference to Louis XIV.

The entire complex is aligned along a single, extremely long axis, with the succession, from the Paris direction, of great triumphal entrance avenues, the palace, and the gardens. The very long *Allée de Paris* crosses the town of Versailles, punctuated by the characteristic tridents of tree-lined avenues, to arrive at the Place d'Armes and notionally continues through the palace along the axis of the gardens as a succession of *parterres*, fountains, avenues and canals. The layout is reminiscent of Vaux-le-Vicomte, but at Versailles Le Nôtre was working in a vast dimension, varying the set pieces and redoubling the decorative elements.

Work on this majestic complex dragged on for over thirty years, but Le Nôtre's first plan, put in place between 1662 and 1668, already included almost all of the most important features. Although the gardens today are actually the outcome of various different phases, they still reflect the original over-

At Versailles the design unfolds symmetrically to either side of the central axis but, unlike at Vaux, the dimensions are vast, and the vista extends as far as the horizon. From the parterre de Latone *the eye runs towards the* bassin d'Apollon, *the core of the elaborate symbolic system and the culmination of the entire composition; beyond the basin, everything is blurred and softened in the light reflected by the long canal. The banks of trees flanking the central axis are now fully mature, and they themselves are members of a third generation: the first planting was done by the Sun King in 1675, but after years of disastrous neglect, Louis XVI ordered the cutting down and replacing of the thousands of trees in the* Petit Parc *as early as 1775. When the life-cycle of the chestnuts came to its end in the second half of the nineteenth century a total replanting was carried out between 1876 and 1883.*

(Opposite, bottom) Versailles. At the start of the first side axis - the allée d'Eau, *which starts from the* parterre du Midi - *before the* bassin de Neptune *the visitor comes upon the* bassin du Dragon. *The central dragon, carved in 1667 by the Marsy brothers, sends a mighty jet of water some 27 metres (29 ft.) into the air.*

arching vision of their creator.

From the château, the visitor comes first to the huge terrace of the *parterre d'Eau*, where great pools of still water effect a transition between the architecture of the palace and nature; from here the eye runs to the horizon in an east-west direction, along a vista of nearly two miles, towards the setting sun. Alongside the *parterre d'Eau*, slightly sunken, are the *parterre du Nord* to the right, laid out *à l'anglaise*, with grassy sections surrounded by flowerbeds enclosed by box hedges, and the *parterre du Midi*, with a *parterre de broderie*, to the left.

Beyond the *parterre du Nord* the view dips down into the *Allée d'Eau*, flanked by the *bosquets* of the Triumphal Arch and the Three Fountains, to reach the large *bassin de Neptune* at its end. On the opposite side, below the *parterre du Midi*, encircled by terracing, Le Vaux created the *Orangerie*, whose garden, flanked by great stairways, overlooks the huge artificial lake known as the *Pièce d'eau des Suisses*, begun in 1678 and named in honour of the Swiss guard who excavated it.

The huge tracts *à parterre* that surround the palace, devoid of vertical features and slightly higher than the park, were designed to give an impression of absolute vastness. There are no trees near the palace, and massive excavations were needed to lower the line of the horizon and to emphasize the sense of depth, shifting the vanishing point backwards towards infinity.

The vista continues with the *parterre de Latone*, reached from the *parterre d'Eau* by two great semi-circular flights of steps, with statues and pyramids of clipped box, solving the thirty-metre (98 ft.) difference in level between the two ends of the central axis: it celebrates the myth of Latona, mother of Apollo, personified by the magnificent fountain in the basin of the same name. The long green carpet of the *Allée royale* now unfolds before the visitor, a grass avenue 400 metres (1300 ft.) ft.) long and 45 (148 ft.) wide, to the sides of which, beyond dense woodland, two straight avenues run, punctuated by four fountains of the seasons, symbolizing the passing of time. Each one is dedicated to a different divinity: Flora for spring, Ceres for summer, Bacchus for autumn and Saturn for winter.

The *Allée royale* ends at the focal point of the whole prospect, with Versailles' most important and famous feature, the *fons et origo* and symbol of the entire park, the *bassin d'Àpollon* (Fountain of Apollo). The sun god Apollo, emblem of the king, is represented driving his chariot to bring the light of a new day, and as the sun rises on the horizon so Apollo emerges from the waters of a large basin. This group — sculptor Jean-Baptiste Tuby's finest work, completed in 1670 — consists of Apollo and his chariot drawn by four horses, with tritons emerging dashingly from the water to announce the sun's arrival.

Beyond the Fountain of Apollo runs the *Grand Canal*, a shining cruciform strip of water, whose arms measure one kilometre (3280 ft.) and 800 metres (2625 ft.) respectively, framed by poplars. Here, at memorable festivities, a miniature flotilla would give brightly-lit nocturnal performances to entertain the king and his court.

Bosquets once stood either side of the *Allée royale* and the *parterre de Latone*, magnificently adorned 'green rooms' with surprise devices and decorations like the water theatre, where

Versailles. Situated to the sides of the central axis, the fountains of the seasons serve as an allegory for the passing of time under the guidance of the sun. Autumn is symbolized by this statue of Bacchus, amidst satyrs and bunches of grapes.

The bassin d'Apollon *is the very emblem of the Sun King's greatness, and of the gardens of Versailles. Passionately devoted to his gardens, continually occupied in extending and embellishing them, Louis loved to accompany his guests on visits there, to which end he wrote at least six versions of his* Manière de montrer les jardins de Versailles.

Versailles. Le Nôtre's last work, the Salle du Bal *resembled a classical amphitheatre with flights of grassy steps, overlooking the exquisite* jeux d'eau *of a fan-shaped cascade which pours down* marble steps, decorated with rocaille *and* coquillages. *The* bosquet *took its name from the dais-like structure in the centre, surrounded by channels of water and used for dancing.*

Versailles. Mansart's colonnade (1684) replaced an earlier bosquet; *a circular peristyle with thirty arches, it stands on a double row of polychrome marble columns interpolated by fountains. The group of statues representing the rape of Persephone, by Girardon to a design by Le Brun, was placed in the centre of the colonnade only in 1699.*

some two hundred jets created *jeux d'eaux* capable of seven different effects, or the Labyrinth where thirty-nine fountains enacted as many subjects taken from Aesop's fables. The best-known was the *bosquet de la Colonnade*, built by François Hardouin Mansart as a circular space with a round marble colonnade, at its centre a splendid sculpted group representing the rape of Persephone.

Other *bosquet* compositions still in existence, though altered, include the Baths of Apollo, Le Nôtre's last work, and the *Salle du Bal* (ballroom), created between 1680 and 1683 in the form of a tiered amphitheatre with jets and little waterfalls.

Taken together, the countless works of art dotted throughout the gardens — fountains, herms, vases, urns — form a paean of praise to the power of the king, each statue playing its part in a complex programme based on the myth of Apollo. This sculptural array was conceived and co-ordinated by Le Brun, and executed between 1665 and 1683 by some seventy sculptors.

In 1687, while work on Versailles was still at its height, Louis XIV decided to rebuild the earlier pavilion of the Trianon at the right-hand end of the canal. Clad in Delft tiles, it was known as the porcelain Trianon, and its gardens were used for cultivating flowers. The king now commissioned Mansart to build the *Grand Trianon*, this time clad in marble, as a secluded place where he could relax away from the pomp and circumstance of the court. The garden in front occupied two levels with the peristyle at the centre of the building and was decorated with *parterres à l'anglaise* and ornamental basins, but its distinctive feature was the luxuriance and variety of its flowers.

The great parterre at Fontainebleau no longer has its decoration à broderie: the largest ever designed by Le Nôtre, it was sacrificed to the growing need for ease of maintenance. The present grassy area completely altered the play of space and colour originally intended by Le Nôtre, being less elaborate, but also completely distorting the feeling of proportion.

The great flowerbeds of the Grand Trianon could accommodate a vast number of flowers, Louis XIV's true passion: surrounded by trellises covered with Spanish jasmine, numerous varieties of bulbiferous plants such as tuberose, narcissi, lilies and hyacinths were grown alongside campanula, carnations, wallflowers and valerian.

The cascade at St Cloud, enlarged by Mansart in 1697 in the form we see today, runs between the Seine and the original site of the château; destroyed by fire in 1870, this château stood in the beautiful gardens created by Le Nôtre for Louis XIV's brother.

The breathtaking Grandes cascades, framed by two immaculately clipped hedges.

At Sceaux the double slope of the terrain suggested the combination of two axes of perspective, one along the Grand canal *and one known as 'of the four statues'.*

The rigours of the climate made the Sun King's real passion, the cultivation of flowers and ornamental plants, something of a challenge in the gardens of the Trianon. Orange trees, grown in the ground and not in pots, were sheltered in winter by temporary greenhouses, and flowering plants of all kinds were transplanted into pots so that fresh flowers were always available, even in winter. It has been estimated that the Trianon's gardeners kept 1.9 million pots ready for transplanting.

As Louis XIV's gardener, Le Nôtre was involved in all the royal gardens, commencing new schemes and sweeping away the earlier sixteenth-century designs. Between 1661 and 1664 he redesigned the main *parterre* at Fontainebleau, giving it the form we still see today, though the *broderie* has disappeared, depriving one of the largest *parterres* he ever devised of its elaborate decoration.

Between 1667 and 1671, in the gardens of the Tuileries, Le Nôtre designed a large central avenue extending beyond its limits, the long axis which was later to become the Champs Elysées. He also marked the boundary of the garden that overlooks the Seine with the *Grande terrasse du bord de l'Eau*.

After various phases of demolition and the building of a railway line, all that remains of the great terraced design of St-Germain-en-Laye to the west of Paris, built by Le Nôtre to link the new château with the old, is the great panoramic terrace overlooking the Seine.

Designing Sceaux for the king's minister, Colbert, and St-Cloud for the king's brother, the Duke of Orleans, both on the outskirts of Paris, Le Nôtre adapted his principles to the natural setting, letting their pronounced natural slopes determine the lie of the gardens. At Sceaux the double slope was resolved with the classical double axis formed by the crossing of a vast canal and a grandiose water staircase. At St-Cloud a prospect of terraces sloped down to the Seine, and the river itself provided the dramatic effect provided elsewhere by canals.

Since Versailles, seat of government and court, was thoroughly official in character, the king also needed a residence where he could receive his private guests, and so between 1679 and 1686 the large complex of Marly was created. Here Le Nôtre designed a water garden as a setting for Mansart's elaborate construction.

At Marly an enormous stretch of water was surrounded by a vast horseshoe of rolling land: around it, slightly raised up, thirteen pavilions were built, with that of the Sun King on one of the short arms, on an axis with the garden as a whole; the other twelve were lined up on the long sides to form an amphitheatre, symbolizing the constellations the sun passed on its course. The demolition of the pavilions and other disfigurements during the Revolution ushered in a long period of decline and very little of Marly's once imposing layout remains today.

Le Nôtre also designed many gardens for the king's relations and court dignitaries: at Meudon for the Grand Dauphin, at Clagny for Mme de Montespan and at Chevreuse for the Duc de Luynes. Among the best-known are the gardens at Chantilly, created for the Prince de Conde, and the delectable garden at Maintenon, for Louis XIV's morganatic wife, Mme de Maintenon.

At Chantilly, where Le Nôtre worked after Vaux but before Versailles, he imposed a geometrical design on a mainly irregular terrain. The château was situated in an eccentric position vis-à-vis any hypothetical central axis: Le Nôtre made an immense garden with sheets of water as its predominant motif. The château is entirely surrounded by a large moat, almost a lake, with the focus of the entire composition, the raised

This aerial view of Chantilly (left) does full justice to the subtle design of the parterres *and basins laid out by Le Nôtre. Despite various alterations, including those which brought the lateral bosquets into line with the English landscape style in the nineteenth century (above), the garden still retains all its original charm. The* parterre d'eau *(opposite) gives the garden the feel of being one vast mirror, one huge reflecting surface.*

terrace, at its sides. Here the garden is of decidedly greater importance than the architecture, and indeed the building — relatively small and laterally positioned — is virtually overwhelmed by the huge area of *parterres* and basins. Serving as an *avant-corps* and distributive centre for the entire complex, the terrace dominates the views on all sides. To the west, it is linked to the château by a drawbridge over the moat; to the south, a broad stairway runs down to a mixtilinear grassy *parterre* — apparently floating on the water — linked to the entrance avenue. Another bridge to the east leads to the service buildings; the garden lies to the north. On this latter side, a short, wide flight of steps leads down to a trapezoidal terrace, with a circular basin at its centre, with two large, rectangular, grassy *parterres* at its ends, incorporating a rich design of rectangular, circular and elliptical basins. Between the two *parterres* the

short side of a large T-shaped canal runs transversally to the whole composition; beyond it, the eye is drawn towards the horizon down a wide tree-lined avenue. *Bosquets* with lavish cascades stand to the side of the *parterres*, separated by avenues of limes. In the nineteenth century, the areas at the extreme edges of the garden were remodelled *à l'anglaise*, in accordance with the fashion for landscape gardening.

At Maintenon, Le Nôtre redesigned the existing gardens, channelling the water into the moat around the château and *parterres*, to feed a large canal. Maintenon is famous in particular for the ruins of its aqueduct, built to carry water to the fountains of Versailles, but left unfinished at an early stage. This massive structure acts as a backdrop to the garden, its reflection in the stretches of water anticipating the eighteenth-century vogue for ruins.

(Opposite) The gardens of the château at Maintenon. On becoming Louis XIV's morganatic wife, Mme de Maintenon was given the estate of Maintenon; she then commissioned Le Nôtre to redesign its gardens, and here too he made use of the original moat, linking it to other basins and a canal, exploiting the dramatic possibilities offered by the great unfinished aqueduct reflected in the various expanses of water.

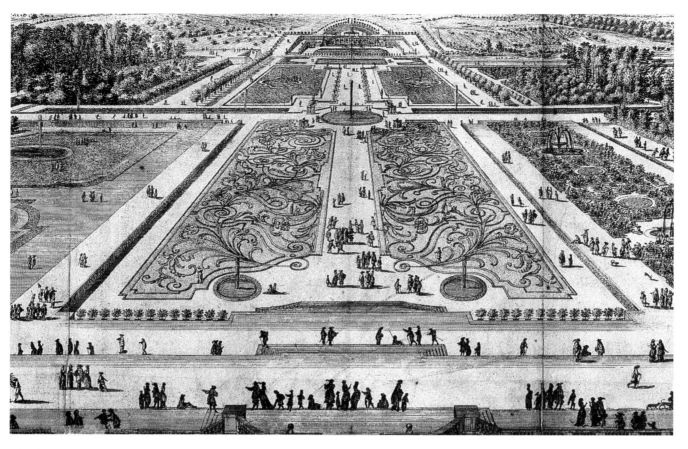

(Opposite, left) The parterre à l'anglaise, *so-called because of its popularity in England, consisted mainly of grass. The simplest form, with grass and sand, was often bordered by sculptures, topiary and flowers.*

(Opposite, top right) Bosquets *were a typical feature of the classical seventeenth-century French garden: they were created from rows of trees and walls of tall hedges, enclosing any variety of ornamental set pieces. This illustration is taken from a German translation of the treatise by Dezallier d'Argenville (1737).*

(Opposite, bottom right) Also from the treatise by Dezallier d'Argenville, this illustration shows a large boulingrin, *a slightly sunken lawn often found in bosquets.*

The classical parterre *was a one-dimensional composition, without trees, its decoration consisting of elaborate designs using box, grass and flowers. This engraving, by Israel Sylvestre, shows the* parterre *at Vaux-le-Vicomte in 1661, with its typical* broderie *decoration — that is, with arabesques remi-* *niscent of the embroidery of the time of Henri IV and Louis XIII. The original baroque* broderie *used by Claude Mollet and Jacques Boyceau had been bordered by slender lines of box; Le Nôtre's design for Vaux-le-Vicomte changed it radically, establishing the new model that would now prevail.*

The so-called parterre de pièces coupées *relied mainly on flowers for its decoration; the term (literally, cut pieces) was used for* parterres *with flowers, divided up symmetrically into variously-shaped beds, with narrow bordering paths enabling the gardeners to tend the flowers.*

Parterre de pièces coupées pour des fleurs

PARTERRES AND *BOSQUETS*

During the seventeenth and eighteenth centuries a series of treatises was published which gradually defined and codified the principles of the classical French garden. After those by Boyceau and the Mollets, father and son, the text which established the French model, and whose popularity made it the inspiration for gardens throughout eighteenth century Europe, was *La Théorie et la pratique du jardinage* by Antoine-Joseph Dezallier d'Argenville. Written in 1709 and reprinted in various editions up to 1747, the most generously illustrated, it collates all the main components of the French garden of the *Grand Siècle* elaborated by Le Nôtre: *parterre, bosquet, plate-bande, boulingrin, palissade.*

The French *parterre* developed from the geometrical and linear compartments of the Italian garden. The best-known is the *parterre de broderie,* the 'embroidered' parterre, developed first by the Mollets and then constantly used by Le Nôtre: its decorative motifs were varied and included vine-shoots, scrolls, rosettes, arabesques, crowns and plumes, created by the expert clipping of box hedges and other evergreens, against a background of coloured gravel.

Other types of *parterre* drew on different garden traditions, for example, the *parterre de pièces coupées,* on the Dutch model of small beds of bright flowers surrounded by low box hedges.

A further example was the *parterre à l'anglaise:* a grassy area, geometrical and regular, based on the English lawn, often with

Parterre a l'Angloise.

Bosquets en quatre.   Prospect eines vierecktigten Bosquets

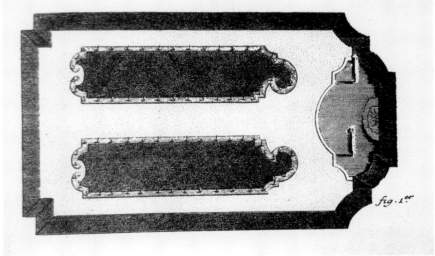

Grand Boulingrin orné d'un Buffet d'eau et d'une Plate-bande d'arbrisseaux et de Fleurs.

statues or the typical *gazons coupées*, (patterns obtained by cutting small areas out of the turf to fill with coloured gravel). Also derived from the English tradition was the *boulingrin*, a distortion of the English term '*bowling green*', like its English equivalent, a flat, slightly sunken patch of grass, with paths, trees, statues and *plate-bandes*.

The *plate-bande* itself was a long strip marking the boundary or acting as a further decoration to the *parterre*, generally of box, either squared or *en dos d'âne*. On other occasions, *plates-bandes* were simple long narrow strips of turf featuring flowers, topiaried yew or rows of citrus plants in pots.

The *bosquet* was the other typical feature of the French garden, its verticality serving to intensify flat areas. *Bosquets* might also house 'green rooms', known as *cabinets* or *salles de verdure*, such as the famous *Salle du bal* at Versailles; they might also be laid out as cloisters or mazes, or contain fountains, statues or basins. The trees in *bosquets* were frequently planted in quincunxes, i.e. arranged like a chequerboard, with their foliage rising above the *palissades*.

Bosquets might also be made up of four simple rows of trees laid out in a rectangle, allowing their elaborate internal decoration to be glimpsed from without: these were known as *bosquets ornées* or *bosquets de compartiment*, divided up symmetrically with geometrical layouts containing the characteristic components of *parterre* or *boulingrin*.

The age of the Baroque in Europe

While in France the political and economic reorganization of the state and the enlightened rule of the Sun King ushered in a period of intensive development, particularly in the arts, the other European countries found themselves in very disparate situations. Specific circumstances caused the art of the garden to develop in quite different ways, and only towards the end of the century did the French model assert itself across Europe.

In England the Tudor tradition of the knot garden persisted, in tandem with Renaissance principles derived, via France, from Italian models: the French model gained ascendancy only after 1660, with the Restoration that followed the Cromwellian period.

One of the many French artists summoned to England was André Mollet, who was appointed royal gardener at St. James's Palace in 1661. As French taste became established, within a few years English gardens were adopting aspects of the great parks across the Channel: long, tree-lined *allées* became particularly fashionable, leading up to great houses or acting as 'telescopes' to direct the gaze into the distant landscape. Despite French influence, English gardens retained certain peculiarities of their own: rather than complicated *parterres de broderie*, simpler grassy compositions were preferred, sometimes with statues; already popular in pre-revolutionary gardens, these were known by the French as *parterres à l'anglaise*. *Bosquets*, too, developed in a freer form, as the so-called 'wilderness', a large wooded area criss-crossed by avenues and tree-lined walks, still formal in design but suggestive of something wilder, mysterious and unexpected, a sort of natural maze in which the stroller could indeed lose and find himself.

With the accession of the Dutchman William III of Orange, for a time English royal gardens adapted to the Dutch taste: traditional yew hedges, clipped into cones and spheres, became increasingly popular. Germany, on the other hand, was a case apart. The Thirty Years War had caused German gardens to remain anchored to the Renaissance model much longer than other European countries. One particularly clear example is the layout *all'italiana* of the famous *Hortus Palatinus* at Heidelberg, created for Elizabeth, daughter of the king of England and wife of the Elector Palatine, Frederick V, between 1615 and 1620, at a time when gardens elsewhere in Europe were moving away from sixteenth-century patterns.

Baroque gardens made an appearance in Germany only after 1680, and even then they bore the mark of the upheavals of the war. On German territory, divided into a patchwork of small principalities each with its own political and dynastic balances and cultural and artistic peculiarities, gardens varied more obviously from region to region than in the rest of Europe. The main differences were dictated by geography: in southern regions, although the Italian tradition remained, elements of the French Baroque crept in, while in the more northerly states Dutch influence was paramount.

Beloeil, Hainault, is the most spectacular baroque creation in Belgium, both for the variety of its decorative repertoire, and the widespread presence of vast stretches of water. It is unique in that its central axis is a parterre d'eau *covering an area of almost six hectares (15 acres), surrounded by long* palissades *of lopped limes.*

Indeed, during the seventeenth century Holland developed her own sixteenth-century tradition along increasingly bourgeois lines. Free of the Spanish yoke, the mercantile bourgeoisie now created gardens essentially for everyday life, with their roots in a decidedly republican and Calvinist culture. The Dutch garden was also a statement of the country's remarkable technical and scientific achievements. Characteristics were the widespread use of water, ubiquitously evident, and a great variety of flowers, the product of Holland's overseas trade. Towards the end of the seventeenth century French elements infiltrated the fertile indigenous tradition to produce the so-called Franco-Dutch garden, which was to become fashionable at the courts of northern Europe in the last two decades.

Spanish and Italian gardens had their own distinctive features, too. As in the rest of Europe, so in Spain absolute monarchy now reigned supreme, though in the Iberian peninsula it was less worldly than in France, more coloured by the austerity and religiosity typical of the Habsburgs. In Italy, on the other hand, fragmentation into small states militated against the breadth of vision fostered by the courts beyond the Alps, and throughout the century fairly small gardens continued as the norm, with fundamentally Mannerist designs, even if, in the second half of the century, the French taste began to prevail and some of Italy's most beautiful gardens as a mature expression of the Baroque were created. In Italy, furthermore,

the particular geomorphological conformation of the landscape gardens made more theatrical and spectacular: the limited availability of water and the predominance of hilly terrain favoured dramatic effects, with garden structures and features like terraces and sculptural groups taking precedence over the natural element.

Theatres of magnificence: Italian Baroque gardens

For Rome and the papacy, the Baroque period was a time of intense artistic activity. While papal patronage was changing the face of the Eternal City with a whole series of ambitious projects, in the surrounding countryside churchmen were giving material expression to their power by the building and embellishing splendid residences. Sixteenth-century tradition and the Mannerist model still exerted a powerful influence, and most of the gardens created in Latium remained closely tied to late-Renaissance design.

Frascati continued to be the area favoured by popes, cardinals and their families. Popular for country villas even in Roman times, the hill of Tusculum had been rediscovered after 1550, and in 1565 Annibale Caro – who devised the extravagant iconography for the Farnese palace at Caprarola — had chosen Frascati for a new villa which, with a *jeu de mots* typical of that era's men of letters, he christened 'Caravilla' (literally 'dear villa', but also an allusion to his own name). More aristocratic families chose this same hill to build on, and in the first years of the

One of the topiaried shrubs in the garden at Twickel. Expertise in clipping and a passion for topiary work were widespread in Dutch garden culture, and such works were omnipresent adornments in the baroque gardens of Holland.

The statue of Fame in the Garzoni garden at Collodi is a typical example of the new-found theatricality of the seventeenth-century

Italian garden, frequently prompted by specific local conditions such as hilly terrain and the availability of water.

seventeenth century Frascati had its moment of greatest glory.

In 1613, a series of canny transactions enabled Scipione Borghese to bring a vast complex of villas together into a single property, overlooking the town of Frascati and the plain below. Land previously belonging to Cardinal Altemps brought him Villa Mondragone and other adjacent villas. Now the centre of a vast estate, the villa — begun to a design by Vignola — was extensively enlarged by Vasanzio; by the middle of the seventeenth century, Villa Mondragone and its adjoining properties was part of an architectural complex unrivalled in Italy. The great building stood on a wide semi-circular terrace overlooking the valley, with four massive decorated columns at its corners and the fountain of the Dragons in the centre. The garden Cardinal Borghese had built on one side of the villa still had the characteristics of a secret garden: a large rectangular courtyard surrounded by high walls, with a portico looking towards the valley and a water theatre in the form of an exedra looking towards the hills. The distribution of fountains, portals and hemicycles was still distinctly late-Renaissance; the organization of the entire complex, on the other hand, was typically seventeenth century, with a sensitivity to the landscape emphasized by the long entrance avenue flanked by cypresses.

Nearby stood Villa Ludovisi, also known as Villa Torlonia, the name of its last owners. For some years part of Scipione Borghese's estate, it too, though less prominent in the landscape, was surrounded by a spectacular garden with rising terraces behind. The villa stood on the site of Caro's 'Caravilla', and around it, between 1607 and 1614, Cardinal Borghese created the very lovely gardens laid out by Carlo Maderno, who also erected the magnificently dramatic water theatre for which the villa was justly famous. After various changes of ownership it passed to the Ludovisi family, who

extended and embellished the garden with important new additions after 1621, the year when Alessandro Ludovisi became Pope Gregory XV.

As is evident from contemporary engravings, an imposing balustraded staircase, to one side of the villa, led to the first area of terracing, divided into sections and crossed by a central avenue leading to the water theatre, into which a long water chain flowed down from the hill. Higher up, in the middle of another terrace, surrounded by *bosquets*, was a large circular *bassin* with a fountain. Below the balustrade the water reappeared, to cascade down tall steps and feed the fountains of the nymphaeum below, with a long retaining wall to the rear, and numerous niches housing statues and fountains. The villa became the property of the Torlonia family in the nineteenth century, and was destroyed by bombing during World War II; the garden was acquired by the Commune of Frascati in 1954, and is now the city's public park.

The most famous of the villas of Frascati, Villa Aldobrandini, was also the last to be built. Having been in the hands of a single family virtually throughout its existence, unlike most of the other villas at Frascati it has survived in an excellent state of repair. With its imposing bulk looming over the town, and the exquisite gardens laid out against the hill behind, Villa Aldobrandini profoundly transforms its setting.

The site was already auspicious when in 1598 Ippolito Aldobrandini, Pope Clement VIII, presented his Cardinal nephew Pietro Aldobrandini with the villa, then known as 'of the belvedere'. Its land, abundant in water sloped gradually down to Rome. Giacomo della Porta was commissioned to carry out the ambitious extensions and subsequently, complete reconstruction. At his death in 1602 he was succeeded by Carlo Maderno, with assistance from Domencio Fontana, a hydraulics expert.

Villa Mondragone occupies a commanding position on Tusculum hill, proof that the planning of seventeenth-century Italian gardens was now fully aware of how the relationship between building and landscape could be filtered through the garden.

The water theatre at Villa Torlonia, Frascati. The Baroque age was quick to recognize the full theatrical potential of the complex water chains that had already made their appearance in the Mannerist era; they were now incorporated into superb water theatres, intricate architectural creations, usually extending upwards, brilliantly exploiting the element's supreme mobility and versatility.

Engraving by Gian Battista Falda from the volume Li giardini di Roma *(1683) showing the great water theatre at Villa Aldobrandini at Frascati.*

The water theatre at Villa Aldobrandini as it is today.

The villa stands above the road to Rome, at the top of three descending terraces overlooking the surrounding Campagna: the result is an elaborately articulated vertical structure, visible from a great distance, though the gardens to the rear are not. On the upper terrace a vast esplanade cut into the hill runs the length of the villa, on an axis with the central approach, of the water theatre.

The gardens are structured as an allegorical celebration of both the world-wide supremacy of Christianity, and the power of the Pope and his cardinal nephew. The might of the Church and its earthly representatives, buttressed by the work of the Counter-Reformation, is embodied in the dominant position and, as the villa dominates the countryside, so the garden behind dominates the villa.

At the top of the hill, two huge twisted columns with mosaic decoration mark the beginning of the water chain; they represent the mythical pillars of Hercules, set at the margins of the known universe and symbolizing knowledge and power carried to the world's end. From here the water —

channelled from Mount Algido to feed the garden's fountains and *giochi d'acqua* — flows over the steep slope down a spectacular eight-step stone stairway. It then re-appears further down to activate the fountains and *giochi d'acqua* of the nymphaeum, which opens up in the centre of a long retaining wall, forming an exedra with several niches containing statues and jets of water. In the centre is a statue of Atlas holding up the globe, an allegory of Clement VIII carrying the fate of the Catholic world in his hands.

Frascati once had many other villas with famous gardens, but little now remains of this one-time splendour, and today those remaining are in a state of disrepair. One interesting garden which has survived, however, that of Villa Piccolomoni Lancellotti, was in fact also the earliest. Hemmed in between two roads, it is rectangular: two tall clipped ilex hedges flank a *parterre* divided into two sections by box hedges, remodelled at a later date with more supple lines in the French fashion, framing a water theatre at its end, making its first appearance here as an independent exedra decorated with statues.

The niches carved out of the great exedra of the nymphaeum at villa Aldobrandini contain statues of various mythological figures and woodland deities.

Villa Aldobrandini. Two richly decorated columns at the top of the cascade symbolize the pillars of Hercules, marking the borders of the known world.

On occasions, the theatricality beloved of the Baroque was heightened by the natural terrain. Possibly the most blatant example of the baroque love of spectacle is the amazing transformation of a lake island into a stupendous garden at Isola Bella on Lake Maggiore, at once a magical stage set to be strolled through from within, and a grandiose architectural composition to be viewed from without.

Isola Bella is deservedly the best-known of the three Isole Borromee, for the marvellous gardens created there by Count Carlo III Borromeo in honour of his wife Isabella — they were begun in the 1620s and completed around 1670. Until the seventeenth century the island, which had long been owned by the Milanese Borromeo family, was just an arid clayey rock: now it was transmogrified into a spectacular floating garden of buildings, terraces, statues, balustrades and stairways. This very lovely garden still arouses as much wonder in today's visitor as it did over the previous three centuries, when it was immortalized in the descriptions of many captivated artists and men of letters.

Huge quantities of earth were transported on barges from the shores of the lake to build the famous terraces, transforming the island into one great construct with distinct architectural outlines, giving the impression of a majestic ship sailing over the waters of the lake.

The exquisitely Mannerist design was inspired by a pervasive sense of space, and the result was a garden with distinctly theatrical connotations. Rising upwards from the waters, it is given its sense of verticality by its pyramidal structures, with ten superimposed terraces bristling with statues, pinnacles, niches and cypresses, all artfully devised to arouse awe and admiration, from the shell-covered grottoes at the base of the palace to the lavish Exedra, outlined clearly against the sky. Access to the island is still from the west, from the landing stage of the small village at the foot of the palace, whose northern façade was left unfinished. The garden lies beyond, to the east, a further projection of the palace's splendour. The complex has survived more or less intact, though the foursquare geometry of the terraces is now blurred and softened

Small and perfectly balanced, the water theatre at Villa Lancellotti Piccolomini was one of the first water theatres to be created at Frascati.

Isola Bella, a commanding terraced composition in the middle of lake Maggiore. Its stilted appearance, particularly evident in this illustration, has now been greatly softened by the foliage of the trees that were planted there over time.

The crowning glory of the theatrical apparatus of Isola Bella is the rocaille exedra, *bristling with statues and pinnacles, topped by the unicorn, the emblem of the villa's owners.*

The vertical thrust of the exedra *is given a sense of continuity by the series of terraces that rise behind it.*

(Opposite) View from one of the terraces on Isola Bella, whose incomparable loveliness is further enhanced by its setting in the middle of a lake.

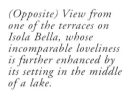

by the foliage of the trees and flowering shrubs added over time. Like many of the gardens on the shores of Lake Maggiore, these of Isola Bella are famous for their ornamental and exotic plants, introduced principally in the nineteenth century. However, there are also great centuries-old trees after which certain landmarks are named. From the courtyard of Diana, where a statue of the goddess looks down from a granite and tufa niche, to admire herself in a *bassin*, the visitor goes up the so-called 'staircase of the Cedar of Lebanon' to the 'terrace of the camphor tree', named after the fine hundred-year-old specimen still standing there. Another flight of steps leads to the focal point of the whole composition, the Exedra, tall and amphitheatre-like, and decorated with shells and niches, obelisks, cherubs and allegorical statues alluding to the lake and the rivers running into it, attendant nymphs and certain natural phenomena. The whole outlandish structure is crowned by the statue of the unicorn, the emblem of the Borromeo family. From the amphitheatre the visitor goes up to the last of the ten terraces, the Upper Terrace, 36 metres (114 ft.) above the lake, with a breathtaking panorama all around.

The garden of villa Garzoni at Collodi was also built as one huge stage set, but in quite a different setting. Here, as at Isola Bella, the baroque principle of theatricality was well suited to the lie of the land: the garden runs up the steep slope to create a magnificently dramatic composition backed up against the hill. First described in Francesco Sbarra's celebratory poem *Le pompe di Collodi*, it was designed completely independently of the villa at the top of the hill, which is positioned eccentrically vis-à-vis

the garden. The visitor first enters a semi-circular esplanade from which rises an orderly geometrical sequence of terraces. From below these accentuate the verticality of the composition. The esplanade has two *parterres de broderie* and two circular *bassins* with high central jets of water. Half way up the hill, below the large central terrace, the visitor comes upon the grotto of Neptune, richly decorated with artificial sponges and mosaics, and devices for various *scherzi d'acqua*. On one side, between high green wings, is a delightful open air theatre. The main central axis continues above the grotto in the form of a water staircase. At the summit, the water pours from the trumpet of a striking statue of Fame, to fill a coloured mixtilinear *bassin* and cascade down steps decorated with highly naturalistic stone motifs. Reaching the grotto of Neptune, it feeds the *giochi d'acqua* and continues through the fountains to link up with the two circular *bassins* in the esplanade. The woodland to the sides of this dramatic axis is entirely terraced and run through with axes perpendicular to the water staircase. If from below the vista continues skywards, from above the steep gradient is broken up by the terraces, and visually softened by a vast array of statues whose iconography — drawing on history, the epic, fairy tales and mythology – has still not been fully deciphered.

By the second half of the seventeenth century French influence was beginning to make itself felt, particularly in Tuscany and the north. If at Collodi the Baroque approach drew upon the Italian tradition of terracing, French practice was now increasingly evident in the villas around Lucca. An independent state and flourishing trading centre, in the seven-

The Garzoni garden at Collodi. Extension upwards, in response to the hilly nature of the Italian terrain, became characteristic of baroque garden design.

teenth century Lucca was going through a moment of particular splendour, with villas and gardens being built throughout the countryside. Many gardens had typically French features, becoming transitional spaces between the villas and the landscape, filtered by a succession of open-air rooms, broad axes of perspective and striking entrance avenues often triumphal in character, as at Villa Torrigiani at Camigliano. Perhaps the most interesting layout, and the closest to the French models, is the garden at Villa Orsetti, subsequently Villa Reale and now Villa Pecci Blunt, at Marlia. Owned by the counts of Orsetti from 1651, the garden was built as a succession of open-air rooms on the *bosquet* model, opening off one another as in a carefully articulated stage set. The Villa is set at a slightly higher level than the garden, overlooking a large expanse of grass. Tall thick hedges wall in the esplanade and the rear of the villa, where a water theatre and a grotto stand in a hemicycle. To the eastern side, parallel to the area of grass, is another room, closed in at its upper end by a small nymphaeum, with a large central *bassin* surrounded by a balustrade and lemon trees. From here the visitor enters the most interesting part of the garden, the open-air theatre of 1652. Crossing another small space between two hedges, a tall jet of water issuing from a circular *bassin*, he enters the little circular theatre, enclosed by galleries cut into the yew and closed in by tall wings with three terracotta statues representing masked figures from the Commedia dell'Arte in their entrances. This unique seventeenth-century work has survived intact despite an extension of the park in the 'romantic' style

Terracotta statues, originally painted, standing on bases decorated with mosaics in coloured stone, give the garden at Collodi a particularly buoyant air.

Garzoni garden. Comedy, one of the statues in the 'wings' of clipped hedges in the open-air theatre, standing to one side of the minor axis.

The Garzoni garden. The pool at the top of the hill, which feeds the water chain from above, is also decorated with coloured pebbles.

The garden at Collodi is linked to the villa by a small bridge, with broad openings in its parapets looking out over the wood below.

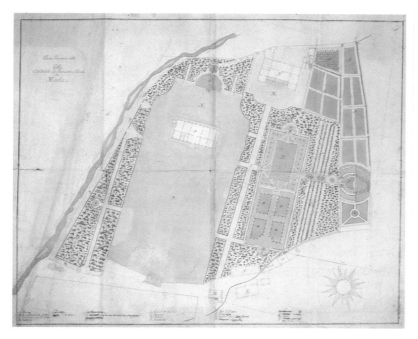

The rigidly structured hedges of dense evergreens, bordering the various spaces into which the garden was divided, are very evident in this plan of villa Marlia.

Villa Barbarigo, now Pizzoni Ardemani. at Valsanzibio. The main axes of the garden are clearly legible in this representation (1717).

carried out by Elisa Baciocchi, the princess of Lucca. At the beginning of the nineteenth century she added further *bosquets* and a lake at the end of the grass to add depth to the view from the villa. Numerous exotic species were introduced at the same time, including species of ginko, thuja and mimosa from the royal gardens in Naples. A further project, which would have destroyed the seventeenth-century gardens was cut short by the arrival of English troops at Lucca in 1814. Various plants were added and replaced in the 1920s during restoration by the new owners, who acquired the complex in 1923. Scrupulously preserved, the garden is actually enhanced by the contrast between the original, unchanged seventeenth-century part, and the later additions.

If gardens of some interest were created in central Italy throughout the seventeenth century, in the north many patrician villas and gardens, including the Savoy residences in Piedmont, were designed on lines increasingly close to the French, though in no way innovative. The Venetian aristocracy continued the expansion across the landscape with country residences modelled on the villa-farm, with rustic outbuildings and an immediate relationship with the agricultural land around them. Only very few broke away from this pattern, but those that did have gardens quite as elaborate as any product of the baroque imagination. In this context the Barbarigo garden at Valsanzibio near Padua is of particular interest.

In 1669 Antonio Barbarigo, procurator to the Serenissima, began to contract a garden reminiscent of the French model of Vaux-le-Vicomte. Even if its smaller dimensions — just four hectares (five acres) — precluded anything like the vast creations of the Ile-de-France, the space was intricately divided up, with the structures and planting arranged around two perpendicular axes to give the garden its unique combination of variety and intimacy. It was partially altered in 1805 to bring it into line with the fashion for the landscaped garden, but its uncompromising classical layout and the rich ornamental apparatus of its detailed iconography remain largely legible. Starting from the villa, a first axis runs in the form of a broad grassy carpet, flanked by tall square-shaped espaliered greenery. The slight slope of a second axis, at right-angles to the first, was used to create a complex vista of water out of a descending sequence of small *bassins*, fountains and little cascades, with mythological divinities and grottoes featuring rustic motifs, overlooked by the pavilion of Diana. The imposing villa, with a prospect out over the garden, rises from the waters of a large pool originally used as moorings for the *burchielli*, the barge-like craft that plied the waterways of the terra firma. Strictly orthogonal, the axes create four quadrants whose 'vaghezze' (embellishments) include a box-hedge maze and the Isola dei Conigli (literally, Rabbit Island), a curious structure where the useful is allied with the beautiful: oval in shape, like the surrounding pool, it has an aviary with a Moorish dome in the centre.

Though Baroque in structure, the garden is thoroughly humanist in mood: the numerous mythological inscriptions on the statues and fountains express sometimes enigmatically an ideal of natural order and other-worldly perfection attained, as in an Arcadian landscape, by this same supremely harmonious garden.

Villa Barbarigo, Valsanzibio. One of the fountains which run along the minor axis of the garden, with Diana's Bath in the background.

Villa Barbarigo. The Garenna, a small island for the rearing of rabbits, with its original aviary perfectly preserved.

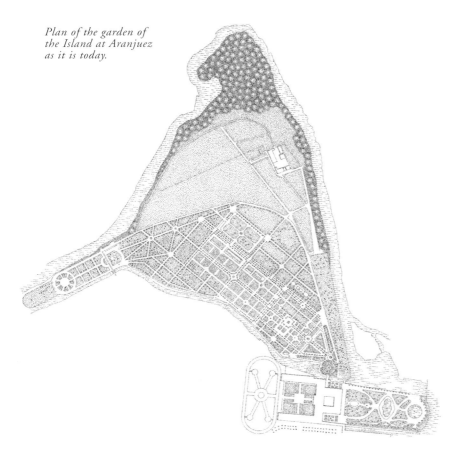

Plan of the garden of the Island at Aranjuez as it is today.

Austerity and tradition in the gardens of Spain

Throughout the sixteenth century, and especially during the long reign of Charles V (1519—56), the first Hapsburg king of Spain, Italian art exerted a powerful influence, particularly in architecture, though without inspiring any very important gardens. Nor did gardens hold a position of any importance in the lives of Spanish noblemen or the Spanish court, which was decidedly austere and little given to lavish entertaiments, apart from starchy court ceremonies and the devotional rituals of the royal monasteries. Even the many patios and courtyards of the imposing and ascetic palace of the Escorial, built by Charles's son Philip II, have no gardens worthy of note.

However, around 1562 Philip did create notable gardens at his residence in Aranjuez. Educated in Holland he preferred the style of the Dutch renaissance garden — divided into small compartments surrounded by geometrical clipped hedges — to the Italian model. Towards the end of the sixteenth century a small island in the river Tagus was incorporated to create the famous *Jardin de la Isla*, though its original design is not reliably documented. Only much later, in 1660, did Philip IV commission a new layout for the garden on the Isla, from Herrera Barnuevo, transforming it into a positive oasis in the plateau to the south of Madrid, whose bare barren landscape is a prelude to the desolate expanses of la Mancha.

The new design was configured along a single main axis, intersected by numerous secondary paths, giving the garden an air of austere grandeur. At Aranjuez, too, water was readily available, and became the backbone of the composition. Also

Aranjuez. Almost hidden by the jets of the fountains, the statue of Hercules towers in the centre of a large bassin on the small island designed by the Italian Cosimo Lotti.

on the central axis, the splendid Avenue of the Fountains was the main attraction, together with the many *jeux d'eau* and *scherzi d'acqua* situated along the so-called *avenida de los Burladores* (Avenue of the Jokers). In 1661 a Florentine gardener, Cosimo Lotti — who had worked on the island of Boboli under the supervision of Alfonso Parigi — was called to Aranjuez to design the spectacular Fountain of Hercules, modelled on that same island. In the eighteenth century certain features directly derived from French gardens, like *parterres, allées* of limes and *treillages* were added, but the seventeenth-century layout remained virtually untouched.

Cosimo Lotti had already been summoned to Spain in 1628 to work on the park of Buen Retiro in Madrid. The last of the Hapsburg gardens in Spain before the coming of the Bourbons, Buen Retiro signalled the end of Italian influence and the adoption of the French model in the style of Le Nôtre. Commissioned by Philip IV and situated on the eastern edges of the kingdom's new capital, Buen Retiro was realized and then extended in successive phases. The absence of any overall plan meant that the gardens never developed in a coherent fashion: a random succession of pools and *bassins* lacks any symmetrical relationship. The largest *bassin*, rectangular in form, is not aligned with the palace, and thus does not constitute the focal point of the main visual axis. Beyond is a large artificial lake, with a small island in the middle, formerly used for court entertainments; a navigable canal leads out of its south-eastern corner to other *bassins*.

On the death of the king the garden was abandoned.

During the eighteenth century various proposals for its renewal were never implemented. But for a long time Buen Retiro has been open to the public and today is Madrid's main public park. At the end of the century, when the Spanish branch of the Hapsburgs died out and the crown passed to Philip V of Bourbon, grandson of the Sun King, the style of the *Grand Siècle* arrived in Spain.

The small bridge linking the gardens of Aranjuez, austerely decorated with vases and statues.

At the Palacio de la Fronteira, near Lisbon, built in the baroque style, the colourful effect produced by the azulejos *combines with the reflective surface of the water to make the garden seem larger than it is.*

The Quinta de Bacalhoa in Estremadura is one of the earliest examples of the use of azulejos *for garden decoration. Used as cladding for both interiors and exteriors, such tiles, of Moorish origin, were a distinctive decorative element in Portuguese gardens.*

AZULEJO GARDENS IN PORTUGAL

With immense fortunes made in Brazil and the East Indies, throughout the sixteenth century the Portuguese built grandiose religious buildings and country residences in the Italian and French Renaissance styles, based on formal structures set in compartments surrounded by box hedges.

But local traditions survived alongside foreign influences. The renaissance use of tiled paving from the Roman tradition persisted, but decoration in *azulejos*, the characteristic Moorish tiles, became widespread. Imported from Spain at the end of the fifteenth century, during the next *azulejos* became established as a dominant feature in Portuguese architecture, thanks in part to the close ties between Portugal and north Africa, where interiors, as in all Muslim countries, were usually clad in ceramic surfaces.

Portuguese *azulejos* soon developed a style of their own, discarding the rigidly geometrical Islamic model with its frequent use of floral motifs, in accordance with Islamic law. Polychrome *azulejos* now began to include a variety of representations, the human figure among them, reminiscent of Italian majolica.

From the end of the sixteenth century Dutch ceramics were the main model, and *azulejos* became strictly monochrome, with the use of blue figures on a white ground. They reached the peak of their popularity in the seventeenth century, becoming the main medium for Portuguese creativity.

Together with *azulejos*, the Portuguese garden was also distinguished by the constant presence of water, with cascades, fountains and water jets derived from the Arab tradition, and large pools and expanses of water, reflecting the colour of the tiles decorating the walls or pavilions, often covered with moss and lichen because of the damp Atlantic climate.

Even when the 'prettier' rococo style caused lines to become more sinuous, exuberant coloured azulejos *still continued to be the prevalent form of garden ornament, as in this view of the* Quinta do Azulejos.

Used for cladding interiors, azulejos *were also used to cover whole outer walls; in this open-air gallery in the garden at Fronteira, they act as surrounds for the series of niches containing the busts of the kings of Portugal.*

One of the oldest Portuguese gardens is the Arab-inspired Quinta de Bacalhoa, in Estremadura. Apart from its formal garden, with four box-hedged compartments around a central fountain, Bacalhoa is also famous for having the oldest examples of polychrome *azulejos* (1565), in green, blue and yellow, inside an arcaded loggia overlooking a large rectangular water-tank.

One archetypal baroque garden with *azulejos* is that of the Palacio de le Fronteira, near Lisbon, created in 1672 for Dom Joao de Mascarenhas, Marquis of Fronteira. Here the blue and white of the tiles is the *leitmotiv*, with a construction entirely clad in *azulejos* standing out as a backdrop to a *parterre* of box, with statues and fountains. Either side of a large rectangular *bassin* two staircases frame an end wall rising from the water, divided into arches, with fourteen large figures of knights on horseback, composed entirely out of tiles, depicting members of the Mascarenhas family. Above, reached by the side staircases, a long terrace overlooking the pool is closed in from behind by a blue-tiled wall, decorated with niches containing statues of the kings of Portugal. Beyond this terrace, on a higher level, is the garden of Venus, also formal in design and decorated with *azulejos*.

Though it did not really have a style of its own, since it more or less followed the classical models, the Portuguese garden nonetheless made a distinctive contribution to the history of the genre, with a special sense of gaiety and Mediterranean sparkle conferred by its *azulejos* decoration.

The Dutch garden: water and colour triumphant

The long struggle for independence from Spain concluded with the peace of Antwerp in 1609, which endorsed the definitive orders of the United Provinces. Holland soon established herself as a fast-developing power: the first successfully to experiment with the notion of the commercial company. With the prototype East India Company, set up in Amsterdam in 1602, she soon became the chief player in international trade. Along with the establishment of international banks like the Bank of Amsterdam, companies founded on a combination of public and private capital gave the Dutch bourgeoisie a distinct economic advantage.

The Dutch garden played a particularly significant role in northern European culture from the seventeenth to the eighteenth century, as well as in her colonies in Brazil, South America and Indonesia. The great garden tradition, established during the sixteenth century on the architectural principles of Alberti, had fostered a philosophical and mystical vision which saw it as an ideal embodiment of the harmony and perfection of nature, a link between man and God. This idea of the garden thrived in a culture steeped in religious austerity, in which there was no place for the representation of the pagan myths and divinities typical of the Italian garden.

The Dutch garden thus cast off mythological allegories in favour of traditional Christian symbols, and developed in an independent manner, reworking characteristic Italian elements into sophisticated structures like wooden gazebos, circular pergolas, pavilions and colonnades. The codification and repetition of such elements gradually developed into a form of Mannerism, most perfectly expressed in the engravings of gardens by Hans Vredeman de Vries published in the treatise *Hortorum viridariumque elegantes et multiplicis formae* (Antwerp, 1583). As pattern books translating this particular concept of the garden into tangible images, de Vries's engravings were extremely popular and made the Dutch garden known throughout Europe.

Having begun to cast off its Renaissance origins at the end of the sixteenth century, the Dutch garden developed generally as a series of rectangular compartments, independent of each other but aligned, surrounded by hedges and pergolas; more complex structures, brought together to form intricate compositions of fountains and *parterres*, were also experimented with. In particular, de Vries's images illustrate one of the features that influenced the northern European gardens of the seventeenth century: the *parterre de piéces coupées* (cut-work). This type of *parterre*, inspired by the Dutch passion for flowers, consisted of an intricate pattern of various elements, each of which, differently designed and separated from the others by narrow passage-ways, created a bed for the cultivation of rare plants and exotic flowers.

This type of garden highlighted Dutch expertise in horticulture. A love of flowers developed alongside an awareness of the colonial markets with which the rich merchants traded.

The architectural vocabulary of the Dutch garden has its roots in the Italian garden, introduced by Hans Vredeman de Vries in his lavishly illustrated treatise published in Amsterdam in 1583.

Twickel, Delden. Over the years, the traditional castle moat gradually ceased to serve a defensive purpose and was transformed, with typical Dutch hydraulic expertise, into a dominant feature of the seventeenth-century Dutch garden.

The Dutch garden was therefore destined to be a flower garden, and consequently it favoured the continued presence of Renaissance elements like topiary and wooden trellises, ideal for showing off flowering species to advantage.

Another key element was water, usually still, in large *bassins* or long canals. This use of water was suggested by the landscape itself: the continual need to drain land reclaimed from the sea, a thorough knowledge of hydraulic techniques and the absolute flatness of the terrain encouraged experimentation with the ornamental potential of this natural element which, used over wide areas, also reflected the blue of the sky and flooded the gardens with light.

The Franco-Dutch garden

Towards the end of the century, the Stadholder William III of Orange, together with his wife Mary, daughter of James II of England, introduced aspects of Le Nôtre's model into the gardens of their royal residences. The combination of the Dutch tradition with French taste was to produce a particular style that came to be known as the Franco-Dutch, embodied most perfectly in the royal gardens of Het Loo, in Gelderland. Such royal gardens, and Het Loo in particular, rapidly became famous, influencing the construction of gardens throughout the Protestant north of Europe. Their style took root particularly in Great Britain after 1689 when William and Mary moved there with their entire court on becoming king and queen of England.

Renamed 'William and Mary' in England, this style in fact amounted to a transition between the renaissance tradition, to which Holland was still bound, and the fully-fledged baroque of the French model. Typically Dutch canals acted as boundaries to geometrical structures reminiscent of the Italian tradition, while the *parterres* now had the flowing lines characteristic of French taste and were brightened by hundreds of bulbs imported to Holland from remote countries. If architecture predominated in the Italian Baroque garden, and if in France special emphasis was placed on the plant element, the 'William and Mary' garden gave particular importance to a balanced though contrasting relationship between geometrical design and natural form, between structures and flowers.

The original project for the royal gardens of Het Loo — realized between 1686 and 1695, near Apeldoorn in Gelderland — by the court architect Jacob Roman was extended and then further embellished by the Frenchman Daniel Marot after 1689, the year when William and Mary came to the throne. Dutch in layout and French in ornamentation, the garden clearly bore the mark of its two designers: at once coherent and complex, Het Loo was the most complete, and resplendent, example of the 'William and Mary' style, and has recently been restored to its former glory.

The geometrical layout followed the criterion of the central axis and a symmetrical structure, with a rich array of fountains, canals and cascades (over fifty in 1699 according to a description compiled in that same year). Nothing

A classic example of the Franco-Dutch style, the garden at Het Loo, in Gelderland, has recently been recreated according to the original layout.

remained of its original design — it had been transformed into a landscape park by Louis Bonaparte in 1807 — until its complete reconstruction, begun in the seventies and completed in 1984.

Aligned with the facade of the palace, the Great Garden covers some six hectares (fifteen acres), over two slightly staggered levels: the Lower Garden and the Upper. Surrounded by canals on three sides and divided up by an orthogonal grid of avenues, the Lower Garden has eight *parterres* with complex arabesque designs, in the style shown in de Vries's engravings, with a double *plate-bande* running around its edge with box bushes clipped into cones aligned along it. In keeping with the French taste for classical iconography, a fountain of Venus stands in the centre, with the fountains of the terrestrial Globe and celestial Globe to each side, along the median axis which crosses the garden. Beyond them, up against the walls of the side terracing, are the cascades of Narcissus and Galatea. From the Lower Garden, still along the main axis, crossing a transverse avenue of oaks forming a sort of green colonnade, the visitor continues to the Upper Garden, which is divided into grassy beds and dominated by the King's Fountain, whose one central jet, naturally fed, is over thirteen metres (43 ft.) high. A semi-circular colonnade rises in the background — a typical feature of the sixteenth-century Dutch garden — its open centre allowing the eye to take in the vista of a distant obelisk, acting as the focal point of the lengthy perspective.

The influence of the Dutch garden in Europe

Over the last years of the seventeenth century, Het Loo became one of the most famous and admired gardens of the time, a model which was to be widely imitated. The Franco-Dutch style was to be very popular in many countries in northern Europe, but above all in England, where it continued to exert an influence for many years. In Germany too many gardens were inspired by Het Loo, and its fame even reached Russia, influencing the gardens of Peter the Great's Summer Palace in St Petersburg in particular.

English gardens, which had already adopted the great tree-lined *allées* and geometrical symmetries of the French style, moved closer to the more inward-looking though still rigidly formal 'William and Mary' style when the Dutch court moved to Great Britain. The English gave a particularly enthusiastic welcome to the use of topiaried evergreens, a recurrent feature of the Dutch garden. This style was especially suited to smaller gardens, and continued to be used almost throughout the eighteenth century, even after the rise of the informal landscaped garden.

When the new sovereigns moved to England, they decided to redesign the sixteenth-century palace and gardens of Hampton Court, Henry VIII's palace overlooking the Thames. With them they brought Daniel Marot, the designer of Het Loo, who now created an elaborate *parterre de broderie* for the Great Fountain Garden, in striking contrast with the simple design proposed by Christopher Wren. Surrounded by a low

Fountain of the Terrestrial Globe at Het Loo. Here a love of jeux d'eau *goes hand-in-hand with an interest in science and the geographical discoveries of the seventeenth century.*

Het Loo, Gelderland. If in the sixteenth-century Mannerist Dutch garden the allusions were mainly religious, with the influence of the French Baroque mythological figures made an appearance, as in the Fountain of Venus in the centre of the garden.

hedge of dwarf box, this *parterre* was decorated with statues, pyramids of yew, and globes of bay and holly; around it were no fewer than thirteen fountains linking the palace and the semi-circular canal to the north. Today all that remains of this design is the central fountain and the canal: Queen Anne, who succeeded to the throne on the death of William, destroyed the thirteen fountains and *parterre*, replacing them with a large lawn, and allowing the yew to grow freely. The same fate awaited the formal *parterre* of the Privy Garden on the south side, Queen Mary's pride and passion: abandoned, allowed to grow undisturbed and remodelled on several occasions, this small garden has recently been scrupulously restored to its original seventeenth-century appearance.

Apart from remodelling the gardens at Hampton Court, William II also commissioned the gardens for his newly-acquired London residence, Kensington Palace, from George London, the well-known garden designer who, together with Henry Wise, ran the famous and well-stocked nursery at Brompton Park. For Kensington Gardens, London designed an elaborate *parterre* with the typical geometrically clipped evergreens and a wilderness, a vast wooded area crossed by avenues and paths. The gardens as we see them today, however, are the result of the numerous extensions and alterations carried out mainly during the eighteenth century: merged with adjacent Hyde Park and accessible to Londoners from the middle of the eighteenth century, they were finally opened to the general public, during the reign of Queen Victoria.

The shell-encrusted rocaille fountain *in the grotto at Het Loo, a masterpiece of its kind.*

View of the garden of Hampton Court, London. The Franco-Dutch taste was imported into English gardens, as we see from

Queen Mary's Privy Garden (left of illustration) and the long canal (bottom) at the centre of the classical layout of avenues à patte d'oie.

The best-preserved garden in the Dutch style in England is Westbury Court in Gloucestershire. The tall, narrow summer-house, overlooking a long canal closed in on both sides by geometrically clipped evergreen hedges, is plainly of Dutch inspiration. The garden is completely protected from the outside world by walls and tall hedges: it has over five thousand yew and holly trees clipped into hedges and topiary figures. Another Dutch characteristic is the prominence given to flowers and fruit trees, espaliered along the walls.

In Germany, where the art of the garden had languished until the second half of the century, the first works making use of the baroque canons now becoming established throughout Europe were particularly sensitive to the Dutch influence. One of the gardens which most clearly reflected Dutch taste was the park of Herrenhausen, near Hannover, which signalled the definitive transition from the Renaissance to the Baroque.

The castle and gardens had originally been created as a summer residence for the dukes of Hanover from 1666, when a pre-existing agricultural estate was transformed with the building of a pavilion and the laying out of the earliest gardens. Around 1673 a new *parterre* was created to the sides of the Schloss, with a Grotto and Cascades, but the real power behind the royal gardens at Herrenhausen was the Electress Sophie, the wife of the Chief Elector of Hanover. From 1680 Sophie devoted herself passionately to the decoration and later extension of the gardens, calling upon Martin Charbonnier, the French gardener already in her service. Their collaboration produced a park whose layout was clearly French-inspired, but

reflecting the Dutch love of water and flowers Sophie had brought to Germany from her childhood in Holland.

A first phase of some ten years saw the implementation of the new design, based on the layout of the pre-existing garden. The area was divided up with strictly orthogonal axes to create various rectangular sections, symmetrically arranged to the sides of the main axis. In front of the castle eight compartments with *parterres* were built, following the French criterion requiring that decoration become sparser the further its distance from the main building. The four innermost *parterres*, around the circular *bassin* placed in line with the central axis and the so-called Fountain of the Bells, were therefore laid out *à l'anglaise*, that is, treated as grassy surfaces crossed by small orthogonal avenues, brightened by flowers and framed by *plate-bandes*. The four outermost *parterres*, on the other hand, were less ornamental and simply surrounded by flower-filled borders. To the sides of the *parterre* area were two large garden rooms: a maze to the right and, to the left, the beautiful hedge theatre, made between 1689 and 1693, which soon became the garden's crowning glory. The two fish ponds marking the limits of the garden in front of the Schloss were transformed into four square *bassins* edged with rows of trees clipped into geometrical shapes; a series of hedged rooms was added, later altered in a variety of styles and these, together with the *bassins*, completed the perimeter of the garden.

By the beginnings of the nineties, however, the Schloss and garden no longer fulfilled the needs of life at court, and a new extension was embarked on. Still intent on giving

Westbury Court, Gloucestershire. With its Dutch-style pavilion, this is the best-preserved English garden inspired by the Dutch tradition.

Bird's-eye view of the gardens of Herrenhausen. In Germany, Dutch taste found expression mainly in the use of canals to encircle the entire composition with water.

Herrenhausen the mood of the Dutch gardens she had so loved, Sophie now sent Charbonnier to Holland for a second time to study the gardens of the court of Orange. On his return he began work on the so-called *Grosser Garten*, joined to the earlier one by prolonging the central axis, and doubling the depth of the perspective. This new, broader avenue starts from a semi-circular space annexed to the old garden, and runs towards a large circular *bassin* with a central jet over eighty metres (260 ft.) in height, today the highest in Europe. The avenue ends with a large round open space surrounded by trees. One single broad canal, the *Graft*, rings the entire garden. Star-shaped oblique paths branch off the central avenue, through *bosquets* and orchards with tall hedges; the intersections are punctuated with *bassins* and fountains.

The Dutch character of the garden is seen most clearly in the canal, in the use of flowers in the *parterres*, and in the still rigorously rectangular compartmentalization typical of Dutch tradition. French influence, on the other hand, is evident in the general layout, conceived as a single large *bosquet*, and in the star-shaped paths and rich complement of statues; unlike the classical French gardens, however, Herrenhausen has no adjacent hunting-park.

But it is the hedge theatre which is Herrenhausen's greatest glory, not just for its sophisticated design but also its size. Trapezoid in shape, it is basically an elongated composition whose depth is further accentuated by the perspective wings formed from tall beech hedges, and by the gilt-lead statues brought from Holland. It has all the feel of a real architectural structure forged out of greenery: in front of the stage is an orchestra pit, and the public could watch performances from an auditorium in the shape of an amphitheatre. The theatre is still used in the summer months.

Sadly, the Schloss was destroyed during World War II, but a wide-ranging and complex restoration, begun during the thirties and resumed after the war, has restored the garden to its original state. Fortunately, unlike that of many European gardens, the baroque layout of Herrenhausen never suffered the landscape alterations so in vogue from the end of the eighteenth century. From 1714, in fact, on becoming George I of England, the Elector of Hanover moved his entire court to London, and the spectacular gardens of Het Loo were left essentially untouched.

Royal Gardens at Herrenhausen, Hannover. In accordance with the traditional Dutch passion for flowers, the parterres *are made up of elaborate flower-filled beds.*

Herrenhausen's real jewel is the hedge theatre (bottom, left), whose depth is heightened by the irregular arrangement of its 'wings', and the statues brought especially from Holland. Here, too,

water is a powerful presence, with a soaring jet of water (below) rising from a large circular bassin *placed on the central axis.*

Endlessly varied, bulbs have always been particularly popular in Holland, and vast tracts of flowering and bulbous plants are still found throughout the Dutch countryside today.

The frontispiece of the treatise Hortus floridus *gives an idea of the importance of flowers in seventeenth-century Holland, their number and variety making the structure of the flowerbeds almost illegible.*

SEVENTEENTH-CENTURY HOLLAND: FLOWERS WORTH THEIR WEIGHT IN GOLD

The sixteenth-century interest in science and botany, which led to the making of the first botanic gardens throughout Europe and particularly in Italy, burgeoned during the seventeenth century. Together with the thirst for exotic curiosities, it was to have a crucial bearing on the development of the garden.

The creation of the botanic garden at the University of Leiden in 1587, and the studies of Carolus Clusius — whose Flemish name was Charles de l'Ecluse — marked a turning-point in the history of Dutch horticulture. Clusius was the first European scholar to concern himself with botany and taxonomy in a truly scientific manner. The director of Leiden's botanic garden from 1594, he took an interest in ornamental as well as the traditional medicinal varieties, introducing numerous species native to the eastern Mediterranean and importing plants from Spain, Portugal and Hungary.

By the seventeenth century a passion for botany had taken hold in Holland, and was fast becoming a distinctive facet of Dutch culture. In 1614, Crispin Van de Pass published the *Hortus Floridus*, a herbal cataloguing almost a hundred species to be planted in gardens, lavishly illustrated and organized on a seasonal basis.

Bulbous plants in particular now became one of the mainstays of every Dutch garden. Not only the ubiquitous tulip, but also fritillaries, hyacinths, sunflowers, crocuses, lilies, anemonies, gladioli, belle-de-nuit, narcissi and marigolds ornamented *parterres* of small flowerbeds separated by paths, modelled on the *parterre de pièces coupées* shown in Vredeman de Vries's engravings from the previous century.

The passion reached such a pitch that flowers became indisputably the main

A pearl among flowers, the tulip is virtually the emblem of Holland. Seventeenth-century tulipomania saw speculators and collectors ruined in the tulip trade.

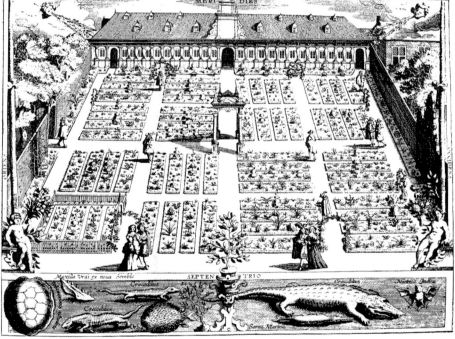

The botanic garden at Leiden, in an engraving of 1655. Most of the species newly introduced into Europe were first grown at Leiden so that their ornamental qualities might be assessed, then passed on to other European gardens. In 1633 the garden's index seminum *numbered a little over a thousand species, which had risen to six thousand a century later.*

attraction, particularly in the small gardens of the urban bourgeoisie where they were found in the *parterres de broderie* copied from the French. Many varieties of exotic flowers became collectors' items, but the one that above all fired the passion and imagination was the tulip. According to tradition, in 1554 the Holy Roman Empire's ambassador to the Turkish sultan, Suleiman the Magnificent, saw tulips for the first time in Turkish gardens and decided to take some bulbs home with him. On his return to Vienna, the ambassador presented the flower, naming it 'tulip', having misunderstood the Turkish term *tulipand*, meaning turban, used by his

guide to describe its shape. It was Clusius himself — prefect of the imperial gardens in Vienna during those years — who disseminated the tulip bulb throughout Europe.

In Holland, tulips became a positive mania, with companies formed simply to speculate on their trade. Prices climbed to dizzying heights, on a par with diamonds, particularly in the case of specimens displaying a strange tendency to develop unexpected colours and iridescences, which we now know to have been caused by a virus. In 1637 the frantic rise in prices precipitated a crisis that brought some speculators to the

verge of bankruptcy.

Botanical collecting spread rapidly from Holland to other nations with vast empires, and scholars and artists were commissioned to collect and illustrate the most decorative species. Collecting was particularly in vogue in Britain, which in the eighteenth and nineteenth centuries became the chief importer of exotic plants.

The concept of self-aggrandizement and the passion for the 'marvellous', inherent in the gardens of the sixteenth century, assumed yet more influence during the seventeenth century, and the baroque age gave them tangible form in vast, grandiose and stupendous works. The garden became immense, merging into the countryside, with endless vistas drawing the gaze towards the distant horizon. This sense of immensity could only be rendered by very broad views, with infinite perspectives: a single overall picture could only be obtained from a very distant vantage point, and a bird's-eye view was the natural answer. The resulting image could take in compositions *à perte de vue*, at a glance.

The bird's-eye view — already used to represent late-renaissance gardens — was thus the best means of representing the baroque garden, closely linked as it was to the theatre, and created with specific scenographic techniques that made it possible illusorily to expand real space. Widely used in both France and England, bird's-eye views often focused on a central vanishing point, characteristic of the classical French garden in the *Grande Manière*. Logically enough, it was to remain in use throughout the eighteenth century to depict the vast geometrical and symmetrical creations of the baroque.

With the arrival of the landscaped garden bird's-eye perspective, unsuitable for the representation of informal gardens, was gradually discarded. It returned again in the middle of the nineteenth century with the revival of interest in the *grand siècle*, when the natural association between the bird's-eye view and gardens in the *Grande Manière* was re-established to be used, for instance, for the restorations of the gardens of Le Nôtre and the depiction of various new creations.

THE REPRESENTATION OF THE GARDEN: THE BOUNDLESS GARDEN AND THE BIRD'S-EYE VIEW

1. Wilton House, Wiltshire. When the Italian style began to give way to the French model in England, the bird's-eye view, already widely used during the Renaissance, became de rigueur *for the representation of the increasingly vast spaces involved. Although the Italian model was largely retained in the general structure, French taste was already evident in the decoration of the* parterres, *while the broadening of the central axis served to heighten the sweeping sense of perspective.*

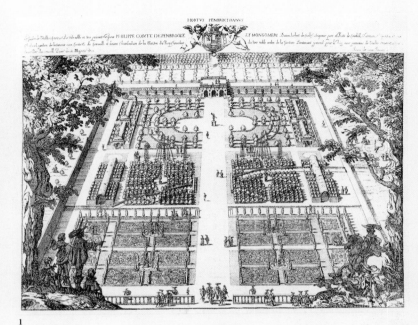

1

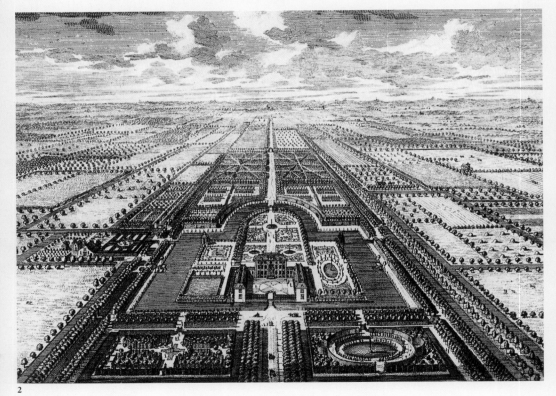

2

2. Zeist, Utrecht. Here the French model has clearly been established, and the central perspective typical of the Baroque era becomes predominant. The whole complex runs mainly along a median axis, whose length is emphasized by the technique of the drawing. Of particular interest is the strict grid of the trees in the surrounding fields, the unremitting regularity of which underlines the garden's axial development.

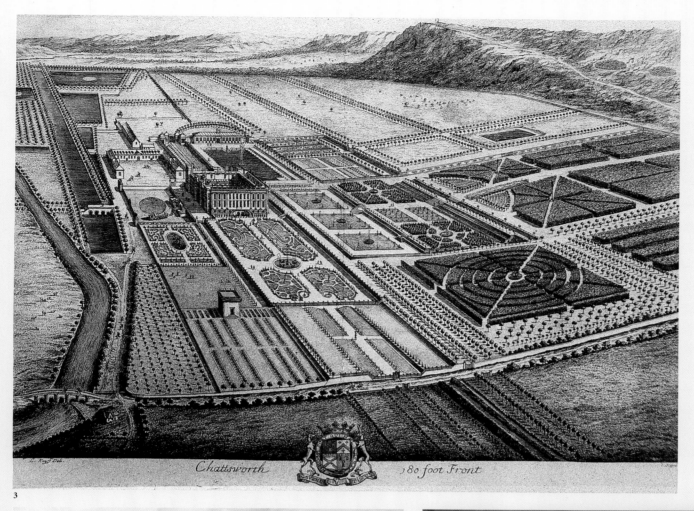

3. *Chatsworth, Derbyshire. When applied in England, the French rule was somewhat softened: the layout had a freer, less absolutely monoaxial lie, and there were already signs that the project was more sensitive to the contours of the landscape. Here the water-course was not diverted, nor higher ground flattened, as had happened at Versailles.*

3

4

5

4. *At Versailles, the epitome of the French classical model, the perspective was absolutely central: in this painting, to emphasize the monoaxial layout, Pierre Patel has given particular emphasis to the higher ground to the sides of the level area, as though to draw attention to Louis XIV's immense programme of excavation to level the terrain. The dauntingly vast dimensions are further heightened by the painter's skill in rendering the distinctive light emanating from the great expanse of the Grand Canal.*

5. *St-Cloud, Hauts-de-Seine. Here the perspective is not centred along the main axis of the garden, with the cascades: rather, Le Nôtre chose to exploit the landscape possibilities offered by the Seine at the foot of the rise, using it to replace the long wide canals he was making in his other gardens. That the bird's-eye view of St-Cloud should be oriented along the flow of the Seine, following its sinuous ribbon of brightness as far as the horizon, would therefore seem in keeping with the underlying principle of Le Nôtre's project.*

The eighteenth century

The return to Arcadia

Signs of the political, social and cultural developments that would so thoroughly revolutionize the complexion of Europe towards the end of the eighteenth century, were in fact already visible during its first years. The wars of succession and the expansionism of the great nation states saw the emergence of new powers, and led to the birth of colonial empires; scientific progress and enlightened thought fostered a different vision of man and society; at the threshold of the nineteenth century the crisis of monarchical absolutism and the rise of the bourgeoisie, culminating in the French Revolution, were to lead to the terminal collapse of the *Ancien Régime*.

After the death of Louis XIV in 1715, French hegemony began to crumble, to the benefit of the other European powers, constantly battling among themselves to maintain an international balance, however precarious. Yet the French cultural model remained the chief point of reference for the ruling houses, and Versailles, symbol of power and the lavish and worldly manifestation of a centralizing court, endured as a myth to be emulated, above all among the many German principalities.

While naturally retaining a strong aesthetic component distinguished by the pomp and grandiosity of the Baroque, eighteenth-century art gradually shed the ethical content and celebratory messages, and assumed the previous age's stylistic and formal preferences of a cynical hedonism. Emulation of the French style found expression in excessive decoration, affected, mawkish and frivolous. Towards the middle of the century such whimsically exaggerated forms led to the flamboyant excesses of the rococo, particularly in German-speaking countries.

Throughout the eighteenth century the compositional principles of the French garden — by now canonical — continued to be re-worked. The *Grande Manière* had long since reached its apogee with the works of Le Nôtre; now on the wane, it had crystallized into a static image whose components were reproduced as though immutable, codified and glorified by innumerable treatises.

Comparison of the plan of Versailles by Le Pautre, 1710 (left), with the engraving by Jacques Rigaud of the park at Stowe (right), as a pointer to the extent to which the gardens of the Sun King served as a model throughout Europe, though at Stowe the elements derived from Versailles are less rigidly distributed.

Opposite) The ice-house in the park of the Desert de Retz, Yvelines.

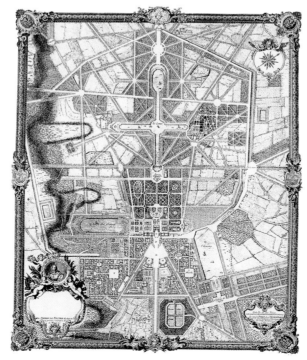
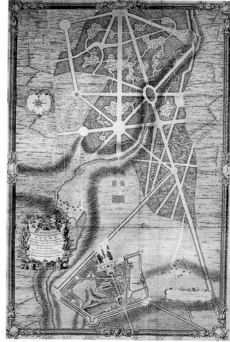

The Chinese pavilion at Sanssouci, Potsdam. The fashion for chinoiserie erupted in the eighteenth century as an imaginary interpretation of China and its gardens, though the often bombastic results were far removed from the mood of the original.

The garden of Villa Arconati Crivelli, known as il Castellazzo, Lombardy. Designed by the Frenchman Jean Gianda, it adopted the typically French palissade with elegant topiary work, seen to great effect in this engraving by Marc'Antonio dal Re (1743).

As previously mentioned, the best-known and most popular of these was Dezallier d'Argenville's *La Théorie et la pratique du jardinage* which became a veritable planners' manual, disseminating the style of Louis XIV throughout Europe.

Since all the great art and architecture of those years bore the hallmark of the ambitions of princes and rulers aspiring to build themselves palaces worthy of comparison with Versailles, buildings old and new alike were inspired by the French works of the *Grand Siècle*, albeit in many and differing 'interpretations'. The fruit of emulation rather than imitation, in every country the model was filtered through the most disparate factors, such as the configuration of the terrain, local cultural peculiarities or simply the taste of the person commissioning the work.

For some years the English — who were among the first to adopt the French style in the seventeenth century — continued to create baroque gardens in the *Grande Manière*, combining Le Nôtre's model with Dutch influence. But with the passage of time a new philosophy of art and nature gained ground, in striking contrast to Baroque contrivance and exaggeration, ultimately leading to a completely different concept of the garden.

In France, in the meantime, in the wake of the technical and scientific progress begun in the previous century, a boundless faith in human reason, in man's abilities to probe and grasp the universe and nature, was taking root: enlightened thought was born, and then exported throughout Europe through the work of, among others, Rousseau, Voltaire and Diderot.

With its new understanding of man's relations with the world and nature, enlightened rationalism — whose sociological and libertarian drift prepared the ground for the French Revolution — was to have a significant bearing on the art of the garden. But while the emergent English attitude to nature was laying the foundations for the future landscape revolution, in the rest of Europe the baroque aesthetic and the classical layout of the garden — particularly in Germany — were moving towards the more contrived and precious forms of the rococo.

Splendour and originality in the German garden

After a slow recovery from the devastation wrought by the Thirty Years War, the German principalities began to show a growing interest in gardens as elaborate settings for the pomp and circumstance of their courts. The baroque garden in the French mould became the height of fashion, and Versailles remained the chief model for almost the whole of the eighteenth century. The German princes were wealthy and cultured, and they lavished their resources upon splendid works of architecture and town-planning. But their main passion — which continued into the nineteenth century — was gardens.

The courts attracted artists from all Europe: the gardens that resulted combine Italian, French and Dutch features with local innovation. The obligatory grandeur and sheer scale of French baroque was variously influenced. In southern Germany the Italian baroque was more in evidence, while in the north the French model combined with borrowings from the Dutch, as we have already seen in late seventeenth century gardens like Herrenhausen. Although the German princes continued to employ almost exclusively Italian and French artists, their designs developed, despite the reiteration of Baroque features in a highly original and independent direction; indeed, the gardens of the German rococo are some of the most fascinating creations of European garden culture. The creators of German gardens were keenly aware of their potential as theatrical spaces, and accordingly they scattered their gardens with open-air theatres, together with pavilions and similar structures suitable for performances. Even the *orangeries* which sprang up everywhere often became auditoriums for musical and theatrical entertainments. With the passion for chinoiserie and all things oriental, many such buildings came to look increasingly exotic, and were decorated with Indian or Chinese motifs.

The waning of the baroque

Clearly inspired by Versailles, Charlottenburg — the great Schloss built in Berlin for his wife Sophie Charlotte by the Elector Frederick III of Brandenburg, crowned King of Prussia in 1701 — had one of the first German baroque gardens. The daughter of Sophie of Hanover, the creator of Herrenhausen, Sophie Charlotte had the good fortune to commission her garden from Simeon Godeau, a pupil of Le Nôtre; the layout, however, was still broadly dependent on the Dutch model, particularly well-suited to this garden's situation on the banks of the Spree.

The design followed the classical scheme, with a broad central vista: a long *parterre* divided up into eight sections, reminiscent of Herrenhausen, ran from the Schloss flanked by avenues and four rows of trees. At the end of the *parterre* was a large *bassin*, beyond which the view, crossing the transversely flowing river, continued *à perte de vue*. The garden continued on the west side with a series of garden rooms and *bosquets*, using hedges in the French style.

After 1786 the park at Charlottenburg was completely remodelled as an English landscape park, with the transformation of the great *bassin* into a natural lake and the addition of a number of buildings. The garden suffered extensive damage during the Second World War, but the *parterre* has now been painstakingly restored to its original baroque design.

Augustusburg, Bruhl. Here the components of the typical baroque parterre *are utterly faithful to their models, with* broderies, plate-bandes, bassins *and* topiary.

Further south at Assia, where contact with Italian culture had remained closer, in 1705 Carl, Landgrave of Hesse-Kassel, began work on the grandiose garden on the southern slope of mount Karlsberg, taking the baroque gardens of Frascati as a model. Known as Wilhelmshöhe after the Chief Elector Wilhelm I who undertook its final rearrangement as an English landscaped park, Karlsberg bears witness to the persistence of the Italian idea of the garden even forty years after work had begun on Versailles. The project was actually commissioned from an Italian artist, Giovanni Guerniero: an immense terraced garden was to be created against the hill, undoubtedly inspired by the theatrical cascade at villa Aldobrandini at Frascati which Landgrave saw when in Italy between 1699 and 1700.

Unlike at Charlottenburg, at Wilhelmshöhe — partly because of the uneven terrain — cascades and *jeux d'eau* in the Italian style featured more than flowerbeds and *parterres*. The project included a vast water staircase, fed by a monumental octagonal reservoir known as the Octagon, which was to flow from the hill to the foot of the Schloss. But this ambitious project was only partly realised: after the first stretch of the cascade had been completed in 1715, work broke off below the Octagon. The shape of this reservoir was dictated by the typically baroque love of contrast between natural setting and artificial superstructure: from its base — in basalt to give it a craggy appearance — rose a two-storey structure reminiscent of palazzo Farnese at Caprarola. The Octagon is crowned by a soaring pyramid topped with a gigantic copy of the Farnese Hercules, over eight metres (26 ft.) high. The long axis serving as a visual link between the Octagon and the Schloss, while still formal in layout, was cut through the heart of the woods, leaving the park with an untamed look and the general feel of a game reserve.

Franco-Dutch influence, on the other hand, is evident in the gardens of Maximilian II, Elector of Bavaria. As governor of the Low Countries between 1692 and 1701 Maximilian had become familiar with Dutch gardens and their sophisticated hydraulic techniques. Later, during his years of exile in France, where the War of the Spanish Succession had driven him to take refuge, he had come into contact with French garden culture. This, coupled with hopes of seeing his son on the throne of Spain, moved him to build himself splendid palaces at Schleissheim and Nymphenburg, both near Munich, and to devote himself passionately to their gardens.

In 1701, on his return from the Low Countries, Maximilian embarked on the sumptuous new residence of Nymphenburg, and a second, the Neues Schloss, to be built at Schleissheim in front of the existing sixteenth-century property, the Lustheim, drawing inspiration for both projects from what he had seen in Holland. Work was suspended when he was driven into exile, and resumed only after his return in 1715. At Schleissheim the gardens, occupying the restricted space between the two castles, adopted the Dutch approach, while the larger gardens at Nymphenburg conformed to the more expansive French tradition. Indeed at Nymphenburg the general plan followed the classical scheme — a typical vista with a sequence of *bosquets* and a *grand parc* — though the generous use of canals to underline the axis confirms an original Dutch inspiration. The entire design originated around a pair of very long canals, interlinked by two arms extended so as to enclose the palace and entire *petit parc*: one runs from the main façade towards the city; the other, behind the building, runs along the central axis of the perspective 'telescope' that crosses the park. The *parterre* to the rear, which originally had *broderie*, has a large circular *bassin* in its centre, with gilded statues and classical *bosquets* along the sides.

Later, Maximilian built three small 'castles' on either side of the great canal, in the densely-wooded park intersected by avenues *à patte d'oie*: the Badenburg, the Magdalenenklause

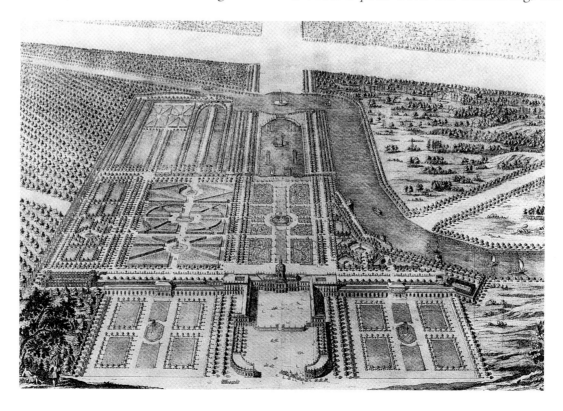

Bird's-eye view of Charlottenburg, Berlin. One interesting feature of the composition is that the river Spree has been incorporated into it, along the main axis.

and the Pagodenburg, a small pagoda-like pavilion reflecting the contemporary passion for chinoiserie. In 1739, before the park was redesigned in the landscape style, a lavish hunting-lodge was added, the Amalienburg, a true gem of German art marking the transition between the baroque and the rococo.

At Schleissheim, on the other hand, the original baroque layout, which has survived unscathed, already prefigured rococo developments in the German garden. Its small size precluded the classical scheme, and the result was a secluded space, projected inwards rather than outwards. Here too water plays an important role in the layout. Two canals mark the limits of the whole garden, while a third forms the main axis of perspective, linking the two castles to end in the monumental cascade in front of the Neues Schloss. A ring of water surrounds the Lustheim and its *parterre*, giving them the appearance of standing on an island. A succession of *bosquets*

lines both sides of the main axis, with circular and star-shaped paths bordered by hedges. The *parterre* of the Neues Schloss, further confirming its Dutch inspiration, is set slightly below the level of the garden, and has round *bassins* at the ends of its two long sections. The decoration of the *parterre*, by the Frenchman Dominique Girard, was originally *à pieces coupées*, with flower-filled borders; very little now remains of the lavish array of statuary that once completed the ornamentation. At Schleissheim the classical scheme is deployed for the first time in a less rigid and patrician way — with the experimental use of new, more imaginative forms of decoration rightly causing the garden to be seen as anticipating the new rococo.

The rococo garden

By the end of the second decade of the eighteenth century, the rigidly formulaic French model had been conclusively super-

The cascades at Wilhelmshöhe, Kassel, centred on the long visual axis that includes the Schloss and proceeds beyond it towards the city.

Wilhelmshöhe includes a number of Italian quotations, particularly from the gardens of Frascati: the statue of the Farnese Hercules, the structure of the Octagon, reminiscent of the palazzo at Caprarola, and the statues of woodland creatures like the centaur, visible on the right, recalling the figures in the nymphaeum at Villa Aldobrandini.

The use of canals at
Nymphenburg is typi-
cally Dutch, though
here, unusually, the
canal runs along the
axis of the entrance
from the city.

Nymphenburg, Munich.
Beyond the Schloss, at
the end of the petit
parc, the canal contin-
ues in the form of a
severe cascade decorated
with the typical statues
of river gods.

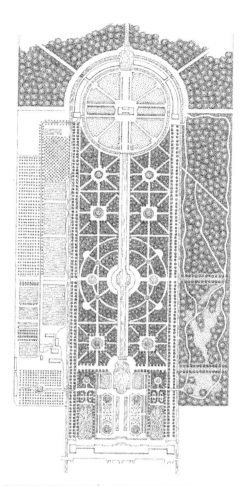

The plan of Schleissheim, Bavaria, indicates a shift away from the baroque model, with circular paths and canals the first signs of a new tendency.

Unlike its baroque equivalent, which heightened the sense of an infinite perspective, the parterre of the Neues Schloss at Schleissheim is laid out as a built element at the end of a vista.

At the end of the vista (below) stands the old castle, the Lustheim, with a parterre of gazon coupé.

(Over page) The Indianisches Haus (Indian House) at Augustusburg. The fashion for all things oriental was an integral part of the rococo outlook, less classical and patrician, and more sensitive to specific decoration.

seded, and the German garden was beginning to discard majesty in favour of prettiness: if the rococo garden retained the regular layout and compositional elements of the Baroque aesthetic, it also ushered in changes in design and spatial distribution. The basic structure became more varied and inventive, the decorative elements lighter and prettier, in accordance with the contemporary passion for extravagant and exotic forms. The demands of self-celebration — associated with the monoaxial and central structure — were gradually set aside, and interest in prolonging the vistas out over the countryside waned. Gardens retreated into themselves, drew inwards. Symmetry, formerly utterly unbending, now adapted to less static forms, giving movement and variety to the opportunities the garden itself had to offer: no longer conceived as a vast composition to be taken in at a glance, each part was now planned as an individual independent unit. Each element, studied and decorated in its every detail, became an inducement for a lighter, playful use of green space, more intimate and welcoming. The vogue for chinoiserie and the Orient prompted the creation of Chinese pavilions, pagodas, tea-rooms and other structures inspired by distant places or simply decorated in the oriental style; these were dotted throughout the garden and its *bosquets,* to lend the composition a more worldly and exotic tone.

One of the most intriguing rococo gardens is Schwetzingen in Baden-Württemberg. The court's summer residence, Schwetzingen, like many contemporary castles, stood on the ruins of one destroyed during the Thirty Years War. In 1748 the Elector Karl Theodor entrusted the construction of its huge garden to the court gardener Johann Ludwig Petri, who designed the original circular *parterre* that is Schwetzingen's main feature and innovation. Its peculiar design was inspired by the two semi-circular wings of the castle, built by Alessandro Galli-Bibiena and Nicolas de Pigage, which housed *orangeries* and drawing-rooms for various entertainments. The yoke of Le Nôtre's rigidly marshalled schemes had been comprehensively cast off.

The circle of the *parterre,* emphasized by orthogonal and transverse axes, flanked by rows of Dutch limes, is bounded on the opposite side by two semi-circular pergolas constructed of wooden trellises. The great axis of the central perspective, with the fountain of Arion standing out triumphantly in the centre of the *parterre,* originally ended in a large rectangular *bassin.* The *bosquets,* with cross-shaped and star-shaped paths,

open out into little clearings with *bassins*, statues, fountains and small structures. After 1761 they were further extended and the gardens completed with new buildings richly decorated with statues and fountains, and in 1776, with the addition of area of grass in the English manner. The rococo *Orangerie* and theatre were now joined by a bath-house set in a romantic 'natural' *bosquet*, the ruins of a Roman aqueduct, a temple to botany, another to Mercury, and a Turkish Mosque. A sense of the 'natural' was thus grafted on to the original rococo conception, turning each *bosquet* into an independent, more intimate garden.

However, it is the garden of Veitshöchheim, the residence of the prince bishops of Würzburg, which is rightly regarded as the rococo garden par excellence. Its definitive layout was the brainchild of the prince bishop Adam Friedrich von Seinscheim, who created it between 1763 and 1776. The garden parallels one side of the castle without any axial connection to the main façade, overlooking a *parterre* dating from an earlier period. Completely surrounded by walls whose perimeter is an almost perfect rectangle, the garden is divided up by three straight main axes, which do not mark out any one area as being pre-eminent, and are intersected at right angles by

transverse axes; short oblique walks break up the regular design. Hedged garden rooms are placed at the intersections of the axes, with niches, fountains and pavilions; the spaces between the hedges are filled with fruit- and other trees. The garden's main decorative feature is its rich complement of statues, originally numbering at least 300, mostly by the sculptor Ferdinand Tietz and representing gods, allegories of the arts and seasons, and noblemen and ladies of the court. To the right of the avenue of limes that constitutes the median axis the visitor comes upon the so-called *Grosser See*, at once the focal point and main attraction, a large, irregularly-shaped *bassin* with a sculptural group by Tietz in its centre, depicting Mount Parnassus with Apollo and the nine Muses, surmounted by Pegasus about to fly off towards Olympus.

The garden has all the variety typical of the rococo: to the left of the avenue of limes, in a central position and on an axis with the Parnassus group, is a large round clearing surrounded by hedges, with a circular pergola. To the north, beyond an avenue of Norway spruce, is a wood containing the Theatre, the Hedge Room, the Lime Room and *bassins* with statues representing the fable of the fox and the stork. Along the paths in the wood stand other sculpted ornaments, including

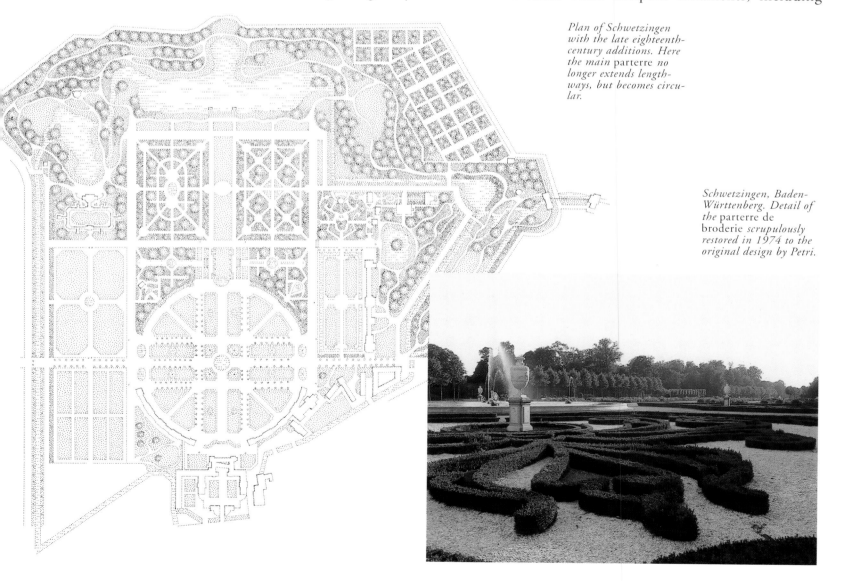

Plan of Schwetzingen with the late eighteenth-century additions. Here the main parterre *no longer extends lengthways, but becomes circular.*

Schwetzingen, Baden-Württenberg. Detail of the parterre de broderie *scrupulously restored in 1974 to the original design by Petri.*

The various spaces which make up the garden of Schwetzingen no longer have the pompous feel typical of bosquets in the French style, but are softer and more intimate, as in the Fountain of the Birds seen here, and in the temple of Apollo (right).

Veitshöchheim. The desire for more intimate spaces, on a human scale, is clearly visible in the positioning of the Chinese pavilion in this garden, regarded as quintessentially rococo.

benches, urns, statues and the delightful Chinese Pavilion.

Fortunately, the garden escaped the fate of so many others, and was never redesigned as a landscaped park; for this reason, despite the losses and damage incurred during World War II, we can still see it in all its original glory.

Another jewel of the German rococo is Sanssouci, its very name – 'carefree' — bearing witness to the frivolous and worldly spirit of the age in which it was conceived. Sanssouci was a place to withdraw to from the oppressiveness of court ceremonial where one could embrace leisure and pleasure.

Commissioned by Frederick II of Prussia, its garden and Schloss were created at Potsdam from 1744 onwards. First to be laid out was the vineyard, descending over six curving parabolic terraces, all ornamented with clipped pyramids or globes of yew. Each retaining wall had 28 niches, closed in by movable glazed panels containing vines and fig trees; between the niches were espaliered apricot, cherry and peach trees.

The following year, at the top of the vineyard, Frederick II built the one-storey Schloss, intended as a summer palace. To its sides run porticoes of greenery *à treillage*, leading to two small pavilions. To the south, at the foot of the terraced vineyard, a *parterre* with eight compartments was added, with the Fountain of Thetis in its centre completed in 1748. Flanked by avenues of five rows of walnut and chestnut trees, after 1750 the garden was extended in the direction of the adjacent game reserve and gradually embellished with buildings like Neptune's Grotto, the *Orangerie* and the delightful Chinese tea-house.

The other pavilions at Veitshöchheim, of wooden construction, are given an added sense of seclusion by the tall hedges surrounding them.

The rococo sense of space altered the very structure of the garden: at Veitshöchheim, for example, the focal point, the Grosser See, with the sculptural group of Pegasus taking flight from Parnassus, is to the side of the central axis and no longer part of any main vista.

The terraces of the vineyard at Sanssouci, where vines and Mediterranean species of tree have recently been planted, following the original design.

Diana's cave and the Rock of Love at Sanspareil, Bayreuth, in a 1793 engraving. The rococo passion for rocaille *and ruins led the Margravine Wilhelmine to create an entirely 'natural' composition based on French Enlightenment ideas. The result was probably the earliest landscaped garden on the continent before the English fashion swept Europe.

(Opposite) In the Eremitage, too, Wilhelmine's other garden at Bayreuth, the archways surrounding the Untere Grotte *have a ruined appearance. The wonderful group of nymphs in the centre of the fountain, and the water-jets spouting from its outer edge, combine to form an exquisite* jeu d'eau.

The Schloss itself formed the nucleus of an immense 290 hectare (700 acre) park, the Charlottenhof, which continued to grow until 1908. The terraces were destroyed in World War II, but restorations begun in 1980 have restored them to their original state.

Among the most outlandish examples of the German rococo garden are the Eremitage and the park of Sanspareil, the two gardens created by Wilhelmine, the eccentric Margravine of Bayreuth. Here rococo exoticism reaches its apogee, anticipating certain features that were subsequently to typify the landscaped garden.

The Eremitage had been laid out in 1715 as a retreat for the Margravine and her retinue to withdraw from court commitments and live in perfect seclusion; here Wilhelmine added an *orangerie* and a new garden extending the earlier one. The surrounding *bosquets* now received a wealth of ornamentation and *jeux d'eau*, together with a number of typically rococo mock ruins, like the Roman Theatre, where open-air performances took place. Equally characteristic of rococo style was the spatial conception of the garden, with each element given equal weight and no main axis to link the individual parts. Anticipating the love of the 'natural' that was to spread over the next fifty years in the wake of the English garden, in the Eremitage we already find the juxtaposition of untrammelled nature and formal design. The regular *parterres* are incorporated into casually composed clumps of trees, while panoramic openings skilfully arranged along the irregular lie of the paths link the garden with the surrounding landscape.

But Wilhelmine exceeded herself with the garden of Sanspareil. A natural beech grove with picturesque rocky formations and casually strewn boulders was transformed into a place of utter enchantment. In a striking natural setting she built a garden-theatre, as a backdrop for episodes from *The Adventures of Telemachus*, a didactic novel by Fénelon (1699). The beech grove became a stage for the adventures of Ulysses' son, imbued with educational and moral allusions in the spirit of the German Enlightenment.

The Belvedere of the Gloriette, the culminating point of the main axis of the gardens of Schönbrunn, was added later, during the reign of Maria Theresa.

Bassin and Roman Theatre (in background) in the gardens of Hellbrunn in Salzburg. Classical allusions in the Italian mould were frequent in Austrian gardens throughout the seventeenth century.

View of the palace of Schönbrunn, painted by Bernardo Bellotto around 1750, flanked by the typical hedges à palissades.

FELIX AUSTRIA

With the exception of the seventeenth-century gardens at Hellbrunn and Mirabell at Salzburg, the great masterpieces of Austrian garden art emerged only after the long Turkish siege of Vienna, the capital of the Habsburg empire. From 1688 Austria entered a period of artistic fervour that was to make Vienna the capital of the Baroque, with a plethora of sumptuous palaces and grandiose gardens. As emperor of the Holy Roman Empire Leopold I set about celebrating victory over the Turks by commissioning a prestigious palace and spectacular new gardens by the river at Schönbrunn, giving the ancient Habsburg dynasty a palace to rival Versailles.

The first ambitious design by Johann Bernhard Fischer von Erlach was soon replaced by a second, equally grandiose, but less onerous for the royal coffers. Despite the reduction in scale, the cost of completion still proved enormous, bespeaking all too eloquently the importance of imperial residences as symbols of monarchical power.

One vast *parterre* runs the length of the façade: eight sections, elaborately decorated and flanked by *bosquets*, create a long vista that ends with the great fountain of Neptune, erected during the reign of the empress Maria Theresa. Indeed, after a long period of neglect during the reign of Charles VI, it was she who encouraged work on the gardens to resume. The immensity and triumphalism of Versailles were abandoned and now Maria Theresa's gardeners, under the supervision of the Dutch Adrian van Steckoven, created a garden of greater sobriety, more in keeping with the enlightened bureaucratic approach. Unlike the French model, and more in line with the German rococo feeling for space, at Schönbrunn the gardens do not stretch vast

Bird's-eye view of the Belvedere, Vienna, clearly showing its rigid structure on the French model, with bosquets and parterres arranged symmetrically in relation to the main axis. Here again the view is closed in at the end by a building, a relative novelty at the time.

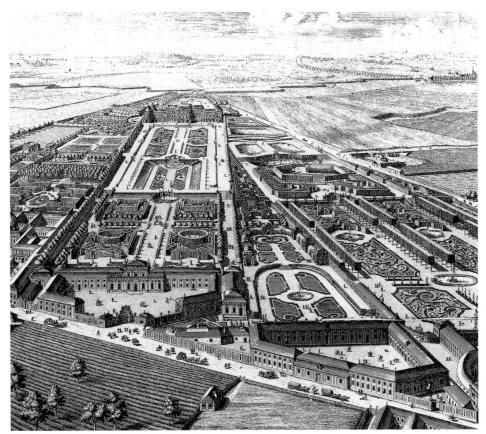

At the Belvedere, the spectacular effect is heightened by the skilled fashioning of the gradient: each part is visible from a distance and disappears as it is approached. At the foot of the cascade, for instance, the Upper Belvedere is hidden from view, to emerge from the water as the visitor climbs the flights of steps leading to the upper level.

distances, *à perte de vue*, with great tree-lined *allées* disappearing into the open countryside, but are concluded by a built element, as already the case at Kessel or Schleissheim. Here this was provided by a small hill behind the fountain of Neptune, the Gloriette, a theatrical belvedere built in 1775 as an airy loggia with a splendid view of the gardens and palace. The mound itself, despite numerous plans to turn it into a monumental series of stairways, fountains and cascades, was left as a gently inclined expanse of grass.

As a symbol of the might of the Habsburg empire, baroque taste persisted in Austria almost throughout the eighteenth century, and its other great masterpiece is the splendid complex of the Belvedere. Built by Prince Eugene of Savoy — the heroic victor over the Turks and Louis XIV's great antagonist on the battlefield — the Belvedere consists of three vast terraces linking the two castles, the Lower and Upper Belvedere. The splendid garden designed by Lukas von Hildebrandt runs between the two sumptuous buildings, completed in 1716 and 1723 respectively. Rectangular and enclosed by long clipped hedges, it lies on three levels: the lowest, at the foot of the Lower Belvedere, has an elegant layout with *bosquets*; the second has a large *parterre* with areas of grass and two *bassins*, and is closed in dramatically by the beautiful stepped cascade, a highly effective visual link descending to the last terrace, with the façade of the Upper Belvedere beyond a *parterre* formerly *à broderie*.

The development of the classical garden in Europe

At a time when the idiosyncrasies of rococo were transforming the art of the garden in a Germany still divided up into a multitude of small principalities, in Louis XV's France gardens were acquiring a more intimate and introverted character, in keeping with the emergent enlightened thinking that tended to prefer spontaneity to ostentation.

In the rest of Europe, however, garden design was still shackled to the inflexible French model of the classical era, a symbol of the absolutist regime which the great European monarchies were bent on maintaining. In Vienna and elsewhere, rulers were investing huge sums in building themselves immense gardens and palaces as emblems of their power. Echoes of French grandeur even reached distant Russia, and Peter the Great was seized by a desire to emulate the splendours of the Sun King. Returning home after a stay at the Trianon in 1716, he commissioned the French architect Jean-Baptiste Le Blond, his Architect-General at St Petersburg, to construct the gardens at Peterhof, the Romanov summer palace. The spectacular result was intended to celebrate the reconquest of the Baltic territories, and the gateway to Europe this had opened up. In a commanding situation on a wide natural terrace, Peterhof is the only palace in Europe that overlooks the sea, to which it is linked by a long canal. Between the palace and the canal a monumental cascade flows into the large *bassin* of the Fountain of Samson, a sumptuous grouping of gilded statues and tall jets of water, one of which rising twenty metres (66 ft.)into the air from a lion's jaws Samson is prising apart.

The great palaces of European monarchies, like Spain's and Italy's, continued to be modelled on Versailles. In England the situation was somewhat different: here, following the French Enlightenment, the rejection of formal precision and a greater sensitivity to nature encouraged the concept of the garden to move away from the classical respect for geometry towards what actually became the English landscaped garden.

Cupid and grapes, *painted panel by François Boucher. With its gaiety and delicacy, the pastoral mood of the rococo lent itself to the typical* fêtes galantes *that became fashionable in gardens.*

The spectacular cascades at Peterhof, or Petrodvorets, the palace built for Peter the Great on the shores of the Baltic Sea, is yet another example of the long shadow cast by Versailles.

(Opposite, top) Bramham Park, Yorkshire. The classical French garden still remained the main point of reference at the beginning of the eighteenth century, though it was already moving towards more flexible forms, as we see from the oblique lie of the T-shaped canal shown here.

(Opposite, bottom) Bramham Park. The dense woodland and broad avenues surrounding the park reflected the desire to emulate the great forest of France.

The waning of the Grande Manière

During the first years of the eighteenth century, English gardens were still designed along French lines, in the *Grande Manière*, long axes of great tree-lined *allées* their main feature. Two outstanding examples are the park of Badminton House, belonging to the Duke of Beaufort, and Blenheim Palace, built by John Vanbrugh for the Duke of Marlborough in 1705 and swept away fifty years later by the designs of Capability Brown.

The use of regularly-shaped *bassins* and canals for grandiose effects of perspective continued to be extremely fashionable, but gradually the inflexible classical schemes were replaced by freer layouts. New gardens devoted less space to great formal *parterres* in favour of large wooded areas — an attempt to recreate the atmosphere of the shady forests that ringed the châteaux of the Ile-de-France, with their long avenues *à perte de vue*.

During the eighteenth century most of the numerous gardens in the *Grande Manière* were remodelled and transformed several times. One of the most alluring of the few to have retained their original monumental design is Bramham Park in Yorkshire. Despite a commanding succession of wide tree-lined avenues, canals, *bassins*, structures and vistas with backdrops, clearly of French derivation, Bramham offers a completely novel sensitivity to landscape — a calculated positioning of openings and panoramic vistas that prefigured the emergent landscape revolution of the following decades. Designed and built by its owner, Lord Bingley, from 1699 onwards, Bramham's park was based on an intricate system of

Bramham Park, Yorkshire. Sensitivity to the landscape and panoramic views as integral parts of the garden can clearly be seen in the great bassin *overlooking the surrounding country-side.*

Vistas and sculpted elements are framed by tall hedges, contrasting strikingly with the frequent openings onto the landscape, in order to make them even more spectacular.

Garden pavilions — early signs of the Gothic revival — do not have any decorative setting but stand, to great effect, on simple grassy expanses.

A characteristic feature of the eighteenth-century English land-scaped garden, the ha-ha was a ditch surrounding the park, making it possible to dispense with walls and enclosures, thereby extending the view over the countryside.

(Top) Harewood House, Yorkshire;
(centre), Stowe, Buckinghamshire;
(below), Hardwick Hall, Yorkshire

straight avenues: intersecting to form several axes centred on as many focal points, they were not forced upon the landscape but adapted to the site. Indeed, the avenues intersect at any number of angles, giving great variety to a layout whose main vistas alone are determined by symmetry.

Similarly, only the main axis is orthogonal, running as it does at right angles to the façade of the house and framing a very long vista. At the end of the avenue is a wide grassy slope with a large square *bassin* reminiscent of a terrace, overlooking on one side the immense expanse of surrounding countryside — a view that contrasts sharply with the long vistas framed and hemmed in by tall beech hedges. On the opposite side of the *bassin*, as though in counterpoint to the panoramic view, a highly original Gothic temple is silhouetted at the centre of the grassy slope.

Beyond the *bassin* the axis continues for almost a mile towards a classically-inspired rotunda; behind it, in the middle of a woodland clearing, ten avenues radiating from a tall obelisk.

Marking the transition between an absolutist formalism *à la française* and a more natural approach, Bramham anticipated the work of Charles Bridgeman, one of the first proponents of a freer garden design. While retaining many formal aspects with its use of *parterres*, straight avenues and geometrically positioned *bassins*, Bridgeman's work also introduced rides — avenues cut through woods to be ridden at a gallop — and

paths exploiting especially panoramic views. But his most important innovation, crucial to the development of the land-scaped garden in the second half of the century, was the ha-ha, a retaining wall running around the property or just along particularly panoramic stretches to create a ditch that was impassable from the outside, avoiding the need for other forms of enclosure while invisible from inside the garden.

Bridgeman's gardens reflect a careful observation of the countryside, with paths, views and buildings positioned accord-ingly, and proceeding from an analysis — in accordance with the writing of Alexander Pope — of the so-called *genius loci*, the spirit of the place. Alongside went a growing interest in mythological, historical and literary references, linking the garden to the perfect heroic landscapes of antiquity.

As Royal Gardener from 1728 to 1738, Bridgeman created memorable works like the Round Pond and the Serpentine in Kensington Gardens and Hyde Park. He also designed many other gardens, sometimes in collaboration with established architects like John Vanbrugh and William Kent, creators of the first real landscaped gardens. He worked at Blenheim, Claremont and Rousham, but his most important work was the park at Stowe. Though no longer in existence, having been completely remodelled by Kent around the middle of the eighteenth century, his impressive design is scrupulously documented by a vast series of views he himself commissioned from the French engraver Jacques

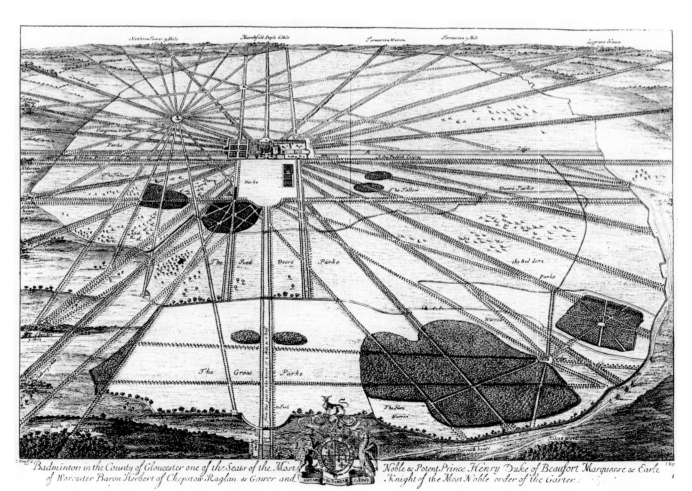

In Great Britain, the fashion for allées *reached exorbitant proportions. The long tree-lined avenues designed at Badminton for the Duke of Beaufort extended liter-ally* à perte de vue, *but the woods through which they ran had more regular borders than their French coun-terparts.*

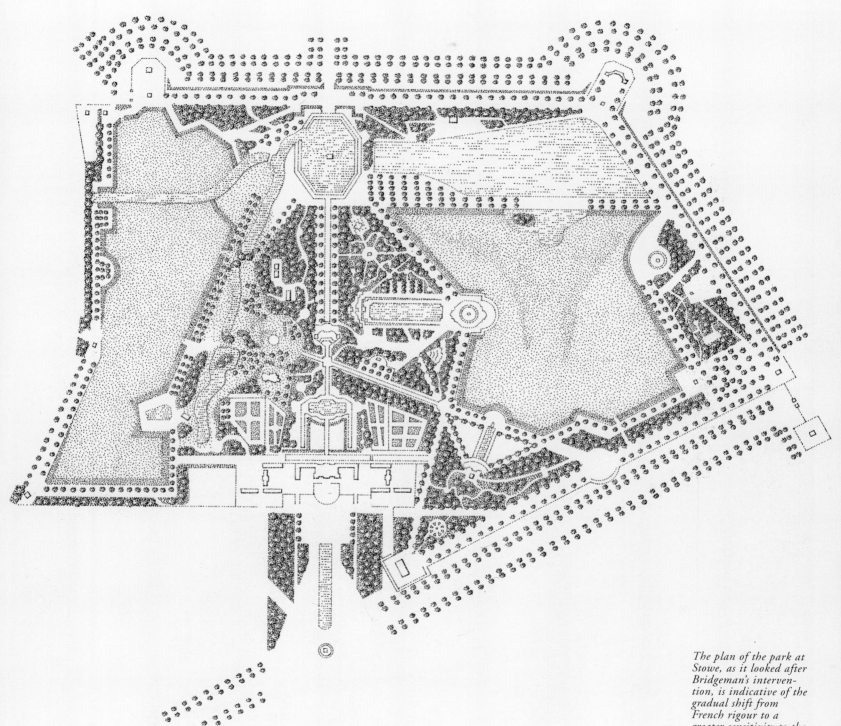

The plan of the park at Stowe, as it looked after Bridgeman's intervention, is indicative of the gradual shift from French rigour to a greater sensitivity to the configuration and character of the place, with the various axes no longer at right angles, but conforming to the lie of the land.

The wonderfully evocative pre-existing ruins of Fountains Abbey were incorporated into the garden at Studley Royal in a manner inconceivable prior to the new approach to understanding the garden.

(Opposite) Studley Royal. The proportions and design of the great bassins *are baroque in style, but the dense woodland surrounding them looks forward to the 'natural' approach adopted in later parks.*

The heart of the garden at Studley Royal is the formal composition of this exquisite parterre d'eau, *designed to be viewed from above, from the route running through the gardens as far as the ruined abbey.*

Rigaud, from which the transitional nature of his work emerges very clearly.

This same period saw the creation, also in Yorkshire, of the gardens of Studley Royal. Although inspired by the great French water gardens, here the English garden was clearly moving toward harmony with the landscape. After retiring from public life in 1722 John Aislabie, a former Chancellor of the Exchequer, devoted himself to the construction of Studley Royal, confining the waters of the River Skell into a long, somewhat irregular canal before allowing them to flow down a French-inspired cascade and out into a large lake. This canal, together with three pools dug out of the grassy woodland clearing, created an enchanting *parterre d'eau*. A round *bassin*, with a pool in the shape of a half-moon to either side, was laid out in the middle, reflecting the neo-classical outline of the temple of Piety.

The garden was enlarged several times over the years. Various structures — a Banqueting House, a Gothic temple and a Rotunda, set along the winding boundary of the wood surrounding the *parterre d'eau* — were added to this first and still essentially formal layout. In the second half of the century, with the growth of the romantic penchant for ruins, Studley Royal assumed a distinctly landscaped appearance. Aislabie acquired the adjacent land, together with the ruins of Fountains Abbey, a glorious twelfth-century Cistercian building that would now become the romantic culmination of the vista, as well as the focal point of many other evocative views.

The great palaces of the Bourbon and Savoy courts

While England was already discarding the rigours of formal baroque design, the countries of southern Europe, after their long subjection to the traditional Italian layout, were only now adopting the French concept of space at its most all-embracing. Le Nôtre's model won the day, above all in the great francophile courts that could afford to create gardens the size of Versailles, namely those of the Bourbons in Spain and of Savoy in Turin.

In spring the Spanish court traditionally moved to Aranjuez, but Philip V, grandson of the Sun King and the first Bourbon king of Spain, decided to establish a new summer residence near Segovia, at an altitude of over 1200 metres (3940 ft.), as a refuge from the heat of the capital. The exquisite rococo jewel built from 1721 at La Granja, on the site of a Jeronymite hospice, drew on the king's childhood memories, since he had grown up at Versailles. The result was a beautiful palace in rose-coloured marble, with a sloping garden enlivened by *bassins*, lakes and statues and framed by wooded hills.

The problematical terrain — a rocky, uneven escarpment — entailed huge feats of earth-moving, but the abundance of water more than compensated, facilitating marvellously inventive *jeux d'eau* with fountains, *bassins*, a canal and a splendid cascade whose steps were made of pink marble and jasper.

The main façade of the palace, where the king's apartments were located, overlooks a *parterre* with statues, and the great cascade, which in an effect of *trompe-l'oeil* appears to lengthen the short distance actually separating the palace from the hills.

La Granja, Segovia. The great European monarchies were still faithfully following the model of Versailles in making their gardens.

At the top of the cascade, the Fountain of the Three Graces — exquisitely reflecting the delicate outline of a small circular pavilion — feeds a veil of water that flows down the polychrome marble steps of ten descending *bassins*, into the Fountain of Amphitrite at the foot of the *parterre*. Another vista, a succession of *bassins* and fountains with statues, opens beside the cascade making up a long *parterre d'eau*, the *Carrera de Caballos*, where five rectangular *bassins* form a sequence of little cascades flowing into a larger one, known as the Half-Moon. From here part of the water runs into a side canal, while the rest feeds the Fountain of Perseus and Andromeda and the Fountain of Neptune, surrounded by sea horses. On another side of the palace, the Fountain of La Fama (Renown), astride Pegasus, stands in the centre of a *parterre*, sending a 47 metre (154 ft.) jet of water into the air. Reaching into the surrounding woods with a series of straight and star-shaped avenues, the gardens are punctuated by a whole array of fountains, including the Fountain of the Frogs, clearly inspired by the Fountain of Latona at Versailles.

With its succession of typically eighteenth-century spaces, sculptures, fountains and mythological allusions, the whole garden is based on a tried and trusted classical repertoire — including the maze, built to the specification found in Dezallier d'Argenville's treatise — without any coherent or indeed original criteria. Nonetheless, the carefully gaged spaces and the

The great cascade at La Granja, with its exquisite decoration in coloured marble, stands out against the superb *mountain background, giving this Spanish Versailles a uniquely atmospheric appeal.*

beauty of the landscape, together with the poised rhythm of the countless sculptures and the colourful architectural structures, combine in an unusual blend of French prettiness and Spanish austerity.

Meanwhile, in Italy, French taste was asserting itself alongside the more theatrical baroque, and here Le Nôtre's use of vistas cutting deep into the landscape through lengthy axes of perspective was particularly popular.

The Savoy monarchy had set about restructuring its territory as early as the second half of the seventeenth century, with a series of royal residences encircling the capital: the castles of Rivoli, Mirafiori, Moncalieri and il Valentino, the vineyards of Villa Madama, the parco dei Cervi and Venaria Reale date from this period. Control over their territory, after the example of the Sun King, demanded the imposition of a geometrical structure on the flat land around Turin, with long straight avenues leading to the various residences, and the creation of large parks and hunting reserves. The last great palace to be built was the hunting-lodge at Stupinigi, designed by Filippo Juvarra for Duke Victor Amadeus II. Linked to Turin by a straight avenue over three long miles, the entire complex is inspired by a rigorous and patrician demand for centrality: as it approaches the hunting-lodge the avenue is hemmed in by two long wings that flank it up as far as the main entrance. The large central drawing-room, with its elliptical ground plan, is

The Fountain of the Frogs at La Granja, symbolizing absolutism, is derived from the Fountain of Latona at Versailles: the peasants who rebelled against Latona were turned into frogs.

The delicate portrayal of these stags, against the mountain woodland at La Granja, already implies the rococo idea of nature as more gentle and responsive.

The long cascade at the palace of Caserta, whose enormous length emerges particularly clearly from this aerial photograph.

View of the Reggia di Caserta (1756). The layout follows the classical scheme of bosquets and parterres, though today the latter have been replaced by an expanse of grass.

the pivot of the whole composition, beyond which the axis of perspective continues, highlighting the elaborate *parterres* and the intricately circular *bosquets* in a manner reminiscent of contemporary German rococo. With its lively, mixtilinear wings, this highly complex building's close relationship with the landscape was achieved through a continuous interplay of references, with voids and solids, unexpected vistas and sudden obstructions, finished off by the grandiose perspective of the park itself.

In southern Italy the Bourbon passion for gardens, which had signalled the decline of the Italian model under Louis XIV, led to the most grandiose garden in Italy. Following in his father's footsteps at La Granja, from 1752 the King of Naples, Charles III, laid out the splendid gardens of the palace of Caserta, a hundred-hectare (two hundred and fifty-acre) park stretching lengthways behind the massive palace designed by Luigi Vanvitelli, the spectacular ribbon of water forming the longest cascade in the world. From the back of the palace the garden follows the classical pattern of an ordered sequence of *parterres de broderie, bosquets*, canals and *bassins*. The cascade begins almost two miles from the palace, forming a long narrow axis of perspective 120 metres (394 ft.) wide, cut through the wood and flanked by hedges of clipped ilex.

At the top, the fountain of Diana and Actaeon collects the waters that flow down from the hill towards the palace, guid-

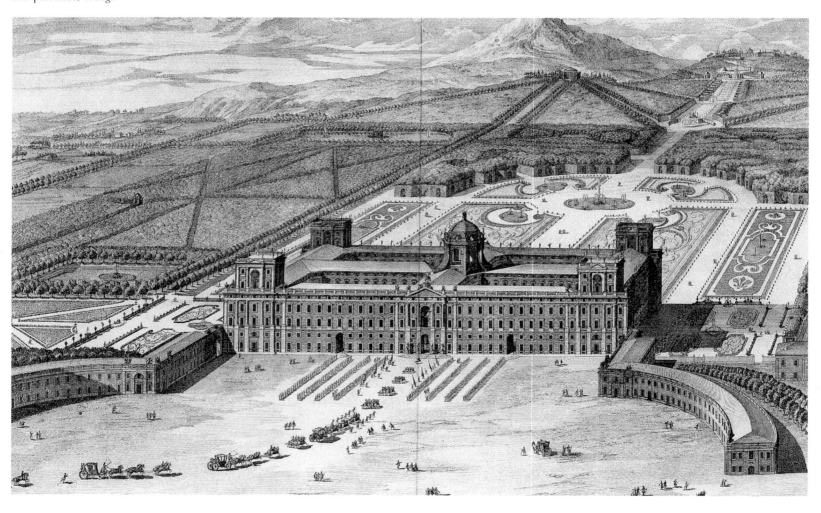

ing the eye towards its majestic rear façade. The cascade is punctuated by a sequence of *bassins* and fountains, with sculpted groups of divinities and figures from classical mythology unified by the theme of water.

In the first fountain Diana is surprised while bathing by the young hunter Actaeon, who is transformed into a stag for his impudence and torn apart by his own dogs. Next is the stepped cascade with the Fountain of Venus, the goddess born of the waters captured in the act of imploring Adonis not to go hunting and meet his certain death. Then comes the Fountain of Ceres, goddess of the harvest symbolizing Sicily, flanked by two male figures symbolizing the island's rivers. Halfway along its course the long ribbon of water widens out to form the *bassin* of the Fountain of Aeolus, god of the winds, and then flows on downwards towards the fountain of the Dolphins; it then continues along a stretch of canal, finally to reappear in the Fontana Margherita below the *bosquets*.

Caserta. Looking downhill from the Fountain of Ceres the visitor can enjoy the spectacle of the incredible ribbon of water which, thanks to a brilliantly planned succession of bassins and flights of steps, seems to flow down from the hill in one continuous billowing line.

Caserta. The monumental group with Diana and Actaeon is the most ambitious fountain in the gardens: to the right, surrounded by her nymphs, Diana is bathing, seeking to escape Actaeon's prying gaze.

The garden of Vrtba Palace, Prague. Its terraced structure is evidence of the Italian garden's long-lasting influence in Bohemia.

The baroque garden of Buchlovice was given a landscaped addition in the nineteenth century, and is the best preserved garden in Moravia.

EASTERN EUROPE: MASTERPIECES RECLAIMED

The fraught political and cultural situation in eastern Europe hampered the development of any autonomous garden style. Of even greater import is the complete absence of interest in garden heritage over recent years, which has inevitably led to the devastation of the Slav countries' significant gardens.

Bohemia's rich garden tradition, dating back to the twelfth century, flourished during the Renaissance; in the sixteenth century many terraced gardens were inspired by the Italian style, well suited to the hilly land around Prague. But many were redesigned in the Baroque period, after the ravages of the Thirty Years War. The Baroque was another glorious age for Bohemia and eastern Europe.

Towards the end of the seventeenth century, Prague's district of Malá Strana was earmarked by the aristocracy for the construction of palaces with terraced gardens. Apart from the late-renaissance Valdstejn garden, by Italian artists, the best-preserved is that built around 1720 for the noble Vrtba family, which has a typical terraced structure.

The classical style reigned supreme throughout the eighteenth century, with the fashion for the landscaped park becoming established only in the nineteenth in Bohemia and Moravia, where many baroque gardens were created. One is the perfectly preserved garden of Buchlovice, originally designed in the Italian manner by the Roman architect Domenico Martinelli, and remodelled in the French style at the beginning of the eighteenth century. Its complex and original design recalls several gardens in the German-speaking countries: two palaces with semi-circular courtyards symmetrically enclose a terrace and a garden of classical inspiration; it has a central axis and topiaried greenery decorated with fountains, statues, and stone urns.

Apart from various baroque gardens, Poland also boasts the romantic park of Arkadia, the summer residence of the powerful Radziwill family.

The Baroque design of the parterres in the garden at Milotice has been lost, but the general structure, and the clipped hedges to its sides, have been preserved.

Another Moravian garden created at the beginning of the eighteenth century is Milotice, though its structure is closer to the French style. Despite the loss of the original floral decor of its *parterre*, Milotice still has a stately baroque design, based on a central axis emphasized by fountains and wide squared hedges. In the nineteenth century both gardens were flanked by an area of English style parkland.

Poland, too, has a great garden tradition dating from the Middle Ages, the era of monasteries and cloisters; during the Renaissance gardens of varying degrees of importance were established, mostly in the Italian mode.

But the greatest Polish gardens came out of the Baroque period, during the reign of Jan Sobieski, King of Poland from 1674 to 1696. The Polish baroque garden preserved an Italian influence: in the royal garden of Wilanów, in Warsaw, for instance, this link with Italy is evident in the terraces, oriented symmetrically along the central axis of the palace and decorated with box hedges, and in the retaining walls, originally decorated with statues and fountains within niches. By the early eighteenth century, however, the English taste for the picturesque was gaining ground, and in Arkadia, Poland has one of the loveliest landscaped parks in Europe: its allusions to the mythical landscape of ancient Greece bear witness to a love of untrammelled nature, and the pastoral mood of Romanticism.

The Arcadian landscape

As we have seen, in the eighteenth century an aesthetic and intellectual trend emerged in England that was to effect a revolution in the art of the garden. The English landscaped garden was underpinned by a strong theoretical imperative, with men of letters — both landowners and politicians — its true proselytisers.

One of the most influencial factors was the great landscape paintings of the seventeenth century. By depicting 'ideal beauty' the Arcadian landscapes of Claude Lorrain (1600—82) and Nicolas Poussin (1594—1665) had quickened a sensitivity to nature, propounding a more spontaneous expression of the natural world. Meanwhile, poets and writers argued for a new communion with nature, seen now as both simple and perfect, as in the garden of Eden in Milton's *Paradise Lost*.

The burgeoning number of nature poems contained substantial descriptions of landscapes and gardens no longer as mere background, but rather the true protagonists. Philosophers, too, were formulating a new set of moral values, permeated with a sense of nature, at, as it were, its most natural. As early as the seventeenth century Sir Francis Bacon had written about gardening, rejecting symmetry, topiary and formal *bassins*, calling for less constrained design, and extolling the beauty of the landscape that opened out spontaneously around the garden, to become an object of contemplation in itself.

Further fuelling this novel conception of nature, the countryside and the garden, was the Grand Tour now bringing a new generation of British travellers into contact with the classical landscape, particularly that of Italy, often dramatic and picturesque, its vistas strewn with temples and ruins. The treatises on Chinese gardens written by the many travellers to the East also played their part in fostering the new attitude.

This new sensibility, with man as the master no longer, but at most seen as the co-ordinator, of a 'wild' nature, was consolidated by two more factors. The first was the rise of a class of large landowners, the bastions of the English constitutional monarchy, with strongly libertarian values: anti-absolutist, anti-French, anti-Baroque and, all in all, anti-formal. With their considerable means they could afford to turn '..their whole estate into a kind of garden...' The second factor was an economic policy that favoured such great landowners as aimed at optimizing timber yield from their woodland and exploiting their pasture land to the full, with consequent influence on the appearance of the English agricultural landscape.

Another vital source of inspiration for the development of the landscape movement was the poet, treatise-writer and literary critic, Alexander Pope (1688—1744). Pope championed the beauties of unadorned nature, vigorously rejecting the balance, regularity and artifice of formal gardens and topiary work. He also set great store by the *genius loci*, the

With its ideal of lofty serenity, heroic landscape painting was one of the chief sources of inspiration for the early landscaped garden, as in this illustration with Aeneas at Delos, *by Claude Lorrain.*

Spirit of Place, which had to be heeded, indeed consulted, in order that nature should have her say, and required that the character of every garden be brought out from hints within its own topography. The art of the garden, like landscape painting, was to include temples, columns, statues and a great variety of plants grouped pleasingly together in an entirely 'natural' fashion.

Pope put his principles successfully into practice in his garden at Twickenham, where scrupulously composed clumps of trees and shrubs created effective areas of light and shade, and vistas dense with classical allusions.

One of the earliest phenomena produced by this new feeling for nature was the wilderness, or wildness, a large wooded area. Until the first decades of the new century it was still crossed by broad, straight avenues, but gradually took on freer forms, with regular paths replaced by winding ones as a prelude to the romantic mood of the second half of the century.

From the heroic landscape to the classicism of William Kent

The desire to recreate the Arcadian landscapes of heroic painting in the parks of their houses had attracted many landowners to an ideal garden that would be less shackled by formal schemes. The initial design for the park of Castle Howard in Yorkshire, one of the very first examples of a landscaped park was still based on broad canals and long tree-lined avenues but soon replaced by a less rigid layout. The traditional baroque

centrality was subverted by an entrance avenue parallel to the castle, creating an unexpectedly broad view across the countryside. Similarly, the wood to one side of the castle was not given the regular classical complement of straight avenues, a definitive shift in the direction of the 'natural'. Furthermore, the street of an existing village was used for a long walk along the edge of a natural terrace situated at an oblique angle to the house. On a promontory at the end stood the temple of the Four Winds, a classical building overlooking the sweep of hills, where sheep and cattle roamed. In this way, the animals too would seem part of a vast artificial landscape, created as closely as possible in nature's image. Years later, an enormous mausoleum in the form of a rotunda, was added some distance away, to complete the panorama as though it were a painted set.

If the great panoramic views of Castle Howard recalled the heroic landscapes of myth and antiquity, the real shift towards a layout unambiguously inspired by the harmony of Arcadia — a mythical landscape of primitive simplicity — was made by the work of William Kent (1685—1748).

Kent was moulded in that theoretical school whose most famous proponents were Alexander Pope and Joseph Addison. While taking painting as the real model for the planning of a garden, they also made a clear distinction between art and nature, enhancing the latter with the instruments of the former, in particular by a carefully judged and revolutionary use of perspective. This indeed was the real novelty of Kent's

The Chinese pagoda at Kew Gardens, designed by William Chambers. The freedom and spontaneity of the Chinese garden was particularly well-suited to the emergent naturalness of the English garden, with its taste for orientalizing decoration.

The shape of the landscape itself now inspired the form to be taken by the garden. The glorious view from the broad natural formation of Rielvaux Terrace, Yorkshire, made it the natural destination for walks and entertainments, for which purpose two temples were built at the garden's outer edge.

(Left) An example of a wilderness in a design by Batty Langley. Here the course of the paths within the *bosquets is* becoming increasingly free and winding.

(Right) View from the Temple of the Four Winds over the surrounding country-side. The sight of cattle always played an important part in the land-scaped park.

The Temple of the Four Winds at Castle Howard, Yorkshire, is set on a high spur, three of whose sides overlook the surrounding countryside.

(Opposite) The heroic ideal is very much in evidence in this view of the great mausoleum, designed by Nicholas Hawksmoor as the scenic climax of the landscaped park at Castle Howard.

The rotunda at Chiswick House, London, is a consummate example of the quotation of classical ideals championed by its owner, Lord Burlington.

innovation: abandonment of the formal scheme once and for all. In the garden at Chiswick House, created around 1725 for his patron, Lord Burlington, Kent arranged a large number of elements in a relatively restricted space, without any strict controlling symmetry between the various parts. Beside a river spanned by a small rustic bridge he set out a classical exedra made up solely of statues and urns, an avenue of cedars and an enchanting little circular lake with a tall central obelisk, facing a classical temple. Within this small space the various architectural elements inspired by Palladianism — a return promoted by Burlington and his circle to the fastidious rigour of Palladio — were arranged as a counterpoint to the vegetation, to conform with painting's compositional ideals of the classical landscape.

Pictorial compositions in the manner of Lorrain and Poussin were referred to as 'picturesque', and from here the term passed to the garden, as an explicit reference to the scenes represented in the major arts, confirming the affinity between poetry, theatre and painting and the newly-flourishing art of the garden.

This implied that the garden should appear as an explicit representation of historical or mythological texts. By singling out painting as their model and literary references as their informing criterion, the theorists of the new art furnished the garden — still regarded as an artificial creation — with an

This engraving by Piranesi, of various Roman pillars, urns and vases, with inscriptions, reflects the taste for classical quotation and allusion which was fashionable again in the eighteenth century.

Tom II *LVII*

URNE CIPPI E VASI CENERARJ DI MARMO NELLA VILLA CORS. I FUORI DI PORTA S. PANCRAZIO

invaluable *raison d'être*. For all the world like a poet or painter, in planning his gardens Kent conferred the greatest importance and centrality upon the 'stage', with man as protagonist, and nature providing backdrops and side-shows. Starting with the text — that is, meaning and classical quotation — as the garden's *sine qua non*, Kent laid out clearly defined paths along which buildings and structures steeped in classical symbolism were positioned as though so many stages in a journey. Illustrious precedents inspired names and inscriptions, such as the Elysian Fields at Stowe, or the Terrace of Praeneste at Rousham. Indeed at Rousham, completed in 1738, Kent deployed a judicious admixture of historical, technical and representational allusions to the painting he had studied in Italy, together with the fundamental principles of the stage and stagecraft. In creating places with evocative names, like the Venus Vale or the Terrace of Praeneste, Kent employed precisely those teachings on pictorial perspective he had learned in Rome during the Grand Tour, to draw attention to an arrangement of scenes of great diversity and naturalness based on a highly localised, sidelong vantage-point. Now it was no longer possible to take in the whole composition at a single glance, as it had been in the baroque garden, where the focus of the perspective had been dependent on the eye of the beholder. Here he was led to follow a route along which scenes presented themselves to his gaze in sequence, as happened in the fictive world of theatre, and in nature. This new approach allowed Kent to intervene upon natural space without force or aggression, rather by ordering and respecting its salient features.

Another of Kent's masterpieces is the park at Stowe, a particularly important element in the history of the English garden. Constantly enlarged over a number of years, with each development reflecting the growth of aesthetic theory, it remained for nearly a century the most significant and influential model of garden style.

Lord Cobham called in William Kent to remodel Bridgeman's earlier eleven-hectare (27 acres) garden and also commissioned a design for a recently-added area. For the extension to the south-west, Kent designed a temple of Venus and a hermitage, while to the east he created a truly Arcadian landscape, the so-called Elysian Fields. Each component was characterized by a water course named after a real or mythical river like the Alder or the Styx and included a large number of buildings and small temples clearly of classical derivation to form an unbroken sequence of idyllic views along the water. On the left bank stood the Temple of British Glories, with portraits of the most illustrious names in English history, while the Temples of Ancient Virtue and Modern Virtue faced each other on the right.

As at Rousham, so at Stowe the scheme was based on

Chiswick House. William Kent was the greatest exponent of the return to antiquity: in the garden he designed at Chiswick the clipped hedge — with its arrangement of urns, sphinxes and herms — is reminiscent of a classical exedra.

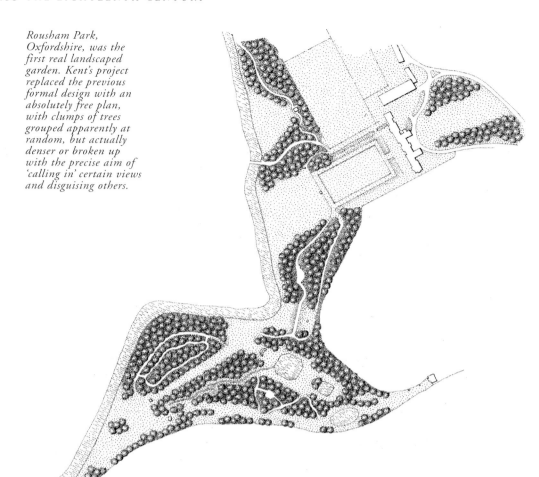

Rousham Park, Oxfordshire, was the first real landscaped garden. Kent's project replaced the previous formal design with an absolutely free plan, with clumps of trees grouped apparently at random, but actually denser or broken up with the precise aim of 'calling in' certain views and disguising others.

Rousham Park. Here, a rill running along the centre of a path leads to a pool with a little grotto known as the Cold Bath, reminiscent of the baths of ancient Rome.

repeated allusions to places mentioned in the classics, and had its own elaborate iconography. The whole garden, in fact, had been conceived as a geographical and artistic statement of the political ideals of the Whig faction, the emphasis on cultivation of personal and political freedom rooted in the Glorious Revolution of 1688. Kent's monuments were therefore, in fact so many homages to the great classical civilizations, in yearning for a heroic society to counterpoint the moral decadence of contemporary life. In the Elysian Fields the Temple of Ancient Virtue — inspired by the Temple of the Sibyl at Tivoli — which contained busts of great men of the past was juxtaposed with the now vanished Temple of Modern Virtue, deliberately constructed as a ruin to symbolize contemporary decline and featuring a headless bust of Robert Walpole, then prime minister and great political rival of Lord Cobham, the Whig leader. Another highly original building with a triangular ground plan, was put up later: known as the Gothic Temple, it too paid tribute to the lofty moral values and love of freedom attributed to the Saxon civilization.

The gardens at Stowe continued to be extended and were updated in the mid-1740s, when Lancelot Brown, the head gardener from 1741, was commissioned to lay out a new area of grass adjacent to the Elysian Fields: the Grecian Valley, shaped like an amphitheatre, with a Greek temple at its head.

When Lord Cobham died in 1749 most of the work had been completed, and the entire planned landscape now covered a vast area of some 360 hectares (890 acres). Stowe House itself and the surrounding gardens and landscaped park were crossed by numerous avenues flanked at the entrances to the pre-existing village with lodges marking the boundary of the estate. Laid out along the main panoramic views were focal points such as Wolfe's Obelisk and Stowe Castle, a mock battlemented ruin with the dual purpose of concealing a farm and creating a picturesque viewpoint.

From the romantic landscape to the 'place-making' of Capability Brown

Around the middle of the century, before Lancelot Brown and his parks had won their enormous subsequent popularity, an increasing number of landowners began to build landscaped parks, to their own designs, less rigidly referential and codified than Kent's.

One early and remarkable example was the park at Stourhead, begun by Sir Henry Hoare around the 1740s by damming a river running through a small valley to make an artificial lake. Over time, its shores were gradually lined with a series of temples and monuments inspired by specific classical works, such as the Pantheon and Temple of Flora, or the Grotto, from a painting by Salvator Rosa in which a nymph

The Venus Vale at
Rousham is particularly
idyllic, with the statue
of Pan giving added
poignancy to its evoca-
tive Arcadian atmos-
phere.

The small grotto of
Venus, providing the
water that fed the pools
in the Venus Vale, is a
wonderfully genuine
version of a woodland
fountain from classical
myth.

Rousham. The portico of
Praeneste shown here is
reached by a path
approaching from the
side, looking down over
the landscape. As its
name implies, it was
inspired by the Temple
of Fortune at Praeneste,
now Palestrina.

reclining above a waterfall, was a more recent classical allusion to Alexander Pope, whose lines were quoted alongside. Such references were intended to stimulate the poetic imagination rather than promote the moral values of classical civilization. Other buildings, for example those in the Gothic style, were stylistic curiosities rather than historical symbols, and foreshadowed a changing attitude to literary references that was to be characteristic of gardens of the second half of the century.

The park at Painshill was also the work of an amateur. Here Sir Charles Hamilton's very ambitious undertaking was to create a garden with a masterly picturesque and landscaped character. At Painshill the buildings had far less importance: no longer vehicles for symbolic messages, they were built to give definition to scenes less freighted with meanings and allegories, but more emotionally intense. Here Sir Charles forged himself a garden of haunting, almost illusionistic spaces, for instance the Alpine Valley, entirely planted with conifers, the Grotto with 'natural' stalactites and cascades, and the ruined Gothic building on the edge of the lake. This was a garden where coherence came from a freer association, as a pleasing sequence of images framed by a series of vistas opening up unexpectedly, along established paths, with gaps in the trees and judiciously organized glimpses of distant views. By the middle of the century the concept of the garden had been completely revolutionized: learned and exclusive allusion was no longer the aim, and a more popular taste now prevailed, with aesthetic enjoyment to the fore.

A combination of socio-cultural factors also came into play in this second phase of the eighteenth-century English garden, modifying the original criteria of the picturesque. A thoroughgoing knowledge of classical iconographic sources could no longer be taken for granted, and the new sensibility spread among a class of lesser landowners, lacking the means to go on the Grand Tour. Nor could they afford to create gardens with buildings illustrating such a wide range of subjects, which favoured the inclination already expressed by certain poets, such as Joseph Warton, to return to woods with purely natural

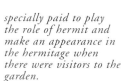

Love of the primitive and the rural made a model hermitage very popular in the gardens of the time, such as this one in the grounds at Stowe. People were specially paid to play the role of hermit and make an appearance in the hermitage when there were visitors to the garden.

Stowe. Entrances to great parks were still usually monumental, with lodges for the gatekeepers, reminiscent of ancient gates, marking the boundaries to the property.

(Over page) The Elysian Fields at Stowe, designed by William Kent, where the requisite Arcadian mood is conveyed by various structures on the banks of the so-called river Styx.

forms, and landscapes no longer 'decked out and partially concealed by the vain ostentations of art...'

A new way of approaching the garden was establishing itself: The visitor was to be free to attribute more personal and private meanings to his encounter, without being forcibly spurred on by epigraphs, statues or temples. Almost of necessity, the garden was cleared of the elaborate system of meanings that had characterized it for centuries, leaving room for a more 'natural' and individualistic approach than the first phase of the 'picturesque'.

The last great exponent of the English eighteenth-century garden was Lancelot 'Capability' Brown, whose concept of the landscaped garden was extremely radical and decidedly unlike his predecessors'. Paying particular heed to the characteristics of the site where the garden was to be created — as his nickname 'Capability' implies, he often referred to its 'capabilities' — Brown regarded symbolic structures and intellectual references as distinctly superfluous, adopting respect for natural appearance as his axiom, banishing all that was not completely natural, and often disregarding many features of the previous design.

The landscapes created by Brown were therefore of the utmost simplicity, structured on three basic components to simulate an immense natural landscape: gently rolling ground, extensive water courses and vast artificial lakes, and plantings of tree, artfully grouped and arranged. His compositions no longer implied any symbolic concern: he stood for the pleasing panoramic effect, uncluttered by pointless frippery. His use of clumps of trees was particularly telling,

Over time, other buildings were added elsewhere in the park at Stowe, signalling the points of view and main panoramic vistas. The enchanting Gothic temple has a triangular ground plan with a single large circular room occupying two levels, and several small rooms in the corner towers.

Stowe, Buckinghamshire. The Temple of British Worthies, built as a classical exedra, *still has a memorial tablet to a much-loved dog, buried here proudly alongside busts of distinguished Englishmen.*

At Stowe, the various phases of the English landscape style co-exist side by side. Capability Brown's Grecian Vale has nothing of the Arcadian strivings typical of Kent's projects, but expresses a feeling for nature that has now shed any claim to cultural authenticity.

particularly with the recreation of dense woodland around the park, like green belts *avant la lettre*, with views through them at particularly panoramic points. Inside the park itself he would group vast clumps of trees together into small plantations, giving the landscape a sense of rhythm with the glancing shade cast by their leaves. The result was a gently rolling vista, vast, apparently spontaneous, but in fact minutely planned. His were no longer parks to be strolled through on foot during long meditative walks. Here there were no eye-catching elements to distract attention from the three basic natural elements. The result was a grandiose landscape where human involvement was artfully and totally concealed, yet which was also a garden, and as such, in all its 'naturalness', worthy of aesthetic consideration.

After his first important, and successful, commission at Stowe, within the space of a few years Brown was at work on the parks of Warwick Castle and Petworth House, soon proving himself the rising star in his chosen art.

His most important work was at Blenheim Palace in Oxfordshire, the property of the Duke of Marlborough, on which he worked from 1763, with a lavish budget and a large team of assistants. Here Brown decided to divert the waters of a small river, the Glyme, in order to create a large expanse of water in the deep valley basin separating the palace from the rest of the park. The pair of large lakes thus created enabled the imposing bridge built some years earlier by John Vanbrugh to link the two sides of the valley, thereby fulfilling

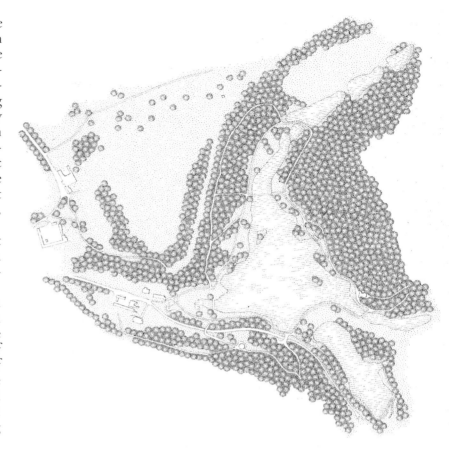

The grounds at Stourhead, Wiltshire, around an apparently natural lake, that was actually created ad hoc by damming up the end of a river running through a deep valley.

At Stourhead the heroic and classical ideal has been discarded in favour of a sentimental romanticism: the buildings dotted along the walk around the lake are no longer stages on a classical itinerary, but atmospheric ornaments to the landscape.

(Opposite) The Pantheon at Stourhead, clearly inspired by the painting of Claude Lorrain.

Painshill, Surrey. Another Gothic building, not far from the Gothic ruin, serving as both an eye-catcher (left) and a belvedere (right).

The lovely grotto at Painshill, built across an arm of the lake and hung with a mass of stalactites.

(Opposite) Painshill. Since ruins had now cast off any pretence at classical allusion, they were built in other styles, particularly the Gothic, like the one on the shores of the lake illustrated here .

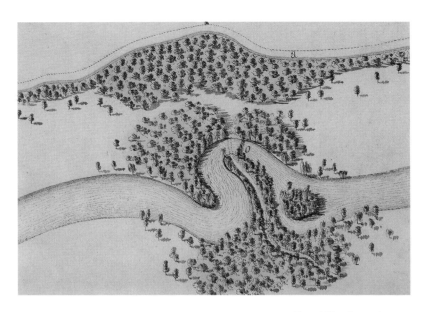

Capability Brown's main concerns — a careful modelling of the terrain, the regimentation of water-courses, and painstakingly assembled clumps of trees — emerge particularly clearly from this drawing.

Petworth House, Sussex. The park was designed by Brown as an absolutely 'natural' landscape. In point of fact, hundreds of men were set to work to create its gently sloping surfaces, and the siting of every single tree was the object of careful thought.

a function more suited to its size. Elsewhere in the park Brown remodelled the rolling terrain, softening his compositions with carefully distributed clumps of trees, building a rockwork cascade tucked away in a corner of the garden where the river-bed narrowed, and generally confining himself to enhancing the few pre-existing elements like the impressive Column of Victory at the top of the slope in front of the Palace.

One of Brown's most successful gardens was the park at Harewood in Yorkshire (1772). A wide hilly terrace was particularly suited to layout as a landscaped park, and here Brown arranged his characteristic clumps of trees to punctuate its vast grassy expanse, surrounding the park with a dense belt of greenery that opened up to allow glimpses of a spectacular and romantic view of the river Wharfe, with the flat rocky outline of Almscliffe Crag looming in the background. He also extended the lake at the bottom of the gentle valley that was overlooked by the house itself.

Brown's work marks both the extremes, and the apogee, of the landscaped garden towards the end of the eighteenth century. Thereafter, fuelled by both precept and example, a heated cultural debate began, waged by such figures as Uvedale Price and Humphry Repton, whose influence was to be crucial to the development of the English style of the nineteenth-century garden. Paradoxically it was these latter, and not Kent or Brown, who were to influence what was subsequently to be known throughout Europe as the *jardin anglais*.

The park at Blenheim, Oxfordshire, still as originally designed by Brown.

Blenheim. One of the carefully laid-out groups of trees known as clumps.

The island with Rousseau's tomb in the grounds of Ermenonville, Oise, given a solemn note by its ring of Lombardy poplars.

The Desert de Retz, Yvelines, on which the Baron de Monville lavished his entire fortune, includes a folly in the form of a gigantic broken column containing apartments on three storeys.

THE *JARDIN ANGLAIS* IN EUROPE

The deeply rural landscape and great forests of the Ile de France had always been central to French culture, a prominence consolidated around the middle of the eighteenth century by the enlightened theories that advocated a return to the simplicity and purity of primitive nature. The scenes painted by Watteau and Fragonard, like the garden described by Jean-Jacques Rousseau in his *Nouvelle Eloise* (1761), were inspired by a more natural and bucolic sensibility. Together with the theories now

firmly entrenched in neighbouring England, this mood was soon throughly to affect the art of the garden in both France and the rest of the world.

Around the 1770s, the writings of the Scottish orientalist William Chambers, in particular his *Dissertation on Oriental Gardening*, as well as the translation of various English treatises and other French publications on the new art of the garden, led several *aficionados* to create themselves gardens in this new style. The taste in landscape becoming established in France was regarded as an English offshoot of the Chinese garden: indeed, the French referred

to the first examples of landscaped parks — dotted with little temples, pavilions, rocky formations and ruins — as *jardins anglo-chinois* The fashion for this type of garden spread rapidly: the *Maison Chinoise*, the first residence the Baron de Monville built for himself in the Desert de Retz, the garden he was constructing near Chambourcy from 1774 — was a Chinese pavilion built of teak, overlooking a pond.

In the Desert de Retz, moreover, Monville created a park where nature, left to her own devices, served to enhance a whole array of outlandish creations intended to stimulate the imagination. The park was dotted with them:

The Temple of Love at the Petit Trianon. The delicate work of Bouchardon showing Cupid making a bow from Hercules' club reflects the romantic attitude inherent in the vogue for the jardin anglo-chinois.

Marie Antoinette's village on the shores of the 'natural' lake at the Petit Trianon, built as a setting for fêtes champetres.

The Bath of Venus in the English garden at Caserta. The iconography of classical allusions altered with the various shifts in taste, and Venus, hitherto portrayed in more austere attitudes, now tended to adopt more spontaneous poses.

the entrance from the forest of Marly was through a rocky grotto, which was followed shortly by a pyramidal ice-house; the *pièce de resistance* was the house itself, on the outside a colossal broken column, but luxuriously furnished within.

The passion for ruins and inscriptions evoking heroic and romantic emotions inspired another of the first landscaped gardens in France, the park of Ermenonville in the Oise. Here, on his return from England, around 1770, the Marquis de Girardin began work on a vast park near the forest of Chantilly where nature was to appeal directly to the mind of man. Apart from its grottoes, monuments, cascades, mills, ponds and greensward Ermenonville is known particularly for the little island set in a large lake with the tomb of Jean-Jacques Rousseau. Here a Roman sarcophagus, surrounded by tall Lombardy poplars, commemorates the last months Rousseau spent at Ermenonville as guest of the Marquis.

The rage for the bucolic now reached such a pitch that Marie Antoinette herself had a landscaped garden created for her own private use in the gardens of the Petit Trianon at Versailles. Some years later, also at Versailles, the Queen indulged another whim, creating a mock village on the edge of a lake, complete with farm, cowsheds and dairies. Here — in a stage village where the ballroom took the form of a barn and the gardens were kitchen-gardens and orchards — Marie Antoinette and her court would frequently dress up as peasants and shepherdesses to give performances in costume.

A few years later, all Europe was seized by the passion for the landscaped garden. Following in Marie Antoinette's footsteps, around 1780 her sister Maria Carolina, the wife of the King of Naples, set the trend for reigning sovereigns to commission gardens in the new style: she had a small 'English' garden made at Caserta, positioned as at Versailles, beside the fountains of the monumental cascade.

In the eighteenth century, with the shift in relations between man and nature brought about by the Enlightenment, the perception of the garden also changed. The theatrical approach that had typified the gardens of the previous century now vouchsafed man a walk-on part, and immense expanses *à perte de vue* were replaced by more contained spaces, more in keeping with the measure of man. The rococo garden tended to divide space up into a sequence of open-air rooms enclosed in greenery, where the individual stroller could enjoy the garden at closer range.

With its sensitivity to man and its analysis of the specific, the spirit of the Enlightenment meant that eighteenth-century gardens were no longer represented with an eye to proclaiming their greatness and vastness, but rather through a series of separate views. Like sketches for stage sets, eighteenth-century engravings represented the garden as a sort of stage in whose various parts man — as both rational organizer and rapt beholder — was involved as absolute protagonist.

The dawning encyclopaedic and didactic tendency encouraged the making of views that were specific, analytic and descriptive, with virtual genre scenes set in the open air. Rigid perspectives with central vanishing points were replaced by oblique and corner views, in keeping with the new way of seeing and experiencing the garden.

Series of views of gardens became very fashionable during the eighteenth century and many owners commissioned engravings of their properties, reproducing genre scenes in avenues or woodland glades, with people walking, talking or pausing to admire flowers or statues, reflecting a new-found sensibility more inclined towards the contemplation of nature. It registered a disenchantment with Baroque formality, with lofty allusions now displaced by the 'natural' and romantic mood of the landscaped garden.

THE REPRESENTATION OF THE GARDEN: MAN AND GARDEN AS PROTAGONISTS IN THE EIGHTEENTH-CENTURY ENGRAVING

1. Versailles, Yvelines. The baroque approach is still very much in evidence in this engraving of the Fountain of Flora on the Avenue of the Seasons. The central perspective and exaggerated dimensions, intensified by the tall green palissades, give the garden the feel of a city square. The figures themselves have something of the anonymity of the undifferentiated city-dweller, and reason and logic predominate throughout.

1

2

2. In this detail from a plate of an Orangery garden by Salomon Kleiner, the carefully depicted figures of the gardeners, transporting the citrus trees in their traditional pots to *arrange them in the open air at the beginning of summer, give the garden the feeling of a space that is lived in, not just by the pair who are strolling in it, but also by those who work* *there. The arrangement of the topiary pyramids, too, suggests a theatrical layout of garden space, a new way of seeing it. The garden is no longer a scenic background, but rather a genuine* *stage on which man lives and moves as a protagonist.*

3. Stowe Gardens, Buckinghamshire. Detail of one of the many views engraved by Jacques Rigaud to illustrate the gardens designed by Bridgeman. In almost every engraving in this series Rigaud slips in Lord Cobham among the figures, always showing him in distinctive poses and attitudes that bespeak his personal involvement.

4. Stowe Gardens, Buckinghamshire. In this later engraving, Thomas Rowlandson mocks the visitors' roguish reactions to the naked figure of Priapus. Over the century the familiarity with the classics underpinning the creations of William Kent had all but vanished, and gardens now became more natural places, as we see from the technique used to depict the trees.

3

4

5

5. Chiswick House, London. This engraving by Rigaud also shows the various visitors to the garden in different attitudes and poses. The garden is now appreciated in a more casual and spontaneous manner: some figures are on horseback, some walking the dog, while others pause to comment on the bas-reliefs of the obelisk. Everyone is enjoying the garden according to their own inclinations, freely and unrestrainedly. Indeed it was this attitude — together with a British libertarianism and anti-absolutism, that abhorred the Baroque stiffness symbolizing absolute monarchy — that was at the root of the English landscape revolution.

The Nineteenth Century

From the picturesque to the eclectic

The defeat of Napoleon and the decline of his empire, the rise of the bourgeoisie and the increasing social pressures of the nineteenth century and the further innovations of scientific progress and industrialisation, brought huge changes in the social order and national politics. Populations became concentrated in the cities, and local authorities faced problems of overcrowding and insanitary conditions. The first constitutions were drawn up, and monarchies found themselves confronting a new era; at the same time, however, industrial development stimulated a general faith in science and the machine. With the broadening of the social base, ever-greater numbers of individuals were involved in public and cultural affairs, and the arts took this lead from the great revolutions of the century.

During the first years of the century, the neo-classical mood associated with the empire found itself challenged by a romanticism that sought to reinstate the spiritual climate of earlier periods and civilizations, and pagan classicism found itself doing battle with medieval and Gothic art. While still inspired by images of a serene and classical harmony, gardens were now increasingly populated by elements, structures and forms of decoration drawn from the most varied sources, from the Gothic to the exotic.

During the nineteenth century a somewhat mawkish sentimentalism emerged, derived from debased romantic ideals, and the cultural and literary allusions which had made it a truly great art form disappeared from the garden. In England a lively debate, already partially vented in the discussions and publications of the late eighteenth century, threw up a proliferation of interpretations which only confused the whole notion of the garden. Travellers and tourists brought back a plethora of new ideas to mimic, the number of species available for cultivation soared, and styles and quotations were piled upon one another in the scramble for novelty.

In the meantime, progress and public health priorities brought about the great nineteenth-century feats of town-planning and the creation of a vast number of public parks. Though not entirely new to the capitals of Europe, in the nineteenth century public parks became vitally important instruments of public propriety in smaller cities, being the main venue for innovative civic projects. The planners' attention therefore shifted to the urban green space, and gardens, while still attracting much creative and academic endeavour were now reduced either to a jumble of different styles,

The urban garden was already beginning to assume importance in England in the nineteenth century as part of a general rejection of the overcrowded and increasingly industrialized city.

(Opposite) Alton Towers, Staffordshire.

or hopelessly overstocked with botanical species. The general uncertainty pervading the art of the garden was further exacerbated by the aesthetic of eclecticism; in many cases the absence of any definite and coherent style, and the mindless repetition of set formulae, undermined any originality and artistic worth such gardens might have had.

The beauty of nineteenth-century gardens arose from their expression of a society that was evolving very rapidly but at the same time still tied culturally to the past: the conventions of the burgeoning middle classes tempered a creativity whose virtue lay in going to extremes, and was therefore capable of creating gardens of great charm, punctuated by either pompous and florid decoration or fascinating exotica. Romantic or eclectic, over-encumbered or pleasantly 'natural', nineteenth-century gardens developed differently from country to country, following the headlong rush of English opinion with varying hesitation. In England the heated debate that broke out over the rival claims of the 'sublime', the 'beautiful' and the 'picturesque' in the late eighteenth and early nineteenth centuries found some sort of resolution in the growing interest in plants from all over the world, but flared up again in the second half of the century in the conflict between 'formal' and 'informal' design. By the end of the century, while the rest of the world was still designing eclectically, oscillating between the landscaped park, the classical revival and the botanical collection, the argument was to some extent settled, again in England, through the works and theories of William Robinson, Gertrude Jekyll and Edwin Lutyens.

The island and temple of Pythagoras in the Puccini garden at Scornio, in the province of Pistoia. In the nineteenth century the canons applied in the design of public and private parks became increasingly similar.

The Grand Cascade at the Bois de Boulogne, designed by some of the foremost planners of the time: Baron Haussmann, Jean-Charles Adolphe Alphand, Edouard François André and Jean-Pierre Barillet-Deschamps.

The development of the English Garden

The debate about the 'picturesque' from the end of the eighteenth century endured into the nineteenth. Uvedale Price and Richard Payne Knight, leading figures in English culture and society, deplored the impoverishment and trickery implicit in the landscape style, but they were not in agreement over the concept of the 'picturesque', whose foremost exponent, William Gilpin, was the author of numerous essays on the subject. If, on the one hand, 'beauty' was said to lie in the clean and flowing lines of a well-sculpted lawn or a skilfully designed path, this concept could not be translated to a 'picturesque' composition. A painter would not be able to reproduce such images: the result would be lifeless and the observer bored. A truly picturesque image would have to be more faithful to nature, more colourful, preferring life-like, jagged terrain to gentle slopes, and reflecting a wilder, more chaotic view of nature. The 'sublime', on the other hand — a romantic intensification of the 'picturesque' — was the term chosen to denote anything which induced strong feelings such as fear, unease, amazement or admiration: jagged rocks, infinite vistas and gloomy caverns were some of its indispensable components.

Out of this controversy different interpretations of what was meant by 'garden', 'landscape' and 'nature' arose: each of the many publications succeeding one another during the early nineteenth century championed one concept or criterion over

The debate over the picturesque was concerned essentially with the rejection of the clean-cut lines favoured by Brown (below), in favour of more evocative forms closer to those of nature (above).

The park at Hawkstone, Shropshire, designed by Sir Rowland Hill, whose craggy rocks and wide vistas are a typical example of the concept of the 'sublime' as applied to the garden.

An illustration from Loudon's Encyclopedia of Gardening *(1822), showing the difference between the 'beautiful' and the 'picturesque' in plan and prospect.*

Views painted 'before and after' the implementation of his designs were a feature of the work of Humphry

Repton, whose Red Books *(so-called from the colour of their covers) depicted the final results.*

the others, resulting in gardens designed in a mixed style, and fully-fledged eclecticism.

Repton, Loudon and the 'gardenesque'

In England the concept of the garden was developed further through the work of Humphry Repton. His career as a garden designer had begun around 1790, at a time — following the death of Lancelot Brown in 1783 — when the profession seemed to hold no new opportunities in garden design.

Repton's designs were broadly in the style of Brown, the main differences being that he created denser thickets and more closely planted clumps of trees, and drew the inspiration for his follies from the rustic and rural, rather than from the classical world.

One particularly interesting aspect of Repton's work was his famous *Red Books*, a collection of before-and-after pictures of gardens he worked on.

Repton gradually moved away from the rigid compositions favoured by Brown, introducing, or rather reintroducing, architectural elements from the Italian tradition, for example balustrades and terraces in the vicinity of the main house. But Repton's creations never reached the grandiose proportions of Brown's, and on many occasions, changes in fashion prompted his employment to carry out modifications to the work of his illustrious predecessor.

During these years the ideas of the Scotsman John Claudius Loudon were gaining ground. Loudon acknowledged his debt to Price's vision of the 'picturesque': his designs were decidedly

'irregular', characterized by watercourses whose banks were left naturally jagged, by a more irregular and natural landscaping and by arrangements of trees that took account of their natural habit. A lover of variety, Loudon took a particular interest in the specific properties of individual plants, especially exotic species which he planted in arrangements designed to allow each specimen to develop its full potential. This method became known as the 'gardenesque' style, to emphasize that these effects were easily achievable in a garden. His planting schemes became extremely influential, and very fashionable, not least because he expounded them in various treatises, as well as in the '*Gardener's Magazine*', a periodical which ran from 1826 to 1844.

Loudon's wife Jane, meanwhile, published books and periodicals about the garden, particularly on the cultivation of flowers and the practical aspects of gardening: their joint editorial activity — one of the first examples of gardening journalism, subsequently to enjoy such success in Great Britain — also contributed to the passion for plants and flowers which was to become an important component of Anglo-Saxon culture, and their ideas continue to be internationally influential throughout the twentieth century.

The Victorian garden

While the 'English garden' was becoming fashionable throughout Europe, in England itself designers were rediscovering the geometric garden and the Italian Renaissance. The landscaped garden had had its day, and from around 1830

Hoole House, with the typical round flowerbeds that were so popular in the nineteenth century because of the passion for the many new plants imported from other continents.

Sheffield Park, Sussex, designed by Brown and altered by Repton. The later introduction of conifers and rhododendrons completely changed the original design.

a 'formal' section was regarded as *de rigueur* in effecting the transition between the house and the surrounding landscaped garden.

The most important feature reintroduced from the Italian classical garden was the terrace, which offered an alternative way of experiencing the space around the house, and a vantage point from which to enjoy the garden and the view. People began to appreciate the joys of the open air, and to use the garden as an extension of the house. Many houses now had terraces on the façade overlooking the garden: in the 1840—50s Sir Charles Barry, the architect of the neo-gothic Houses of Parliament, was responsible for many such layouts. He also introduced the fashion for the popular Italian garden, an English version with formal symmetrical layouts and huge flowerbeds, reflecting the passion for ornamental floriculture rife in England at the time. Nevertheless, the fashion for the 'Italian' garden should be seen in the context of the continuing debate according to which all garden styles were equally valid and applicable.

One particularly remarkable example is the garden of Biddulph Grange in Staffordshire, restored by the National Trust between 1988 and 1992. Here areas of different styles were linked with great ingenuity; they included an Italian garden, a Chinese garden, an English garden, a garden inspired by ancient Egypt, a rock garden and a pine wood. The fashion for the revival of past styles, and the use of exotic plants, reached its peak in the second half of the nineteenth century, with gardens of every period and idiom being created in just a

few years; giant hothouses, both public and private, sprang up everywhere to house the vast collections of ornamental plants culled from around the globe.

Formal design therefore predominated in the Victorian garden, with plants, especially flowers, given particular prominence. Victorian floral bedding became extremely fashionable in the seventies, consisting in the planting and continuous rotation of highly coloured flowerbeds in the most varied ornamental compositions.

Rather like Victorian interiors, the gardens of this period were stuffed with ideas, structures, plants and colours, and as in the interiors the abundance of 'furniture' greatly diminished the remaining space. Less and less room was left for lawns, which were filled with flowerbeds in many shapes, ever more elaborate until eventually they resembled nothing so much as enormous baskets of flowers. The return to geometry also saw the enlargement of the clipped hedges into buttresses and embankments enclosed and created other little gardens, anticipating the interest in 'rooms' and 'thematic gardens' that characterized English gardens in the first half of the twentieth century.

Harewood House, Yorkshire, in a nineteenth-century photograph by Roger Fenton. The terrace overlooking Brown's landscaped park had been added just a few years before this photograph was taken.

An illustration by Charles Rennie Mackintosh showing a typically elaborate Victorian flowerbed.

At Castle Howard, Yorkshire, the revival of the Italian garden inspired a formal parterre *to the front of the house, and the addition of the great Triton fountain, acquired at the Great Exhibition of 1851.*

This 1834 engraving, taken from a French text, shows some of the weird topiary at Levens Hall some years after it was restored.

Levens Hall, Cumbria: the garden has a number of eccentrically-shaped hedges, and these box arches, topped by a crown, are among the most outlandish.

The cultivation of highly colourful flowers was a twentieth-century innovation: in the nineteenth century flowers *were not grouped in single-colour masses, but subdivided according to species in small flowerbeds, contrasting* *with one another rather than creating a uniform background.*

The spiral, on the other hand, was a favourite seventeenth-century form, probably derived from the old tradition of clipping à l'estrade, *or with superimposed layers.*

pattern of cones, pyramids, spheres, arches, birds and spirals unfolds to reveal new vistas at every turn. The charm of this original garden lies also in its wonderful variety of colour: the beds are kept permanently full of very bright flowers, and the dark green of the common yew forms a striking background to the endlessly varied roses in the rose-garden, as well as for the golden yew. A Cedar of Lebanon planted at this same period, now enormously tall, casts its sweeping shade magically over the garden's fantastic hedges.

Other parts of the original late seventeenth-century creation have also been preserved: enormous walls of beech surround the orchard and the bowling green, while luxuriant creepers and generous herbaceous borders in a more recent idiom are a lively contrast to the earlier rigid structure.

Like many other old English houses, Levens Hall is preserved and maintained with passionate devotion by its owners, who open it regularly to the public. The maintenance of the hedges alone is a major undertaking: trimming the long walls of beech is done mechanically between mid-August and mid-October, while the styling of the yews, a more complex and delicate operation, is mostly done by hand, finishing around the middle of December.

The English Garden in Europe

The fashion for the English garden had already reached Europe by the end of the eighteenth century, but it was during the next one that the taste for the *jardin anglais* or *englischer garten* really took hold. Garden style was continuously developing in England, and therefore its influence among European countries varied according to the date it reached them. Russia was among the first to import the landscape style; in France it arrived even earlier, but the disruption caused by the Revolution meant that when the English landscape style was resumed, it was already contaminated by new elements. Furthermore, the purity of the English style was everywhere adulterated by the demands of the terrain and local garden tradition. In Germany the huge acreages available to the German princes allowed them immediately to realize vast landscape designs; in Italy, on the other hand, where the tradition of the architectural garden was very strong, the taste for landscaped gardens only began to take hold in 1801, which also saw the publication of *Dell'arte dei giardini inglesi* (On the Art of English Gardens) by Ercole Silva. The English landscaped garden was, however, adopted everywhere as a model for the public parks springing up in cities throughout the western world.

Gradually the English, or picturesque, garden began to follow pre-established formulae, and the search for variety robbed it of its original ideals. More architectural structures were introduced, and flowers began to predominate, with over-elaborate compositions and excessive attention to decora-

Plan of the park at Wilhelmshöhe, Kassel, after the nineteenth-century landscape transformations, which fortunately spared the rococo Octagon and cascades.

The Treves garden at Padua. The design for this small city garden was by Giuseppe Jappelli, who was one of the first in Italy to create gardens in the romantic English style.

tive appeal. Incorporating ideas from different civilizations, landscapes and epochs, the English garden now embraced an eclecticism far removed from its original inspiration, as had already happened in England itself.

The jardin anglais *in France*

France had been one of the first countries to acquire the English taste, in the second half of the eighteenth century. Initially it was reflected in small spaces adjacent to the large formal gardens – the romantic copses as at Chantilly, for example, or elegant rustic compositions like the *hameau* at the Petit Trianon; subsequently it inspired larger projects like the park at Ermenonville and the Desert de Retz.

The French Revolution decisively consigned the classical French style to history: it was seen as symbolic of the Ancien Régime, and returning exiles found it much easier to redesign their ravaged and abandoned gardens in a landscape style.

Such was the case with the gardens of François de La Rochefoucauld at Liancourt — which have now completely disappeared — and the gardens of Champs, near Paris, which were further remodelled and restored to Le Nôtre's original design at the end of the nineteenth century.

Certain gardens adopted the English style during the First Empire, under Napoleon Bonaparte: some were new projects, others restructurings of existing gardens, they were detailed in Alexandre Laborde's book, *Nouveaux Jardins de France* (1808): most famous was the garden of Malmaison.

Josephine Beauharnais, Empress of France, acquired the

The English style proliferated throughout Europe: here, the eighteenth-century garden of the castle of Fredricksberg in Copenhagen was transformed in 1801 by adopting the characteristic elements of the English garden, like this Chinese bridge.

The Lombard lakes became popular places for holiday villas during this period, and Villa Melzi at Bellagio, on Lake Como, is a typical example of the many gardens created on their shores.

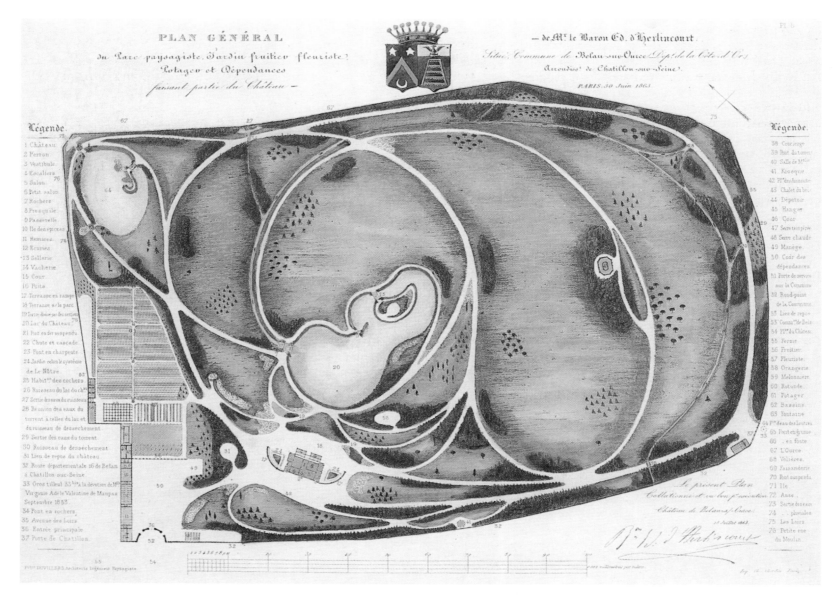

The private garden in France was structured according to the long-codified canons of the *jardin anglais. The avenues now followed a curved, oval layout, and lakes and little islands were* de rigueur.

The rose was particularly popular in France in the wake of Josephine Beauharnais' passion for her rose garden at Malmaison at the beginning of the century. Collections of the rarest and finest varieties were ubiquitous, as seen here in Redouté's illustrations.

The codification of the various garden structures took on the nature of a veritable catalogue, as we see in this illustration from the treatise by Gabriel Thouin.

(Opposite) Fontainebleau. During the Napoleonic Empire, the great royal gardens too were altered or given additions in the romantic style, such as this pavilion on an island in the Etang.

château of Malmaison in 1799. It became her favourite residence and she enlarged the property until it extended over seven hundred hectares (1700 acres), which she then had landscaped into an exquisite park in the English style.

The park included a lake, a stream with elegant little bridges and waterfalls, *fabriques* such as a temple of Venus, a farm and a menagerie for exotic animals. The entire park testified to a passion for exotic and unusual plants, flowers and animals, mostly of Australian origin. There were emus and kangaroos in the menagerie, black swans on the lake, numerous species of cedar and conifer, acacias and grevilleas, and any number of rare plants which Josephine exchanged with the Jardin des Plantes in Paris. Above all there was her vast collection of roses that made Malmaison famous, and, though reduced in number, still give the garden its particular charm and colour. They also provided the subjects for the wonderful illustrations in Pierre Joseph Redouté's book, *Les Roses*, drawn between 1817 and 1824.

Josephine only lived a few years at Malmaison, and during the nineteenth century the park almost disappeared entirely: today, of more than seven hundred hectares (1700 acres) which surrounded the château at the time of the empress, just six (fifteen acres) remain.

The English fashion also came to Fontainebleau: between 1809 and 1812 Napoleon had the original garden — remodelled several times by Catherine de' Medici — re-configured in an irregular style; because of the fountain of Diana placed at its centre it became known as the *Cour de Diane*. Napoleon also built a tiny island with a pavilion in the sizeable lake to take the place of the sixteenth-century Jardin de l'Etang in front of the *Cour de la Fontaine*.

The gardens of Malmaison and the illustrations of Laborde also reveal the influence of Repton's ideas on the particular style of landscaping becoming popular in France, but it was Gabriel Thouin who perfected the formula that dominated French garden design until at least 1870. Thouin's model consisted of a relatively simple arrangement of winding avenues linked by a wider circular *allée*, enclosing ample lawns dotted with groups of trees or densely planted *bosquets*. Because it was functional and easily reproducible, it quickly became very popular — taught in the schools and academies and becoming the backbone of the numerous public parks created in the mid-nineteenth century. Translated to an urban location, the picturesque style invigorated these new parks intended for the entertainment and exercise of city- dwellers, their promenades, circular avenues, miniature mountain streams, little lakes, islets and hillocks all given a sense of unity by their common, sinuously elliptical line. Similarly the use of *fabriques*, already codified by Thouin in his *Plans raisonnés de toutes les espèces de jardins* of 1820, provided a solution for every situation.

Ruins and classical temples, pagodas and oriental pavilions,

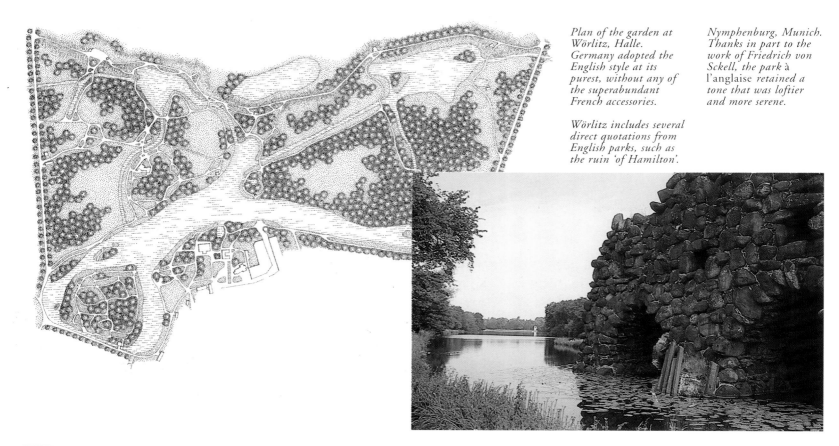

Plan of the garden at Wörlitz, Halle. Germany adopted the English style at its purest, without any of the superabundant French accessories.

Wörlitz includes several direct quotations from English parks, such as the ruin 'of Hamilton'.

Nymphenburg, Munich. Thanks in part to the work of Friedrich von Sckell, the park à l'anglaise retained a tone that was loftier and more serene.

urns and vases, fountains, arches and railings, were all in a great range of styles, available in dimensions, materials and functions that could be adapted to any requirement. Thus for a long time garden design remained tied to set formulae embedded in current taste, with the addition of ever more decorative and ornamental features. This eclectic culture continued beyond the second half of the nineteenth century to influence the academies and the gardens designed to the criteria of the Beaux Arts for many years.

The landscaped park in Germany

In Germany the taste for landscaped gardens took a different turn: romanticism was more firmly rooted, and the German principalities were much more stable than their French counterparts.

By the end of the eighteenth century the ideal of a garden which respected nature, and was designed to resemble some serene Arcadian landscape, already had many enthusiastic supporters in Germany among philosophers and writers, including Johann Wolfgang Goethe. Goethe was a keen student of botanical taxonomy and geology; he was also a traveller, and interested in gardens because of their close connection with contemporary romantic literature. In his novel *Elective Affinities* a garden provides the setting for the plot, which unfolds simultaneously the story of its creation. Goethe contributed to the botanical collections of the Belvedere, the

garden attached to the Duke of Weimar's residence; later he devoted himself to his own garden, after visiting one of Germany's earliest landscape gardens, the park at Worlitz. Like the protagonists in *Elective Affinities*, many German princes of the period took an active interest in developing their own parks in accordance with the new taste: one was Prince Franz von Anhalt-Dessau who began work on the park at Worlitz after visiting various parks in England. It became part of an ambitious project that was to occupy him for more than fifty years — the *Gartenreich*, the transformation of his entire kingdom into one great garden. To indulge his interests in agriculture, forest management and cattle-breeding he devoted himself to landscaping over 150 square kilometres (60 square miles), within which he constructed several parks. Worlitz, the most important of these, was a vast agricultural holding of 120 hectares (300 acres), forty of which (100 acres), laid out between 1765 and 1817 became the park proper. Dotted with buildings, temples and belvederes, the entire park had a serenity that evoked the myth of the Elysian Fields. Goethe was a great admirer.

One of the first professional garden designers to be inspired by a taste for the English style was Friedrich von Sckell, who had studied in England and drew his inspiration directly from Brown. His most important project was the enlargement of the gardens at Schwetzingen between 1776 and 1802, but he is primarily known for designing the Englischer Garten in

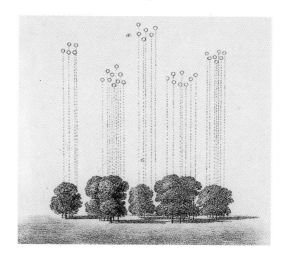

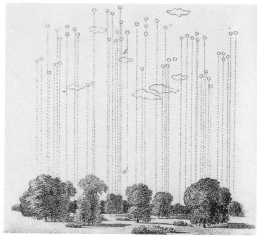

The park at Branitz, Kottbus, the last work by Prince Pückler-Muskau. The prince and his wife were buried under this grass-covered pyramid in the middle of a lake.

Taken from Pückler-Muskau's book, this illustration shows the correct way of grouping trees, with the clustering of their trunks shown in projection above.

The façade of the Schloss known as Charlottenhof, Potsdam, designed by Karl Friedrich Schinkel, standing out at the far end of the great lake.

Munich, the first public park in Europe to be created according to the theories of the landscapists.

The most original expression of the taste for the landscape park in Germany was the garden created by Prince Hermann von Pückler-Muskau. In 1816 he began to create a park for himself at Muskau, applying the teachings and theories of Repton he had learnt about on his first visit to England, and systematized in a treatise, copiously illustrated on the art of the landscape garden . He laid the vast area out as an authentic landscape, using illustrations he had commissioned specially: the park had a vast lake, plantations of forest trees riding the gentle slopes or framing different vistas, and bridges, pavilions and decorative buildings combining into a series of views of a strongly picturesque character. The influence of Repton and the emerging fashion for ornamental floriculture were obvious in the garden proper, situated in the immediate vicinity of the castle. Full of original ideas like extravagantly shaped flowerbeds and trellises for climbing plants, this part was described by Pückler-Muskau as 'a cross between a bazaar and an elegant lady's drawing-room.' The park was enlarged following a second voyage to England, but subsequent economic difficulties obliged the prince to sell the property and move to another residence at Branitz where, in 1846, he began work on a new park of seventy hectares (170 acres), a project to which he devoted himself until his death in 1871.

But the most important figure in the nineteenth-century

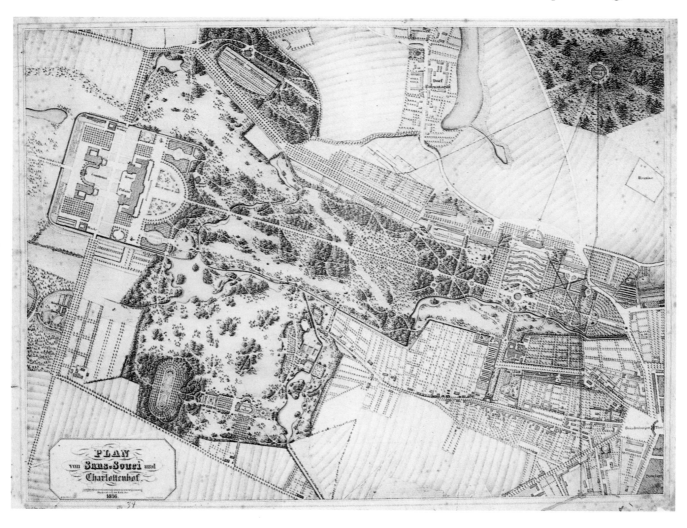

Plan of Sanssouci, Potsdam, showing Lenné's extensions and alterations to the original garden. Interestingly enough, the design of the terraced vineyard dating from the previous century — to the right of the illustration — has been incorporated into the comprehensive design along its central axis.

German garden was Peter Josef Lenné. After studying in Paris under Thouin he worked in the royal gardens at Laxenburg in Austria, and in 1826 started work on the park of Charlottenhof, not far from Sanssouci, a property given to the future king of Prussia, Frederick William IV, by his father. In the vast projects he undertook at Charlottenhof Lenné introduced many formal and geometrical elements from the Italian tradition, a revival soon to become very fashionable. In the enlargement which connected Sanssouci to Charlottenhof Lenné designed a singular form of linkage in the form of three long panoramic axes that cleverly precluded any vistas of the surrounding landscape, forcing the visitor to concentrate on the interior of the park. Modification and addition of new areas to the already huge park continued until 1860, and further work continued right into the twentieth century, ceasing only on the eve of World War I.

But Lenné's most important contribution to the wholesale transformation of the Potsdam landscape was the park of Klein-Glienicke. He began work on it in 1816, summoned by the then-owner, Chancellor Hardenberg, to redesign the existing garden. Here, as at Charlottenhof, he added a liberal sprinkling of buildings and pavilions modelled on the Italian style villa, embracing the ideal of Italy as the exemplar of Western culture.

As elsewhere, huge sums have been spent to return this park back to its original conception, and today Klein-Glienecke is the best-preserved example of Lenné's work.

A view of the park of Klein-Glienicke, giving an idea of the atmosphere created by Lenné's sure touch in the grouping of trees.

Germany too experienced a sort of revival of the Italian model, with many garden buildings following the lines of classical Italian architecture, such as this loggia at Klein-Glienicke, Potsdam.

The mosque at the imperial park at Tsarskoye Selo, also overlooking the lake. Begun at the end of the eighteenth century, Catherine the Great's park became the model for other Russian land-scaped gardens.

The grotto built by Bartolomeo Rastrelli, with masks of Neptune, tritons, dolphins, nereids and sea-horses, by the lake at Tsarskoye Selo, with the gallery by Charles Cameron in the background.

THE FASHION FOR ENGLISH-STYLE GARDENS IN RUSSIA

On the other side of the Urals, the first passionate devotee of the English style in gardens was Catherine the Great, Empress of All the Russias. Catherine was an ardent supporter of the ideals of the Enlightenment, and had corresponded with Voltaire, to whom she had confided her dislike of formal gardens and her enthusiasm for the gentle vistas of the landscaped garden. During her reign she greatly advanced the cause of the English style herself through the works she undertook at Tsarskoye Selo, the imperial residence a few miles north of St Petersburg. The landscape taste became very fashionable, so much so that Prince Potemkin, Catherine's favourite, who shared her passion for gardens, created a garden *à l'anglais* around each of the pavilions Catherine stayed in on her way to the Crimea (where he intended to establish his own residence). At Tsarskoye Selo the tsarina had called a halt to the proposed baroque design for the gardens, ordering that the southern section of the park be laid out in the landscape style instead. A number of buildings were erected in a somewhat haphazard lay-out in keeping with the fashionable taste for the exotic. A great deal of earth-moving was required to obtain the gentle slopes for planting groups of trees; a large lake was dug to the south of the palace, probably the work of the Russian Vasily Neyelov, who had been sent by Catherine to England to study the English parks; a Palladian bridge was also built, similar to those at Wilton and Stowe.

At Pavlovsk, south of St Petersburg, the residence of the future Tsar Paul I, work had begun towards the end of the eighteenth century and continued for more than forty years, on what resulted in the largest landscaped park in the whole of Russia. The Englishman Charles Cameron was the first to

Cameron also worked on the park at Pavlovsk, with a skilful use of the gently curving river and various gradients to enhance the picturesque mood of the buildings.

The Temple of Friendship in the park of Pavlovsk, derived from the round classical temple supported by an order of Doric columns, which became the model for many other garden buildings throughout Russia.

work on it, contributing buildings like the Temple of Friendship, the Colonnade of Apollo and the Temple of the Three Graces, all incorporated into the existing landscape along the wooded banks of the Slavyanka river; grander buildings were added after Paul came to the throne. Vincenzo Brenna was responsible for the architectural elements, while another Italian, Pietro Gonzaga, was responsible for the park. In contrast to Cameron, Gonzaga drew his inspiration directly from the Russian landscape, with its meadows and forests, especially in the vast area known as the 'The Silver Birches.' In Russian parks, in fact, the English model, with its expanses of carefully mown laws so popular elsewhere, was rejected in favour of meadows of wild flowers — occurring in such profusion in Russia — which were cut only twice a year. Gonzaga, a decorator and scene-painter, arranged the trees in almost scenographic groups, taking account of their particular characteristics and the atmosphere they created, arranging them like the wings or flats of a stage to give depth to the whole composition.

Another important Romanov residence remodelled along landscape principles was the park at Oranienbaum, also near St Petersburg, with the pre-existing baroque framework of a large part of the gardens now re-fashioned in the contemporary manner. The so-called Lower Garden was in fact completely replanted during the nineteenth century, but in 1975 the garden was restored to its original eighteenth-century design. The French invasion, and the increasing social tensions caused by anachronistic political and agricultural institutions, brought a halt to the development of the vast country estates and their landscaped parks, which were then gradually abandoned. Recently, after the devastation left by World War II, restoration has begun on a large number of the great imperial gardens of Russia, and they now have something of the fascination of an earlier age.

The *fin de siècle* garden

The eclectic approach, which had been incubating since the middle of the century, reached maturity in the seventies. Peter Josef Lenné, the last great landscaper, died in 1866. The emerging historical revivalism, and the drying-up of ideas in the landscape and picturesque tradition signalled an unconditional abandonment of the 'natural' garden and a return to the 'formal' style, which meant a style whose designs — often symmetrical as well as geometrical — were in essence architectural.

The bourgeoisie was by now well represented in all the cultural, political and social institutions, seeking its own values and redefining those of the former ruling classes. The house and garden were an expression of social status, and this led to a certain uniformity in the rules governing their composition.

In France, treatises appeared harking back to this tradition of design subject to strict architectural rules: one example was the *Traité général de la composition des parcs et jardins* by Edouard André (1879), and there was a strong revival of interest in the gardens of the *Grand Siècle*. In Germany, on the other hand, the call for a return to the architectural garden was seconded by the architects themselves, who now proclaimed the conceptual unity of house and garden, anticipating the modernist creations of the early nineteenth century. In England the industrial and commercial classes signalled their increased financial standing and stability by a return to the landowning tradition of Anglo-Saxon culture, and the garden once again became the subject of a heated debate between architects, with their rigid formal approach, and devotees of the more naturalistic garden, among them several outstanding

A plate from the Rev. Henry d'Ombrain's 'Floral Magazine', which was extremely influential in popularizing flower-growing in Victorian England.

A water-colour of Thomas Mawson's design for an Arts and Crafts garden: the use of the various building materials, particularly *stone for the arches and flight of steps, was influential in the return to the ideal of craftsmanship.*

Pampas grass, and various other grasses were among the exotic but hardy species whose cultivation was suggested by William Robinson.

Design for a garden from Thomas Sedding's Garden Craft, Old and New (1890). The absolutely formal layout reflects the vision of many designers of the time, who were against a more spontaneous type of cultivation.

figures who were to leave a lasting mark on twentieth-century developments.

The naturalism of William Robinson and the cottage garden of Gertrude Jekyll

Spurred on by a desire to legitimize their status, the swelling ranks of the urban bourgeoisie adopted the ways of the traditional land owning aristocracy. A country property was not only a way of asserting one's social standing, it also provided an escape from the overcrowded smoky cities with their increasingly threatening criminal element.

Several factors coincided to favour a return to the countryside. A serious economic crisis in the agricultural sector brought a fall in land prices, and many of the vast landed estates were broken up and sold off. Meanwhile a growing concern about the state of the countryside itself, now under threat from massive country-wide industrialization, saw the land and the countryside reasserted as an important part of the national heritage. The writer and art critic John Ruskin advocated the need for its protection, and it was not long before, in 1875, the National Trust was founded, with the object of preserving the natural beauty and artistic heritage of Great Britain. A little later, in 1897, *Country Life* first appeared, reflecting the new interest in English rural culture.

It was against this general background that the Arts and Crafts movement came into being, with the aim of reapprais-

ing the craft tradition in the applied arts, whose products were in stark contrast to the poor-quality industrial goods to which the Universal Exhibition of 1851 had drawn attention. The Arts and Crafts movement looked back to medievalism and ancient English traditions, paying renewed attention to the concept of the cottage garden, with its vegetables, fruit and flowers. Emblem of individualistic self-expression, of the innate wisdom of the countryman, of the union of the utilitarian and the aesthetic, the cottage garden became something of a cult, influencing the new approach towards arranging and cultivating plants that characterized most gardens at the dawn of the twentieth century.

One logical consequence of this rejection of mass-produced goods and concern for nature under threat, was the sternly 'pro-nature' doctrine of the Irishman William Robinson. In a series of publications Robinson firmly maintained the need for greater respect for nature and a new system of garden cultivation: species should be planted carefully in relation to one another, with attention paid to their individual characteristics, and they should be able to thrive without special treatment. Indigenous plants and those exotic plants which could withstand the English climate could be planted together, provided care was taken that they did not clash in size, colour or foliage. In 1870 the publication of Robinson's *Alpine Flowers for Gardens*, intensified the English penchant for rock gardens with minute alpine flowers Later the same year he published *The*

Gravetye Manor, West Sussex. Robinson's work was fundamental in pioneering the pre-eminence of plants in the design of the twentieth-century English garden.

Wild Garden and subsequently in 1883 his most important work, *The English Flower Garden*, in which he considered the juxtaposition of plants, not just from an aesthetic point of view, but also considering each era's unique characteristics. Robinson developed several concepts of the greatest importance to garden design in the next century: the harmonious combination of colour and flower shape, permanent cultivation through the use of perennials and sturdy rustic species, a reduction in maintenance by respecting the needs of plants, and the garden as an expression of one's own personality. A further feature was the ecological concern which underlay all Robinson's work and was to provide a constant inspiration for the garden designers of the twentieth century.

But this 'natural', informal attitude provoked the opposition of many designers who favoured the formal approach. Most prominent among Robinson's opponents was the architect Reginald Blomfield, who stated his position in his book *The Formal Garden in England*, published in 1892. There was now open war, and the eternal clash between formal and informal continues to dog the debate on the art of the garden to this day, albeit in more muted tones.

Only towards the end of the century did the controversy appear to die down, thanks to the collaboration between the enthusiastic gardener Gertrude Jekyll and the young architect Edwin Lutyens, who collaborated on the design of numerous houses and gardens between 1893 and 1912. Jekyll was directly influenced by the theories of Robinson; Lutyens had been trained as an architect. United by their approval of the ideas championed by the Arts and Crafts movement, they worked together in a perfect synthesis of the various approaches which usually set nature and human intervention at loggerheads. From the social point of view, too, the work of Lutyens and Jekyll was the most comprehensive response to the requirements of the urban bourgeoisie, whose investment in small country residences formally asserted their new social status as part of the traditional life of the countryside.

Jekyll and Lutyens' designs were based on a rigid architectural structure for the garden to set its various parts into relief, though always by free and spontaneous planting. Their built elements — pavings, basins, steps and walls — were constructed in local materials with a strongly vernacular feel and square, clean lines, arranged around Jekyll's splendidly colourful flowerbeds. She herself was a talented painter, with a shrewd feeling for the colours and shapes of plants, combined most effectively in her famous herbaceous borders with their mingling of noble and common plants, such as the iris and the lupin, the rose and the sweet pea. Her expertise in juxtaposing different varieties led her to experiment with planting schemes to splendid chromatic effect, sometimes consisting of monochrome sequences based on her knowledge of the different shades of a single colour. She too published various books, of which the last, *Colour in the Flower Garden*, published in 1908, remains a source of inspiration for designers and enthusiastic gardeners.

The gardens of the Riviera and the fashion for botanical collections

In the second half of the century the Côte d'Azur became a

A water-colour (1901) showing a typical herbaceous border by Gertrude Jekyll in her house at Munstead Wood, Surrey, with a variety of asters in the foreground.

Folly Farm, Berkshire. The Dutch-inspired canal is one of the most inspired creations of the collaboration between Jekyll and Lutyens.

Edwin Lutyens had a particularly good eye for detail, as with this paving at Folly Farm, Berkshire.

Folly Farm. According to Arts and Crafts principles, the built elements followed the structure of the garden, designed by Lutyens and planted by Gertrude Jekyll.

The mixed herbaceous borders in the garden at Goddards, Surrey, on which Jekyll and Lutyens worked in 1899. Contrary to popular belief, such herbaceous borders, which became a leit-motif in the gardens of the twentieth century, are extremely difficult to establish, and require a high level of mainte-nance.

The design of the central pool in the courtyard at Goddards is reminiscent of Indian pools, reached down a series of steps. A recur-rent feature in Lutyens' gardens, it was one example of Indian cultural influence on the British Empire.

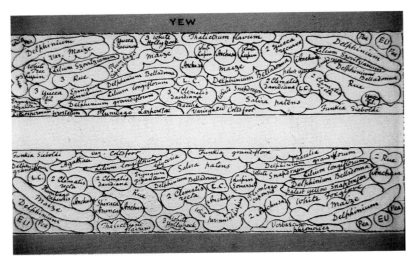

Scheme for a flowering border in various shades of blue, from Jekyll's Colour Schemes for the Flower Garden.

Botanical collecting was greatly encouraged by the large numbers of species that could be imported by means of the small portable greenhouse known as 'Ward's box'.

View of Villa Sylvia at Villefranche, Alpes Maritimes, designed by Harold Peto.

very popular destination for holiday-makers: Russians and Germans, but above all the English, created villas and gardens there, and occasionally settled permanently. The climate was favourable: the mountains offered shelter from harsh winds, and the mild winters and springs made it an excellent place for the cultivation of every kind of plant. The great plant enthusiasts took full advantage to create their own gardens in which they planted and acclimatized the wealth of species that travel and botanical exploration were continually introducing into Europe. Scientific discoveries and technological advances meant that an ever-greater number of amateur gardeners was now taking an interest in growing plants and in botany. Many gardens came into being as early as the second half of the nineteenth century, at Cannes, at Cap d'Antibes and Menton, often containing rich plant collections. Villas and gardens drew their inspiration from many different styles — the Moorish, the Italian, the French — but in all of them vegetation played an extremely important part. As well as many designers like Ferdinand Bac and Harold Peto, the turn of the century also saw the arrival on the Riviera of a number of plant enthusiasts who created wonderful Mediterranean gardens. One of the most famous plantsmen of the Côte d'Azur was the Vicomte de Noailles, the architect of the gardens at Grasse and Hyères. The 'Mediterranean garden' developed a style of its own, characterized by the cultivation and careful juxtaposition of plants indigenous to the south of Europe but not excluding the more exotic species imported from distant lands.

Among the more famous gardens where foreign species were acclimatized was the garden of the Villa Hanbury at La Mortola, near Ventimiglia, just inside the Italian border. Here Sir Thomas Hanbury, a rich businessman, acquired the old Villa Marengo and retired from public life to create a

splendid garden with plants of every kind on his property of over forty hectares (100 acres), with its series of terraces some hundred metres (330 ft.) above sea level. Assisted by his son and brother, who was an accomplished botanist, he commenced an ambitious programme of planting trees and shrubs — acacias, eucalyptus, magnolias, yuccas and many other species — sent from all over the globe. As the Mediterranean became a favourite destination for collectors and enthusiasts, so during the first half of the twentieth century they flocked not only to the Tyrrhenian riviera but also to the less well-known rivieras of the Lombardy lakes.

The Villa San Remigio, an Italian garden begun in 1883, stands on a hill overlooking Lake Maggiore, with splendid terraces and a spectacular assortment of rhododendrons, azaleas and roses. Next to it is the more famous Villa Taranto, whose garden was created in the first decade of the twentieth century by the Scotsman Neil McEacharn. Here McEacharn assembled an incredible collection of plants: not just the more usual rhododendrons and azaleas, but also nearly 200 varieties of camellia which flower slightly earlier, followed at the end of April by a multitude of tulips of every conceivable hue. Both Villa Hanbury and Villa Taranto are run by foundations that keep the gardens in perfect condition and open to the public, allowing posterity to enjoy the glorious array of scents and colours as their owners had originally wished.

The climate and soil of the Lombard lakes were particularly well-suited to the growing of acidophilous species, and many gardens blazed with fine collections of rhododendrons, maples and azaleas, such as those seen here at villa Melzi on Lake Como.

Olive trees and lavender in the Mediterranean garden of Villa Noailles. The passion for Mediterranean plants, and for warmer climates in general, led to the creation of the so-called 'Mediterranean garden', which became fashionable on the French Riviera.

One of the first great hothouses was Paxton's Crystal Palace, built for the Great Exhibition in London to incorporate the trees already growing on the spot.

The hothouse at Alton Towers, Staffordshire. During the nineteenth century hothouses became de rigueur in every self-respecting English garden: what- *ever their dimensions, they were vital for the growing of the increasingly numerous imported species.*

THE GREAT HOTHOUSES

The vogue for collecting and acclimatizing exotic plants peaked in the nineteenth century, leading to the building of numerous hothouses – especially fashionable in England from the middle of the century. Malmaison had had a hothouse since the end of the eighteenth century in which Josephine Beauharnais kept her exotic plants, often exchanging them with several other enthusiasts, including those across the Channel. Indeed, the country that really turned botanical collecting into a national mania was England. Although many exotic plants arrived in Great Britain during the eighteenth century, after 1830 the number increased dramatically, above all thanks to one vital invention: Ward's box. This was an easily transportable, sealed glass box — a sort of miniature greenhouse — which provided plants with the necessary microclimate to survive long sea voyages. The rise in the number of plants reaching British shores in Ward's box saw the English passion for plants and flowers burgeon.

In 1845 the tax on glass was abolished, and there was also a fall in the price of iron, and of the coal used to fuel stoves. Now it was much less costly to build the hothouses needed for growing exotic plants. One of the first big hothouses to be built in Britain was at Chatsworth in Derbyshire, now unfortunately destroyed. Designed by Joseph Paxton between 1836 and 1840 for the Duke of Devonshire, it was an enormous construction, 40 metres (130 ft.) wide, 90 metres (295 ft.) long, and at its centre no less than 22 metres (70 ft.) high. Also at Chatsworth, and still in existence, is the Conservative Wall, a long greenhouse following the slope of the garden and set against the boundary wall; it too was the work of Paxton, and today houses many varieties of fruit tree, including fig, apricot, plum and peach.

The interior of the Palm House at Kew resembles that of a real building, with tall columns supporting its iron structure and spiral staircases leading to the galleries that run right around it.

The Palm House at Kew. Built between 1844 and 1848, it served to house some of Kew's ever-growing collections, especially the various varieties of palm.

Paxton's other great creation was the Crystal Palace, an enormous structure in iron and glass erected in Hyde Park to house the Universal Exhibition of 1851. The decision to build this kind of structure was prompted by his desire to avoid cutting down the trees on the site for the Exhibition pavilion.

Equally enormous, and still in perfect working order, are the hothouses in the Royal Botanic Gardens at Kew — the Palm House and the Temperate House, still two of its main attractions. The former was built between 1844 and 1848; whilst the latter, begun in 1860, was not completed until 1898.

The fashion for hothouses of exotic plants spread to such an extent that no garden was complete without one; houses themselves were now equipped with conservatories, or so-called 'winter gardens'. The use of glazed structures to house exhibitions or events, from the Crystal Palace onwards, led to many iron and glass structures being built as shelters or meeting places in gardens, public parks and, above all, at seaside resorts, though here real trees tended to be replaced by potted plants.

The hothouse tradition lives on in England: and even the smallest gardens have their greenhouses — prefabricated and modest in size, maybe, but never empty.

As ideas of the picturesque evolved in a more 'natural' direction, the eighteenth-century engravings used to depict landscaped gardens began to strike the nineteenth-century observer as somewhat lifeless. The keen interest in plants and flowers, in both the extravagantly-conceived gardens of the Victorian heyday and the more 'natural' fin de siècle gardens, directed attention to the colours used for their depictions. The romantic appreciation of the natural life of trees, and a keener awareness of plants' individual characteristics from foliage to flowers, drew illustrators towards oils and watercolour. Watercolour in particular became a very popular English hobby in the second half of the century. Humphry Repton used watercolour in his before-and-after drawings, to explain to his patrons what he was doing, and many other designers followed his example; Gertrude Jekyll worked out the colour combinations she planned for her herbaceous borders in watercolour. The 'naturalist' mood of gardens from 1870 onwards seemed to find a direct equivalent in the paintings of the Impressionists, whose subtle use of colour enabled them to depict such transient phenomena as wind blowing through leaves, the murmur of water, birdsong, or the sudden shock of bright flowers in the shade of a tree. The Impressionist painters created gardens for themselves, with reflections of light and patches of colour like those of a painting: Monet cherished and painted the water-lilies on the pond and the little Japanese bridge in his own garden at Giverny.

THE REPRESENTATION OF THE GARDEN: THE GARDEN AS DEPICTED IN OILS AND WATERCOLOURS

1

2

1. Hafod House, Dyfed, Wales. From J.E. Smith, Fifteen Views illustrative of a Tour to Hafod, London, 1810. The park at Hafod was one of many inspired by the concept of the sublime; this depiction shows it in the late afternoon, a time often chosen for illustrations of gardens of this period: the sense of the sublime, typical of those places where nature is especially vast or disturbing, was regarded as all the more impressive as twilight approached and the shadows lengthened.

2. View of the Wilhelmshöhe in an oil painting by J. E. Hummel, c. 1800. The heroic character of the place is vividly rendered, with the backlit Octagon on the

3

4

3. Claude Monet, The garden at Giverny. Impressionist painting might almost have been invented for Giverny, a sort of cottage garden with its riot of plants and profusion of shapes and colours. Indeed, Monet planted his garden as he painted, with strong slashes of colour, sometimes delicately nuanced, sometimes discordant.

5

4. Thomas Mawson: the garden at Hvidore. The technique of watercolour became increasingly popular during the nineteenth century, becoming the favourite means for depicting the garden by the century's end, as particularly effective for the rendering of detail and shades of colour. In this Arts and Crafts design, proposed by Mawson for Queen Alexandra's garden at Hvidore, the colours of the borders and the details of the trellises with the climbing roses stand out strongly against the dark of the hedges and the pale sky.

6

top of the hill to the right apparently almost diaphanous. The low-angled light is that of sunset, but the model is that of Claude Lorrain's landscape paintings, with their heroic and mythological connotations.

5. Humphry Repton: the rose garden at Ashridge, Herts. The Victorian passion for flowerbeds emerges almost startlingly clearly from this illustration, as does the late nineteenth-century English love of colour. In the garden, the equivalent of this love of colour in Victorian architecture and decoration was mosaic culture, or patterned flowerbeds.

6. View of the so-called Mon Plaisir, in the garden of Elvaston Castle, Derbyshire. The Victorian fondness for excess evident in flower-gardens also led to more strictly formal gardens being over-burdened with ornaments. At Elvaston Castle, the topiary around the central star-shaped bed is clipped into the most outlandish shapes.

The twentieth century

The bourgeois garden

After the profound social changes of the second half of the nineteenth century, and then World War I, the world seemed to have been turned upside down: the war marked the end of an epoch, and the models upon which pre-war society had been based were no longer valid. Progress, whether technical or scientific, appeared unstoppable, nineteenth-century positivist ideals had been swept away, and the new realities facing twentieth-century man were altogether more complex. The aesthetic canons the middle classes had relied upon at the turn of the century were clearly out of date. The new way of confronting reality – apprehended and expressed by the French Impressionists, who were first to develop an investigative way of looking at things in an attempt to capture their essence — necessarily entailed redefining its very perception.

The desire to break with an irrelevant past led to the emergence of an artistic avant-garde and the rise of new ideologies, determined to explain the new world and confer upon it some rational order. World War II was both symptom and proof that design had failed: the difficulties of the post-war period, especially in Europe, and the hardships of the period of reconstruction, demanded new and harsher sacrifices.

People flocked from the countryside to the cities, now places of immense contradiction, crowded and depersonalized, centres of production and consumption, where information arrived indirectly, and everything was experienced at one remove.

Twentieth-century art — intellectual and bourgeois — was an art instinct with anxiety, engaged in a desperate quest for meaning; it was the voice of a new society faced with a new and different world. It was also an individualistic art, in which man stood alone in the face of social complexity.

After Impressionism's great leap forward, the figurative arts were no longer constrained by the need to be purely representational in their depiction of reality and nature; in the first half of the century artists felt the need to band together in groups and movements, but after World War II they tended towards extremes of individualistic expression, in response to a

Model of a settlement for a 'professional farmer' by the German landscape gardener Leberecht Migge (1926). Migge was particularly interested in the question of the garden and gardening as a means to self-sufficiency, in the context of the housing reform movement of the beginning of the century.

(Opposite) Villa Noailles at Hyères.

Le Corbusier, too, concerned himself to some degree with private green spaces. When applied to the garden, rationalist architecture favoured compositions with clean, pure lines, requiring little maintenance.

society that felt the need for charismatic figures.

The change was just as swift and radical in the sphere of garden design. The nineteenth century had already experienced something of a dearth in creative ideas, and now there seemed nothing fresh to say. Only Art Nouveau, which had brought a breath of fresh air into the suffocating atmosphere of *fin de siècle* art, provided any inspiration.

In Germany, social pressures led to the creation of an architecture responsive to the needs of the working classes, with residential complexes that had their own gardens and vegetable plots, either individual or communal. Bourgeois domestic architecture, on the other hand, developed a philosophy of its own *vis-à-vis* living space utterly in keeping with the spirit of the times. In the first half of the century the garden — as the status symbol of a wealthy bourgeoisie seeking to assert and legitimize itself through art — acquired a new vigour, forging links with the various avant-garde movements that were attempting to give artistic expression to a host of new ideas.

Alongside the avant-garde, with a return to geometric shapes and regular systems of planting, there was also an incipient revival of the classical garden, in its assertion of the old conservative principles. But neither the classical nor the avant-garde had any great success, and the formal gardens of the early twentieth century failed to make any great impact, partly, at least, because of the two world wars. World War II also sounded the death knell for those inferior imitations of the Belle Epoque which, blind to the changes that had taken place, had tried to carry on regardless. Every certainty, however illusory, had now been shattered, and this also cast a shadow over the world of the garden.

In the post-war era, the garden occupied a distinctly secondary position, mainly because designers were turning their attention almost exclusively to the urban environment, the garden was no longer regarded as a theatre for artistic expression, but rather as a superfluous decorative addition; it therefore lost all moral and literary significance, being seen rather as an escapist vehicle for reactionary conservatism. A garden thus became a matter of personal expression, of the individual's response to the times: gone were the days when the garden had been as it had for centuries the subject of debate, and as for the garden so for the designer, who found himself working on his own, and often marginalized. The search for a new identity for the modern garden resulted in a great variety of design, oscillating somewhat desperately between the traditional opposites of formal and informal, geometric classicism and romantic naturalism.

One factor did persist however: Anglo-Saxon culture, which was both deeply pragmatic and intimately related to the garden and gardening. Practical and technical business took the place of all the philosophical, literary, historical and political theorizing of the preceding centuries; it preoccupied people to the exclusion of positivism, scientism and sociology,

J. Lepelmann: garden on the outskirts of Düsseldorf, 1908. The country-house garden of the early twentieth century was composed of a formal structure using vegetation to decorative effect, except for several characteristic built elements like a pergola.

the nineteenth-century values that had provided the theoretical basis of not only the art of the garden (and especially the enthusiasm for botanical collections) but also the whole mission of redefining green spaces, as the city parks and avenues that were prerequisite for civilized, healthy living.

Since the seventies, a practical interest in the garden and the Anglo-Saxon love of nature have fostered a growing awareness of dwindling natural resources and an ecological movement which has spread worldwide.

But the twentieth century has also witnessed a new phenomenon: original gardens of international importance are now being created in America — both in the United States, casting off British cultural hegemony to look towards Europe at large, and in South America, which is looking beyond its own borders to make a key contribution to international culture.

(Right) The parterre *at Courances, Essonne, restored at the beginning of the century by Achille Duchêne. The restoration of the great baroque gardens was a powerful force for the classical revival in new gardens.*

(Below) Dartington Hall, Devon. In the twentieth century, the practice of gardening became an important factor in the relationship between man and nature, giving rise to a new aesthetic of the garden: a bed of irises, cut after flowering, might now take on a new ornamental significance because of the particular effect of the squared-off leaves.

The modern garden in Europe

The debate between formal and informal, already over a century old, has not died down completely, and attempts are continually being made to combine the natural element with the rational outlook, scientific progress and the growing interest in ecology.

The twentieth-century garden is an expression of a totally changed world. Coming as it does after the huge social upheavals which began in the nineteenth century, it has a strongly individualistic character and is on a much smaller scale, affording creative scope to an ever-greater number of people but resulting in a certain repetitiveness in design.

The large-scale movements of population and the internationalist and cosmopolitan tendencies which characterized the last years of the nineteenth century have continued into the twentieth, and both the aristocracy and the wealthy middle classes continue to build their holiday homes and gardens in fashionable areas. The middle classes, still seeking confirmation of their cultural status, have turned to art, becoming collectors and patrons of the various avant-garde movements, and this is reflected in their designs for gardens, whether implemented or merely planned.

Thus the garden falls prey to the dichotomy affecting art and culture generally, drawing inspiration from multifarious sources, many of which can be traced back to the avant-garde. On the one hand, as a predominantly middle class art and a means of asserting social status, the garden made a return to a classical style, with some huge projects harking back to an era when people still had great fortunes at their disposal. On the other, particularly in Great Britain with its deeply-rooted cultural tradition, a more 'natural' approach endured, in which individualism was not to be expressed by adopting any one given style, but rather by personal self-expression, something

the Anglo-Saxon gardening tradition guaranteed. The gardens created in England in the first half of the century have a strongly personal feel, and, as befitted the amateur approach, the owners were also the designers.

The garden and the avant-garde

The early twentieth-century middle classes were generous patrons of the arts, and the garden found a distinctive niche in the artistic panorama. The new economic and social conditions inspired the middle classes with a new self-awareness that also found expression in using industrial techniques and developments in design theory, producing gardens which were a synthesis of art, nature and 'lifestyle'.

In this respect, the garden was closely associated with the visual arts, once again employing forms and motifs derived equally from art and fashionable decoration to express universal values and a striving for the absolute.

With the return to a more formal, geometrical design, the garden was more easily able to adapt to the aesthetic criteria of the avant-garde movements.

Art Nouveau, too — whose vigorous rejection of sterile nineteenth-century historicism had given a new impetus to art — made a brief impact upon the garden, particularly with its passionate concern for detail and all-pervading love of decoration. Its distinguishing features — a wealth of decorative motifs, both geometric and biomorphic, with the sinuous lines of flowers and plants super-imposed on the ornamentation for a kind of emphasis — found expression in similarly intricate gardens with elaborately regimented plants that nonetheless had a sense of unity and harmony sadly lacking in the chaotic, overstocked gardens typical of eclecticism. The Art Nouveau garden was decorated mainly with regular geometric shapes, often rectangular, also used for structures like pergolas, steps, benches, balustrades and pavings. Plants

Artists also created works for their own gardens, as with this fountain at Charleston Farm, home of the painters Duncan Grant and Vanessa Bell,

A. Lilienfein, Jugendstil garden at Stuttgart. The new artistic styles had a great influence on the garden, which now became more formal, particularly in the German-speaking countries.

Modern garden *in a design by Franz Lebitsch. The geometrical forms and linear decoration typical of art deco lent themselves perfectly to the requirements of the emerging middle classes.*

A perfectly preserved art deco garden still exists at Baden-Baden: it is given both structure and decoration by square, linear flowerbeds, small mophead-like bushes and large trained hedges.

were trimmed into geometric shapes like spheres and pyramids, and treated as built objects. Further regularity was provided by gazebos and trellises covered with climbing roses and wisteria, which became very fashionable in the first half of the century.

This regularity and geometricality dominated the most interesting projects of the 'Viennese Secession', which preferred the use of square shapes. Around 1900 the spread of the 'architectural' garden saw the appearance in Germany of gardens inspired by *Jugendstil*, a style in favour with young middle-class intellectuals and used for their gardens by the nobility and the upper classes. This 'architectural' aspect was based on a clear definition of the various spaces, which now took on specific functions, whether aesthetic or utilitarian, following the principles of industrial production, a prevalent influence on the whole of early twentieth-century culture. In gardens which were often rather small, much play was made with different levels, in order to make the space seem larger and give the vistas greater depth. The planted element, whether tree or hedge, acquired great importance, and was treated as a 'one-off' creation, almost as a sculpture. The trees, which were often tall and thin — cypresses, Lombardy poplars or thuyas trimmed into geometric shapes — served to accentuate perspectives, delimiting the spaces and lightening the stiffly geometrical terraces, walls and flowerbeds.

Of particular interest among the few examples still in existence are the projects of Joseph Maria Olbrich at Darmstadt, in the artists' colony on the Mathildenhöhe. The garden he designed for himself is in fact very small, divided up into little spaces decorated with tiny lawns, flowerbeds and trees. At the

Art Colony, on the other hand, he made use of a more complex design: here the architectural element is more in evidence, with regular structures such as chequerboard paving and the geometrical pergola.

The concepts expressed in the private garden are also to be found, on a larger scale, in public works of the time, with city gardens conforming to the same architectonic criteria.

Between the wars, the predominantly 'architectural' conception of the garden meant that it too was susceptible to the aesthetic and decorative theories of the early twentieth century.

Art Deco — characterized by its love of pure line, geometrical shapes and bright colours — made its first appearance in 1910, but began to have an influence on garden design only in the period immediately after World War I. The garden designs of André Véra were initially traditionalist in inspiration, drawing upon classical ideas, yet in their way they were also typical of the aesthetic theories of Art Deco; although influenced by the abstract expressionism of the day, his projects remained firmly in the classical school, with its reliance on a central axis. They were characterized by symmetry, straight lines, flat surfaces and perspective effects in which he applied many of the Art Deco principles of the minor arts like jewellery and fabrics.

In a later phase, the 'architectural' garden was strongly influenced by painting, notably abstract expressionism, with its striving, in the wake of the Impressionists' discontinuous technique, for a new way of perceiving reality.

The visual arts were now acquiring ever greater autonomy, distancing themselves from reality to the point where actual depiction of nature was completely abandoned. This new

A typical Jugenstil design with a pool by Joseph Olbrich in the artists' colony of Matildenhöhe at Darmstadt.

A water-colour by A. Laprade showing a typical parterre *inspired by Art Deco. The use of geometrical compositions with flowers of a single colour was a hint of suprematist developments to come.*

The 'love garden' designed by André Véra. A fervent supporter of the straight line in gardens, his work shows clear evidence of the classical structure on a central axis.

outlook sought expression in pure shapes and colours; in the work of the avant-garde natural forms were dissolved and replaced by forms that bore little relationship to objective reality; substance would be more tellingly communicated by virtue of being pared down to its essence. New relationships were established between form and figure, colour and tone, straight lines, broken lines and circles, and between planes and dimensions. Cubism, in particular, divided the natural world up into a series of regular figures, hitherto a feature of classical garden art. Mondrian's neoplasticism and Malevich's suprematism asserted the autonomy of pure shapes and a limited range of pure colours.

Of the gardens inspired by the avant-garde, the most famous and best preserved is the one Gabriel Guevrekian created in 1926 for Charles de Noailles at Hyères in France. It gives the best sense of how the garden was influenced by the 'années folles' of the artistic avant-garde, since it is in fact a 'cubist' garden, a markedly geometrical structure in a small triangular space, made up of squares and rectangles whose surfaces have been staggered so as to heighten the perspective. The concertina-like flowerbeds emphasize the dynamism of the design, whose vertical features took it out of the purely two-dimensional. Making a clean break with the more classical character of the 'architectural' garden, Guevrekian had already proposed a triangular project for a Garden of Water and Love for the 1925 Exhibition of Decorative Arts. Here the design itself is to all intents and purposes a proper abstract painting,

The 'chalices' in André Véra's 'love garden'. Véra had close contacts with the Cubist movement, and often collaborated with his brother Paul Véra, himself a Cubist.

to be turned into a real garden by assembling living natural elements into a faithful three-dimensional representation of the theories of colour and geometric abstraction. Thus monochrome surfaces are juxtaposed for contrast, with relief effects obtained by using intense colours in a play of voids and solids, geometric shapes and colours, in combinations both contrasting and mutually enhancing.

Reduction to two dimensions and absolute simplicity of line — so characteristic of twentieth-century art — held obvious implications for garden design: plants now tended to be grouped tightly together, blocked and flattened, allowing broader patches of colour to dominate.

The British amateur style

What had happened on the continent — a simplification in the use of form and colour, in line with a view which, paradoxically, saw variety as generated by fewer elements — did not occur in England, where the more practical and 'natural' approach of the cottage garden, and by 'gardening' individuals, led to some of the most interesting projects of the century.

Two centuries earlier, a certain number of 'amateurs' Like Sir Henry Hoare at Stourhead or Sir Charles Hamilton at Painshill, devoted themselves full-time to tending their gardens. Vita Sackville-West, for example, or the architect Laurence Johnston, both passionate gardeners, showed a commitment to their gardens, and a personal involvement, increasingly impractical as the century wore on. Their gardens,

Plan of the Noailles garden at Hyères by Gabriel Guevrekian, in whose gardens the Cubist influence is particularly evident.

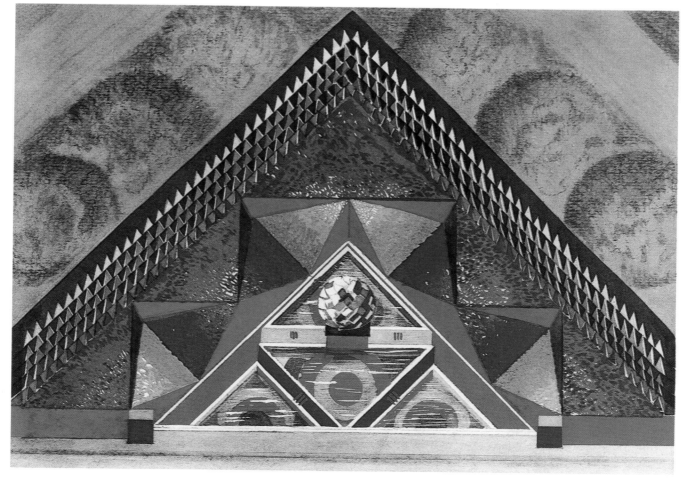

Garden of water and light, *water-colour by Gabriel Guevrekian, based on a careful study of the forms and theory of colour.*

Garden at Villa Noailles by Gabriel Guevrekian, seen from above. The beds alternate with similarly-shaped coloured surfaces combined on different levels.

The relative two-dimensionality of the parterre *is countered by the vertical of the corner beds.*

(Opposite) A typical expanse of crazy paving, scattered with small rock plants. This quintessentially English form of decoration came into fashion at the beginning of the century.

generally consisting of an informal planting system within a formal structure (a style that had already emerged at the end of the nineteenth century), were characterized by a certain rugged individuality that turns them into expressions of their owners' character, and of the relationship between the individual and nature. Henry Duncan, the second Lord Aberconway, created a marvellous garden at Bodnant, a property he acquired in 1875, with splendid views over the valleys and mountains of Snowdonia. Duncan devoted himself to his garden for some fifty years, until his death in 1953. Major restructuring work commenced in 1905, starting with the broad slope on one side of the house, where five terraces were set into the rocky hillside. In descending order from the top there is a rose garden, linked by steps to a baroque-style fountain, flanked by white wisteria; then a croquet lawn; then the magical Water-lily Terrace, with a rectangular pond, semicircular at one end, full of dozens of varieties of water-lily; then another rose garden with pergolas, and finally the lowest terrace, known as the Canal Terrace because of the long narrow stretch of water which runs down the middle, reflecting a delightful eighteenth-century garden pavilion. Above all Bodnant owes its splendour to its incredible variety of ornamental plants; worthy of special mention is the spectacular collection of rhododendrons and the Laburnum Arch, Bodnant's best-known feature, which was planted at the end of the nineteenth century by the first Lord Aberconway.

Perhaps even more famous than Bodnant is the garden at Hidcote Manor in Gloucestershire, created from 1907 onwards by its owner, Laurence Johnston. At Hidcote Johnston combined a beautifully gauged spatial composition (something he had learned while training as an architect) with an inspired deployment of plants and flowers. On a gently-sloping piece of land planted with just one ancient cedar, Johnston created a series of high hedges, offering shelter from cold winds but also serving to form a number of green 'rooms'. Here Johnston could give full vent to his passion for gardening, fired by his admiration of Jekyll and Lutyens, in whose works indigenous and exotic plants were freely combined. The garden at Hidcote is composed around a central vista leading from the original cedar through a cottage-style garden to a circular bed of lilacs and hellebores. From here the visitor enters a corridor of trees and shrubs with bright red flowers and foliage; at the end is a gazebo, and beyond that an avenue flanked by typical hornbeam hedges, cut square in the French style, their trunks bare. At the end of the avenue a view of the surrounding countryside is visible through an iron gate. Around the central axis Johnston created a number of surprising spaces: a *parterre* of fuchsias enclosed by a mixed hedge of hornbeam, yew, holly and beech, providing with the changing seasons a continually varying counterpoint of colour; a little enclosure containing a round pond reflecting the sky and the surrounding plants, and other little gardens brightened by the varying shades of blue and yellow of violets and veronicas, or towered over by the solemn shapes of fastigiate yews.

The incredible variety of species used at Hidcote, its huge number of hybrids, like the famous varieties of lavender and hypericum that bear its name, and their skilful combination, in a subtle interplay of expertise and spontaneity, make Hidcote

a model garden and, in some sense, a paragon of the English garden in the twentieth century.

The example of Hidcote — where flowering shrubs grow together with roses, herbaceous plants with bulbs, with coloured creepers trained over evergreen hedges and flowers allowed to grow where they have seeded themselves — was an important source of inspiration for Vita Sackville-West in her garden at Sissinghurst in Kent. From 1930 onwards, on the land around the ancient manor house they chose for their home, Vita and her husband Harold Nicolson created a marvellous garden of coloured 'rooms'.

When they purchased it, the castle was in a disastrous state of disrepair and the surrounding land virtually a rubbish tip. The Nicolsons had to spend three years clearing the ground, and another seven planning and planting the new garden. Sissinghurst was opened to the public in 1940, and soon became internationally renowned as a 'classic' of the English twentieth-century style.

Sissinghurst fulfils the ideal of harmony between formal and informal, as had already been achieved at Hidcote: a rigidly formal design — by Harold Nicolson — is combined with an absolute freedom and spontaneity in the planting, for which Vita was responsible. Like Hidcote, Sissinghust is a garden of open-air 'rooms', some planted to achieve maximum effect at a given season, others based on specific colour schemes, but the symmetry and regularity of the design in no way hinder the free growth of the plants. Roses, clematis, daffodils and fritillaries brighten the various compartments, with a rose garden followed by a cottage garden, a hazel wood and a herb garden. The most famous 'room' of all is the 'white garden', which consists solely of plants with white flowers or silver leaves: white climbing roses, delphiniums and gypsophila flower alongside the silvery grey of artemisia and the omnipresent *Pyrus salicifolia pendula* that dominates the scene.

Bodnant, Hidcote and Sissinghurst have all the elements typical of the twentieth-century English garden: a regular structure of walls, expanses of water, squared evergreen hedges and pathways, giving a sense of form and framework to the garden, softened and to some degree confused by an overlay of plants, which are allowed to grow freely to demonstrate their

Bodnant, Gwynedd. Canal terrace and eighteenth-century pavilion. Patches of water-lilies are grown to the sides of the pool, but the centre is kept clear so that the pavilion can be reflected in it.

Bodnant. At the other end of the canal, a series of evergreen hedges are arranged like theatre wings as a backdrop to a splendid old seat.

Apart from more formally designed areas, Bodnant also has a magnificent collection of ornamental trees, and was one of the first gardens to be acquired by the National Trust.

*Hidcote,
Gloucestershire. Avenue
with border of perenni-
als. Hidcote was given
to the National Trust in
1948.*

ornamental possibilities. Careful attention is always paid to the juxtaposition of species, which are suitably marshalled according to flowering season, colour, ornamental characteristics and cultivational requirements. The garden as a whole thus has an intense vitality in which colours, scents and seasonal variations combine to soften the underlying rigid framework in a masterly blend of formal and informal.

The efforts of such amateurs, and the superb gardens they created — now peerlessly maintained by the National Trust — made no small contribution to England's predominance in garden creation this century; they have also ensured that the practical and individualistic attitude characteristic of the British tradition is still well to the fore in the nature-loving culture of the second half of the twentieth century, with a crucial influence on garden culture throughout the world.

*Hidcote. Yew hedges
and topiaried box form
the framework of the
'white garden', one of
several gardens themed
according to colour,
where all the plants
have white flowers.*

Plants climbing freely over the old wall at Sissinghurst, with the enchanting wooden bench designed at the beginning of the century by Edwin Lutyens, the model most often reproduced by firms making garden furniture.

The 'white garden', Vita Sackville-West's pièce de resistance *at Sissinghurst, where only plants with white flowers or silvery leaves are grown: the well is overshadowed by a* rosa longicuspis *(left). The tall yew hedges provide a perfect backdrop for the white of the flowers.*

Villa La Foce, Chianciano. Cecil Pinsent created several gardens in Tuscany as reworkings of the Italian Renaissance style. The wisteria in the foreground, very popular at the beginning of the century, was therefore not an anachronism in this context.

Perspective view of a garden project for Monsieur Weiller at Versailles, *from a design by Achille Duchêne. The revival of the classical style led many private individuals to commission gardens in the style of the* Grand Siècle.

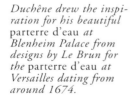

Duchêne drew the inspiration for his beautiful parterre d'eau *at Blenheim Palace from designs by Le Brun for the* parterre d'eau *at Versailles dating from around 1674.*

THE REVIVAL OF THE CLASSICAL GARDEN

The first three decades of the century also saw a reintroduction of classical styles, especially in France. There, the historicist and nationalist mood so widespread after 1870 saw a return to the *Grande Manière* of Le Nôtre, notably in the work of two great garden architects, Henry and Achille Duchêne, father and son. In addition to time-consuming restorations of the great Le Nôtre gardens, Vaux and Courances for instance, and wholesale reconstruction of those that had vanished, such as Champs-sur-Marne,

the Duchênes also produced an enormous number of designs for new gardens.

The name of Duchêne was associated with a truly astounding number of gardens — over 380 worldwide — and its reputation made it possible for Achille (1866—1947) to take over from his father, on Henry's death in 1901, and to carry on working for over forty years. The most famous of his projects was the *parterres* to either side of Blenheim Palace, created for the Duke of Marlborough in 1930. For the one to the east he employed a classical Italian layout, while for the one to the west, by the banks of the river Glyme, he created a splendid *parterre d'eau* in the manner of classical French gardens.

Various side *bassins* with whimsical mixtilinear borders, set among intricately patterned low box hedges, send up slender spouts of water, which then flows into other *bassins* and finally into the larger central pool, the whole resembling an elaborate mirror framed in lace.

In Great Britain — where a reaction against the suffocating atmosphere of the nineteenth century had caused the house to open up to the outside, and the garden to be transmuted into a sort of open-air room — formally designed gardens were once again in vogue The special popularity of Italian Renaissance gardens was due in no small measure to the large number of Britons who had decided to

To the rear of Blenheim Palace, Duchêne designed what he called an 'italianate garden', though it included a parterre de broderie in the French style.

Villa Le Balze, Fiesole. Here too Pinsent used plants particularly popular at the time — geraniums and oleander — to decorate this niche, with its mosaic of coloured pebbles.

settle in Tuscany. There men of letters, upper-class gentlemen and assorted eccentrics set about reclaiming old gardens, or constructing new ones, drawing directly upon renaissance models. One such Englishman was Sir George Sitwell who, after completing the layout of his garden at Renishaw Hall in Derbyshire along Italian renaissance lines, moved to Tuscany, to the Castello di Montegufoni, where he worked on his garden from 1925 until 1940. This colony of ever more garden-conscious 'Anglo-Florentines' was now joined by Cecil Pinsent, a garden designer who worked on numerous projects, mainly in Tuscany, but elsewhere in Italy and England as well.

Pinsent's projects were essentially homages to an earlier age: he borrowed not only the formal layout and enclosed spaces typical of the renaissance Tuscan garden, but also its decorative additions —the statues, niches and *exedras*, and lily-ponds adorned with mosaics, coloured stones and artificial sponges. In all his projects Pinsent observed the Italian tradition of an orderly series of terraces and geometrically shaped enclosures, long hedges of box clipped into square or rounded shapes, and the typical terracotta vases containing lemon trees.

Most distinctive is undoubtedly the garden of Villa Le Balze at Fiesole, which was built as a twin to the adjacent Villa Medici. At Villa I

Tatti too, in the garden created for the art critic Bernard Berenson, he again worked to a regular design emphasized by wide borders of box and gigantic hedges of cypress. Pinsent took tradition's classical elements and endowed them with a vision derived from the Arts and Crafts movement, so that the decorative elements are treated with great freedom and variety. At Villa La Foce near Chianciano, Pinsent designed in conjunction with its owners a garden in the spirit of an open-air room, created out of nothing on the dry clay soil, buffeted by the wind from Val d'Orcia, and punctuated by the chiaroscuro of dark box hedges and the luminous yellow of the lemons in pots.

The contemporary garden in Europe

The wars, social disruption and economic crises that have afflicted most of the twentieth century gradually marginalized the art of the garden. More attention was paid instead to open spaces and the countryside. Designers widened their horizons, and in place of the city parks of the nineteenth century they now set to work designing areas of green around residential estates, schools, city centres, car parks and factories, as well as city terraces and roof gardens. In the process, the design of the garden proper was affected. Technological progress and the invention of labour-saving devices, coupled with a gradual decrease in the availability of manual labour, brought a change in the very idea of a garden. Huge lawns, easily maintained by powered lawnmowers, no more planting of annuals, a reduction in the use of herbaceous perennials requiring intensive maintenance, and the widespread use of plants for ground cover, are some of the characteristics of the contemporary garden.

With the economic recovery after World War II, the influences of garden design were many and varied. The development of communications and the facility for rapid exchange of information played their part in this, but no one overarching style or direction emerged, for reasons including local cultural traditions, the discipline of landscape architecture and Land Art.

Thus the style of the individual designer took on greater importance, the desire for novelty resulting in some very fine personal creations, like the gardens of the two Belgians René

Ernst Kramer, The poet's garden. *The structure of the garden was now increasingly influenced by rationalist architecture and design, and abstract art.*

Gunnar Martinsson, Roof garden for an insurance company at Karlsruhe. Garden designers were now frequently employed by public bodies and

private industry to work on public open spaces, and the heated debate that had hitherto typified garden culture was now dying down.

Richard Long, Grass circle, *garden at Celle, Pistoia, 1985. The phenomenon of Land Art emerged in the 1960s, with artists now making a crucial contribution not just to the culture of the landscape, but also to that of the garden.*

(Below) The popularity of gardening as a hobby, and developments in communications, put a wide range of products on the market, not least of which were the numerous do-it-yourself manuals appealing to an ever-wider constituency of aficionados.

Pechène and Jacques Wirtz.

In the second half of the twentieth century we therefore find a whole range of voices, sometimes discordant, advocating different paths, though a few constants are discernible. The profound influence of the visual arts (especially abstract art) reinforced the complementary relationship between structure and nature that English gardens of the first half-century had stimulated. On the other hand, designers were paying great attention to the location of the garden and its idiosyncrasies, which in turn required a sound knowledge of 'botanical technique'.

The debate between formal and informal: the garden as a work of art

As we have seen, much of the twentieth century has witnessed a lively interest in the culture of the garden, in horticulture and in outdoor activities, with gardening becoming a very popular national hobby in England. Many English designers, who received their training in the first half of the century during the rediscovery of the classical and formal garden, had the widest influence on twentieth-century garden culture. They worked all over the world, creating gardens of the greatest diversity which at the same time shared a thoroughly open-minded attitude and respect for the *genius loci*.

One of the most important figures was Geoffrey Jellicoe (1900—96). He made a particular study of Italian renaissance gardens and, at the early age of 25, after two years of research and observation, published with C.J.Shepherd *Italian Gardens of the Renaissance* (1925). His work as a designer is distin-

guished by its strictly formal quality, and the careful attention paid to any pre-existing elements. One of his first commissions was Ditchley Park in Oxfordshire, to redesign the formal terrace originally planned by James Gibbs in the first half of the eighteenth century but never built. His project included stone paving, a complex *parterre* enclosed by curving box hedges and an expansive lawn flanked by two corridors of squared lime trees, closed off at the end of an imposing *allée*, by a large classically-inspired *bassin*. On each side of this composition he constructed 'green rooms', small enclosures surrounded by high yew hedges. At Ditchley Park the lightness of the design, based on formal grouping, is combined with great attention to colour in the selection of plants: the differing shades of green of the limes, yews and box, and the lavender/senecio borders, contrast subtly with each other and give the rigidly formal whole a surprising liveliness.

Jellicoe's activities were not restricted to private gardens, but also included city parks. He designed green spaces surrounding business premises and reclaimed scarred landscapes like old quarries. His concern for the countryside and involvement with the major schools and associations of the United Kingdom inspired his universally acknowledged contribution to England's cultural heritage in exposing the necessity for architectural criteria in managing the countryside. His passionate interest in the art of the garden and landscape also produced a book of fundamental importance to the landscape culture of the twentieth century, *The Landscape of Man*, which he and his wife Susan published in 1975. Susan was also responsible for many of the planting schemes in the numerous gardens

Formal, informal and dwarf hedges

Ditchley Park, Oxfordshire, one of the first projects by Geoffrey Jellicoe, realized in 1936. The classically designed box hedge on the terrace was kept at a height somewhere between a parterre and a labyrinth.

The avenues of limes — a typical feature of the classical French garden — to either side of the lawn in front of the terrace are also a blend of tradition and innovation, with the completely informal senecio border creating a highly effective colour contrast.

(Opposite) Dartington Hall, Devon, one of the most successful twentieth-century English gardens, on which Beatrix Farrand and Percy Cane worked, as well as other internationally-recognized designers.

designed by Jellicoe all over the world. Besides their strongly structural quality, with a leading role played by the plants themselves, Jellicoe's designs are also remarkable for his frequent use of water, as at Shute House near Shaftesbury, where in 1970 he created a 'musical' waterfall. One of his last projects, regarded as his masterpiece was the garden at Sutton Place. Called in by the industrialist who bought the property in 1980, Jellicoe created a series of gardens with a strongly symbolic content: the Moss Garden, the Paradise Garden, the Music Garden, the Fish-pool Garden and the Surrealist Garden, forming an allegorical stroll through life and creation, blending the more mysterious elements of man's subconscious with classical art-historical values.

Although no longer conducted in the vehement tones of the nineteenth century, the debate about the garden has continued into this century as various designers have written their own books expounding their theories and recounting their experiences. One such is Russell Page's *The Education of a Gardener*, published in 1962, in which Page (1906—85), who worked with Jellicoe briefly before the war, describes the fundamental principles underlying his work. With his fine understanding of plants — their shapes, characteristics and combinations — and his instinctive feeling for the 'genius' and possibilities of a particular place, Page takes his place in the history of the garden as a 'gardener' (as he liked to call himself) with a sound botanical background, rather like

Jellicoe's design for Sutton Place is a clear example of the relationship between the contemporary garden and the visual arts, as indeed we see from the so-called Miró garden, its pool decorated with a series of tiles reminiscent of a Miró painting.

In the Paradise Garden a series of stepping-stones across the little lake symbolize the difficulty of attaining paradise.

'Musical cascade' in the garden of Shute House, by Jellicoe. In the twentieth century water continues to play a crucial role in garden design.

The garden at La Mortella, Ischia, the home of the English composer William Walton. The exuberant omnipresent vegetation is typical of the work of its creator, Russell Page.

Aircraft-carrier bird-table *by Ian Hamilton Finlay, garden at Stonypath, Scotland. A poet, artist and garden designer, Finlay is something of a figure* sui generis *in the history of the contemporary garden.*

Virgilian Wood *in the park at Celle, Pistoia, for whose olive grove Finlay created a variety of classical, mythological and bucolic allusions, including a plaque, a bronze duck and basket of lemons, a small temple and tiled pathway.*

Gertrude Jekyll. A garden can be approached in many different ways, according to Page, and it is part of his thesis that the art of the garden designer is never static, but rather a continuous attempt to find a balance between nature and artifice. He settled in France between 1945 and 1962, designing many gardens while he was there, not only in France but all over the world.

The Scottish artist Ian Hamilton Finlay occupies a special place in the history of twentieth-century garden art; his work has some affinities with Land Art and falls somewhere between Jellicoe and Page. It is informed with sophisticated literary and intellectual connotations, and has a neo-classical feel to it. Finlay is more of an artist than a garden designer or a landscape architect, who has chosen the garden as the most suitable medium for his art. His culturally suggestive landscapes, recalling the arcadian ideal of eighteenth-century gardens, are strewn with sculptures, allusions and built elements of various kinds, all with a profoundly symbolic content, conceived both as independent objects, and to enhance the vegetation. The essence of Finlay's work can be seen at its clearest in the garden of Little Sparta at Stonypath, not far from Edinburgh.

Finlay's work has its place in that general rediscovery of the garden as a vehicle for the arts which, over recent decades, has inspired sculpture gardens all over the world, sometimes private but more often than not public, true open-air museums.

Tradition and mysticism in the work of Pietro Porcinai

In post-war Italy, a country with a rich gardening tradition, the garden was long neglected by its cultural institutions. The traditional interest in the countryside was now forgotten by a nation busy with reconstruction and the achievement of an unaccustomed economic prosperity. Industrial complexes, massive urbanization and the flight from the countryside, tourist developments and an unbridled building spree all contributed to the despoiling of an exceptionally beautiful landscape that for centuries had been an object of admiration and an inspiration for painters.

Among the earliest impassioned voices to be raised in protest was that of Pietro Porcinai. A Florentine educated in Germany and Belgium, Porcinai was a garden designer whose long career and numerous creations have made an important contribution to twentieth-century garden culture. Over a considerable period, from the early thirties up to 1986, Porcinai designed a large number of gardens and open spaces, in accordance with his profound conviction that 'a garden should always strive towards some artistic ideal.' He belongs to that typically twentieth-century group of talented artist-gardeners who devote their energies to developing their own strongly individual style. Although he worked mainly in Italy, Porcinai's designs form a link between traditional garden culture and the political and social developments of this century, and his work, although carried on quietly far from the academic limelight, takes us by a continuous thread to the threshold of the millennium

Porcinai paid great attention to the surrounding landscape and the peculiarities of the terrain, and his gardens set up an ongoing dialogue between tradition and innovation, between a naturalistic approach with profoundly mystical overtones and a hard-headed practicality in relation to the formal requirements of the design. Possessed of a great respect for the Italian garden tradition, and in particular for Tuscan renaissance gardens, he selected his options to suit the different situations. When working on established gardens with a history of their own, particularly in Tuscany, he maintained a severe formalism, but in his new creations in other parts of Italy he gave free rein to his inspiration. Porcinai would make repeated visits to a site, and then work instinctively, paying close attention to the *genius loci*: his gardens are characterized by their careful use of the lie of the land, a fairly restricted number of species, a preference for evergreens and rather less interest in flowering plants. He took a keen interest in all the elements which go to make up a garden, occasionally designing the garden furniture, the lighting, and structures and artefacts of every kind from fencing to paving, to ensure the design fitted well with the planting. He viewed the garden as a unified whole, in which every element had its part to play; thus in his work the garden regained its importance as a complete work of art, irreducible to a sum of its parts and a juxtaposition of plants.

Villa I Collazzi, Florence. With its pure, clean lines, the large pool designed by Pietro Porcinai fits seamlessly into the problematic setting of an old garden.

(Opposite) The pool at Stonypath, Scotland. Finlay created spaces of extraordinary spiritual tension for his own garden, following the English tradition of eighteenth-century poet-gardeners like Alexander Pope and William Shenstone.

Among the most interesting features in Porcinai's designs are his swimming-pools — those typically twentieth-century adjuncts reflecting its obsession with the open air – which often constituted an integral part of his gardens, perfectly attuned to their settings and wonderfully unobtrusive. At the Villa I Collazzi, near Florence, the square pool with its severe lines fits in marvellously with the character of the ancient villa, as does the stone used for the surround; at Portofino the panoramic nature of the site required a bolder solution, the pool cut directly into the rock rising vertically out of the sea, merges with its surroundings. Elsewhere, swimming-pools were linked to other pools in which aquatic plants were grown. Porcinai also achieved elegant effects by combining plants and built elements, as at Villa Il Roseto, also near Florence, where Tuscan tradition and modern design are combined in a highly innovative *parterre* of lawn and box. The work of Porcinai — a fully-fledged artist as well as a designer – has restored garden design to the level of art, a significant contribution to the recent elevation of garden culture.

(Opposite, top) Castle of Paraggi, Genoa. Porcinai's scrupulous attention to every last detail reveals affinities with the thinking of design culture.

(Opposite, bottom) The entire design of the hedges and grass beds of the hanging garden at Villa Il Roseto is based on the shape of the circle and the curve: here the architectural component is more in evidence than in his other projects.

(Top) Garden of Villa Theobald in Cologne. Conceived as a series of open-air rooms, it is divided up into various areas: a terrace, a solarium, a dining area and a swimming-pool, with an adjacent pool for aquatic plants, as found in other of Porcinai's projects.

(Right) Here the spectacular nature of the site, with its vast view of the sea, inspired Porcinai to design a pool directly above, in some sense a continuation of it.

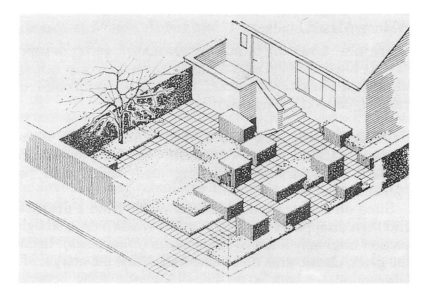

Drawing of the garden Andreas Bruun designed for himself at Lyngby, Denmark. Here the designer experimented with a layout based on a rigid but lively structure made up of squared evergreen hedges.

The dark green of the circular box borders is lightened by the round heads of allium, or common garlic, in the garden at Marna's Have, by Sven-Ingvar Andersson.

DESIGN AND NATURALISM IN GARDENS OF THE SCANDINAVIAN SCHOOL

The Scandinavian countries, with their long-established landscape tradition, have produced some very fine work this century in architecture and design, an inspired naturalism underlying both the use of materials and the relationship between internal and external spaces.

The Finnish architect Alvar Aalto (1898—1976), one of the most important architects of the twentieth century, was one who paid particular attention to the open spaces around a house. At Villa Mairea, near Noormarkku, the building and the garden flow into one another in a perfect balance between artificial and natural typical of all his work. But it was under the guidance of Carl Theodor Sørensen (1893—1979) that a design school proper came into being: all its projects were the fruit of scrupulous research and inventive experimentation, offering an invaluable stimulus to modern design. Sørensen was a firm believer in the importance of shape and colour when it came to choosing materials, and his designs tended to be geometrical, making much use of circular forms. In practice, this led to severe garden layouts with a generous use of plants trimmed into regular shapes and, spareness his watchword, a restricted number of species.

The characteristics of this school are typical of Scandinavian design: clean, simple lines and a firm, clear underlying concept, ever present in the gardens of architects and designers who combined linear shapes and vegetation to accentuate the contrast between nature and built element.

The work of Arne Jacobsen (1902—71) — one of the greatest Danish architects — exemplified the main teachings of Gunnar Asplund (1885—1940) and Gudmund Nyeland Brandt (1878—1945): a natural and irregular design in the planting, combined with

In the garden by Mai-Lis Rosenbröijer at Tapiola, the controlled and linear design of the terrace contrasts powerfully with the free-growing vegetation.

Every element in the garden by Preben Jakobsen at Stanmore, London, whether natural or man-made, is laid out in accordance with a careful arrangement of forms, surfaces and colours.

more geometrical shapes for the house and other built elements. In his own garden at Klampendorg, Jacobsen created during the sixties a regular structure of square larch hedges, which he used to subdivide the space and form a background for a rich variety of flowering plants and shrubs. The Danish landscapist Sven-Ingvar Andersson was equally successful in utilizing typical Scandinavian design elements in his sensitive creations of exquisitely inter-related green spaces, according to the principle of the visual arts. Andersson, Sørenson's assistant between 1959 and 1963, followed him closely in his use of archetypal geometrical shapes for hedge design, to separate clearly the parts of a garden, and enable the visitor to gain a real sense of its component spaces.

Although sometimes used in large-scale landscape projects, this type of planning often achieved its most interesting results in smaller gardens. Preben Jacobsen, a Danish architect who moved to England and set up his own studio there in 1969, took the view that the city garden is actually the place where 'green' architecture comes closest to a true art form. In these small spaces each element — plants, flowers, pergolas and paving — combines seamlessly with all the others in a comprehensive blend of nature and artifice, to create a true work of art.

From revival to modernism. The Americas

The fashion for landscape gardening, imported from Europe, spread throughout North America during the nineteenth century. In 1841 the writer and garden theorist Andrew Jackson Downing (1815—52) published a *Treatise on the Theory and Practice of Landscape Gardening*, popularising the ideas of the *gardenesque* style of John Claudius Loudon, and explaining the subtle differences between a 'beautiful' garden and a 'picturesque' one in an American context.

Downing's theories gave a helpful fillip to the infant American tradition of landscape architecture and the immensely influential public parks it was now inspiring in various states. The major opportunity for the development of garden art in the United States occurred in the last two decades of the nineteenth century, when the rich middle classes created by the recent massive industrial expansion were asserting their claims to status. This nascent bourgeoisie spent immense fortunes acquiring extensive country properties on the European model, and it was to the great European styles that they turned for inspiration when planning their villas and sumptuous gardens. At first recourse was had to the French *Grand Siècle* and creations such as Vaux-le-Vicomte — undergoing a thorough restoration at the time — but as time went by the Italian renaissance style became extremely fashionable. In the plethora of publications on Italian gardens that saw the light of day in the early years of this century (the first being *Italian Gardens* by Charles Platt, published back in 1894), what readers found most impressive about the Italian model, and

tried to re-create, was the harmony between internal and external spaces, and the way in which the house merged so perfectly with its surroundings.

Taking its lead from the revival of classical styles and the restorations of the great historic gardens taking place in Europe, the United States witnessed the building of numerous villas and gardens in the classical mould, the latter with a markedly 'architectural' quality, particularly on the east coast. Today these years are remembered as the Country House Era. In the first decades of the twentieth century the interest in past styles led to some imaginative reconstructions of gardens from colonial times, for example the garden of the Governor's Mansion at Williamsburg, Virginia.

During the thirties, the craze for revival and reconstruction was ousted by the new design theories of the Modern Movement, especially in California. Only one traditionalist, John Paul Getty, held out against the cultural trend, returning in the seventies to the provocative idea of reconstruction by making a perfect replica of the Casa dei Papiri at Herculaneum in his garden at Malibu.

The landscape taste and the gardenesque style also reached the various countries of South America during the nineteenth century, influencing the numerous public parks of the period. Only in the twentieth century, between the wars, did the commercial development of South America set in train a process of disengagement from cultural dependence on Europe and the United States. Around the thirties there was a sudden upsurge in the art of gardens, thanks especially to the work of Roberto Burle Marx in Brazil, a painter and landscapist of

Blithewood, the home of R. Donaldson at Barrytown on the Hudson River, *the frontispiece to* Landscape Gardening *by Andrew Jackson, the greatest nineteenth-century theorist of the American garden.*

international renown, and a notable figure in twentieth-century garden culture.

From the gardens of the Country House Era to the 'Californian style' of Thomas Church

The period known as the Country House Era lasted from around 1880 to the 1930s; numerous country houses were built in the States during this period, many boasting spectacular gardens. One of the most fascinating is Vizcaya in Florida, created between 1912 and 1922. It was designed strictly in accordance with the tenets of Italian renaissance garden theory, with explicit borrowings from the garden of the Casino di Caprarola and the secret garden of Villa Gamberaia above Florence.

Beatrix Farrand was the most renowned garden designer of this period. Farrand was an enthusiastic disciple of Gertrude Jekyll and William Robinson, and fond of combining a free and colourful planting scheme in the Anglo-Saxon manner with the rigid architectural designs of the classical Italian tradition. At Dumbarton Oaks, Washington DC from 1921 onwards, she articulated her theories in a spacious composition of separate areas or 'rooms', blending architectural design with garden practice, alternating informal lawns with geometrical terraces. A wide walk, framed by densely planted trees, extends from the front of the house; a path bordered with box runs parallel, leading to a fountain in the centre of an ellipse of box hedge, now replaced by pruned hornbeam. Much of the garden at Dumbarton Oaks has been altered over time, with continual variations and additions to Farrand's design, but her influence is still much in evidence in the harmonious blending of formal

The garden of the Governor's Palace at Williamsburg, Virginia: rather than a restoration, this garden is a twentieth-century interpretation of the gardens of the colonial era.

House of the Papyrus at Malibu, California. During the seventies, this scrupulous reconstruction of the original at Herculaneum was a genuine gesture of defiance in the face of the prevailing culture.

design and informal planting. One of the most interesting additions is the so-called 'Pebble Garden', a wide *parterre* of curved lines of stone framing an elaborate design of cobblestones from Mexico, which are covered by a thin veil of water that irradiates them in a fascinating version of a classic *parterre d'eau*.

The economic crisis which followed the stock market crash of 1929 brought an end to the vogue for investing large sums in houses and gardens. American society was changing, and a new era was dawning. In the wake of architecture and modern art, the garden too was metamorphosing, responding to new demands and keeping abreast of technological and cultural developments. In the thirties, architecture and design came into the orbit of the Modern Movement, with various designers now expressing a new concept of living and of the external environment. In the meantime, a more intense feeling for the landscape was giving rise to the Prairie Style, which had its origins in an appreciation of typical American open country and the myth of the prairie. Its foremost exponent was Frank Lloyd Wright, who wrote in 1908: 'The prairie has a beauty of its own, and we must acknowledge and enhance this natural beauty, with its restful flatness. So... protective overhangs, low terraces and walls reaching outwards to create secluded gardens.'

The 'Italian' garden at Vizcaya, Florida. Although it was built as a copy of the Casino at Caprarola, here the vegetation is utterly American, and the resulting creation is therefore completely unlike the model.

American gardens were characterized by a blend of tradition and modernity, as we see in the large garden at Longwood, Pennsylvania, created during the first years of the century. Classical quotations combined with modern lines and concepts were widespread, as in the Fountain Garden (right) and the Rose Garden (left), with its striking classically-inspired pavilion.

Dumbarton Oaks, Washington DC Inspired by French seventeenth-century broderies, *the design of the Pebble Garden (below) has one striking novelty: the whole composition is covered by a delicate veil of water, turning a* broderie *into a* parterre d'eau. *In the Rose Garden, on the other hand, the stress is on combinations of colour, with the roses arranged in deepening hues contrasting with the clumps of box in the background (above).*

Back garden of a house
in San Francisco,
designed by Thomas
Church. The garden's
separation into two by
an irregularly-shaped
wooden seat increases its
sense of spaciousness.

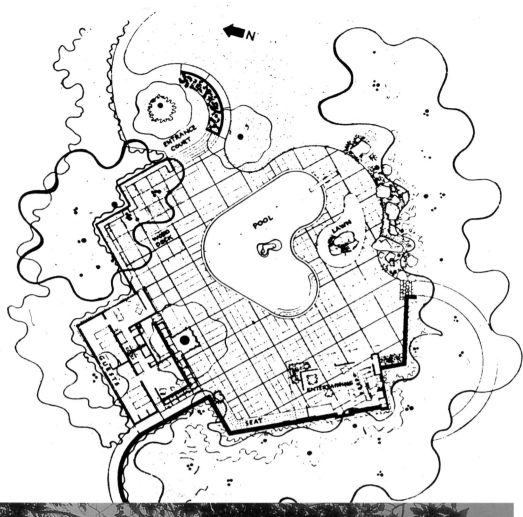

Ground plan of the El
Novillero garden at
Sonoma, California, by
Thomas Church.

The swimming-pool at
El Novillero, given an
added decorative touch
by Adaline Kent's
central sculpture.

Greater attention was being paid to the specific natural phenomena marking the American landscape, a change fundamental not just to Wright's work — as for instance in the lack of distinction between internal and external spaces in the famous Fallingwater (1937) at Bear Run in Pennsylvania — but also to the development of garden design in general, and to what became known as California Style.

Its chief pioneer was Thomas Church, who sought a position midway between classicism and the 'natural' approach. His career began in California in 1930 in open defiance of academic teaching and the decorative tradition that had hitherto characterized garden art. He was a passionate believer in the garden as a work of art and devoted himself mainly to designing gardens for private houses, completing more than 4,000 designs in 56 years of active life.

Church evolved a completely novel approach to the modern garden. Using asymmetrical lay-outs characterized by broken and oblique lines, he experimented with paving in wood rather than stone, and brickwork walls and seats, in response to the new way of experiencing a garden which had now shrunk in size. Now it was far more a place of recreation for the urban family, a sort of extension to the living space that might function as a play area for children, a dining-room or a place for relaxation and leisure activity. Gardens now had to be functional, with plants that needed minimal maintenance: hence the use of creepers supported by stakes, shrubs and flowers in small beds edged with smooth stones and expanses of grass or gravel. Such confined plots were carefully divided up into sections, with designs whose oblique and angular shapes made the available space seem larger.

From the 1940s onwards, after coming into contact with

Simplicity of line and harmony of form characterize the McIntyre garden by Laurence Halprin at Hillsborough, California (1960).

During this century the West has acquired a knowledge and appreciation of Japanese culture, thanks in part to the deeply symbolic work of the Japanese-American Isamu Noguchi (1904—88), whose Japanese garden at the UNESCO headquarters in Paris is shown here.

Ground plan of the garden for Odette Monteiro, Rio de Janeiro, in a drawing by Roberto Burle Marx. The projects of this landscape designer and painter do indeed resemble paintings.

The flowing lines of a creation vaguely reminiscent of the English landscape tradition are given a sculptural feel by the highly-coloured and strongly-shaped flora of Brazil.

Aalto and Scandinavian naturalism, Church produced designs that were less harsh and linear: the lines of the garden of El Novillero at Sonoma in California, although clearly defined, are more flowing than in Church's earlier work. This garden, created between 1947 and 1949, gives the impression of having developed organically, extending itself beyond its borders into the surrounding landscape: here the centre of a wide terrace overlooking the Sonoma plain is occupied by a swimming-pool, with curved edges and a sculpture in the middle. The vegetation carefully arranged around the pool frames the view and leads the eye towards the horizon.

Following Church's example, a number of other landscape architects adopted the concept of the garden as a 'people-centred' work of art: one such was Lawrence Halprin — originally a collaborator of Church's — who concentrated on developing green spaces and gardens in the cities; another was Garret Eckbo, who made a special study of the complexities of the twentieth-century domestic garden.

In the second half of the century American garden design made a crucial contribution to the art of the garden, pointing the design of green spaces in a new direction: less constrained by historical factors, and attentive more to the needs of the individual than the artistic and spiritual values of the past.

The tropical 'paintings' of Roberto Burle Marx
Roberto Burle Marx was an all-round artist — painter, sculp-

tor and garden designer — and a key figure in the history of the twentieth-century garden. The son of a German immigrant father and a Brazilian mother of Franco-Dutch extraction, he was born in São Paulo in 1909 and received a polyglot education, also studying music and singing. From his earliest years he shared his mother's passionate interest in gardening and in plants, first in São Paulo and from 1914 onwards in Rio de Janeiro.

His abiding interest in indigenous Brazilian plants was aroused by a stay in Berlin to study singing and painting: there, visits to the hothouses of Dahlem Botanical Garden acquainted him with the flora of his native country. The plants most commonly found in Brazilian gardens were in fact imports from Europe, the native species growing unremarked in the depths of the dense forests. Apart from his painting, Burle Marx's main interest in life now became the native flora of Brazil and its classification and preservation. On his return to Brazil he concentrated on the study of plants and on the fine arts: one of his professors at the Escola Nacional de Belas Artes was the architect Lucio Costa, who encouraged him in his painting and pointed him in the direction of garden design. Indeed, Burle Marx's first project was a private garden for the house of the Schwartz family at Copacabana, which Costa had designed. It was the start of a long and successful career: as well as numerous private gardens Marx designed the parks for the new city of Brasilia, the grounds of a number of government buildings and, his most famous work, the beach front at Copacabana.

Marx's gardens always bear the mark of his desire to make maximum use of Brazil's native plants which he arranged in powerfully sculptural groups, blending colours and shapes and juxtaposing different masses and volumes. His training as a painter and his botanical knowledge gave him a perfect mastery of the art of garden design. His works are characterized by a very relaxed layout, their fluid lines and compact masses typical of his paintings. Burle Marx designed gardens as paintings, and paintings as gardens.

Burle Marx's work cannot be said really to constitute a 'style', since it entails such a complete fusion of art and nature that they become one seamless whole. His love of plants and his love of art combine and merge in his work as a garden designer, with the explosive vitality of the tropical vegetation contrasting compellingly with the sternly disciplined shapes of the architecture. By placing the various species side by side in massive groups Burle Marx reproduces their habitat and microsystem, in a successful marriage between artistic experience and scientific research. His commitment to the study and preservation of the indigenous flora led him on explorations of the tropical forests in search of new or threatened species; he was an outspoken critic of the rampant deforestation taking place and the consequent devastation of the environment, and built himself a garden-laboratory, the *sitio* or small holding of Santo Antonio da Bica, where he cultivated, studied and propagated the plants he had collected.

Garden at the De Souza Martins house, Rio de Janeiro. A tireless collector and researcher, Burle Marx often used species from the Brazilian forests that he himself discovered, for instance Heliconia burle-marxii *and* Merianthera burle-marxii.

The little lake at the sitio *at San Antonio da Bica. Burle Marx acquired this smallholding in 1948, and here he cultivated, experimented with and protected numerous native species.*

*House-studio, Louis
Barragán. The garden,
entered from the draw-
ing-room through a
large plate-glass
window, is severe and
linear in structure, in
contrast to its vegetation
— apparently wild and
untrammelled, but
actually carefully
contrived and juxta-
posed to give a sense of
calm and serenity.*

*Plaza del Bebedero de
los Caballos, Atizapán
de Zaragoza, where the
water wells up from a
long drain, rather like a
horizontal reflecting
wall, flanked by huge
eucalytpus trees.
Barragán's gardens are
notable for their feeling
of silence.*

THE HISPANO-ARAB INFLUENCE IN THE MEXICAN GARDENS OF LUIS BARRAGÁN

Barragán's work, initially strongly influenced by rationalism and the architecture of Le Corbusier, is closely bound up with the tradition of colonial architecture. His interest in the landscape and the garden sprang from a fascination with the relationship between houses and their surroundings, a feature of both the International Style in architecture and the Mexican tradition of house building. His gardens always bear the mark of Mexico's Spanish origins, and hence of a culture whose roots can be traced to the artistic traditions of Islam. This is clearly felt in his arrangement of spaces, at once enclosed, intimate and communal; in his handling of colour and materials, and in the constant presence of water. A devout believer in the emotional dimension of architecture as a creator of living spaces, Barragán also regards gardens as magical spaces conducive to contemplation, meditation and sociability. Hence his use of simple square shapes, evocative rustic materials, and strong colours establishing links or contrasts, together with a preference for single species of trees or shrubs. Barragán also drew inspiration from the gardens of the Alhambra, with their combination of public and private spaces, and this led him to a re-elaboration of the concepts of the 'open' and 'closed' garden, with the latter regarded as essential for modern man — an enclosed, intimate, private garden, indirect spur to meditation, where he may once again find peace and calm.

In 1951 Barragán wrote: 'I wish I could convey to you the inner peace to be gained from spending a few hours each day in a garden. It is as though you were entering some secret domain, sitting at some traditional fireside. Such gardens enable us to experience beauty regularly, so that it

The stud-farm/stables at San Cristóbal. Barragán's spaces are distinctly sculptural, with each element playing a crucial role: the large pool, the long vertical apertures of the hayloft, the warm tone of the wall and the sparse use of vegetation.

Inner courtyard of the Convent of the Sacramentarian Capuchin Mothers of Colonia Tialpan. The yellow jalousie *above* the small pool acts as a contrasting background, diffusing a lovely light over the interior of the building.

becomes our daily bread; unconsciously, with no particular effort, we begin to meditate, and all stress falls away.'

For Barragan the garden is a place of rest and contemplation, and as such is composed of a few clearly defined elements: geometrical structures like retaining walls, partitions and horizontal surfaces combined with expanses of water like pools, canals and waterfalls. The natural element is handled in a free and spontaneous manner, with trees shading the walls, and light playing over the rocks, to heighten the contrast between light and dark. Light — filtered, coloured, broken up — always plays a fundamental part in Barragán's designs.

The result is a very personal language, in which the simple built elements resemble abstract sculptures, made all the more striking by the use of everyday vernacular materials. Barragán is also very partial to brightly coloured surfaces, and to typical Mexican vegetation, luxuriant and sharply sculpted. His gardens resemble landscapes in miniature: a wall, a sheet of water, a pathway through the rocks, a synthesis of landscape and culture, a primordial paradise: silent, intimate, personal and deeply rooted in the nature of the place.

These are, in a way, minimalist gardens, where the experience of space is pared down to the essentials of spare and simple shapes:

despite the harsh sunlight and dazzling colou they nonetheless convey a feeling of ut serenity and calm.

THE REPRESENTATION OF THE GARDEN: THE GARDEN IN PHOTOGRAPHY

The photograph has changed our perception of the world, leading man to custom himself to 'interpreting', 'focusing', 'specializing'. In the early days of photography the 'objectivity' of the images obtained was enthusiastically received: John Ruskin praised the precision of photographic detail and Charles Platt considered photographs the only true means of representing gardens, as testified by the splendid reproductions in his book *Italian Gardens* of 1894.

At the beginning of the twentieth century the photographer Eugène Atget made a study of French gardens which faithfully reflected their state of abandon. Atget's pictures are a telling demonstration of the photographer's 'artistic' role: he chooses one particular aspect of reality from an infinite range of possibilities, immortalizes one specific moment, and produces a subjective image which nonetheless suggests some sort of absolute finality.

Progress has made it possible for anyone to take a picture, and a photograph may be a record of a visit, precious evidence of a vanished garden, or a work of art in its own right. Perhaps this is photography's real contribution to the twentieth century: despite the mechanical and electronic means at his disposal, man is elevated to the rank of artist, an arranger of nature and 'gardener' of the world. A garden and a photograph have much in common: the garden is a work of art, both in essence and design, to be taken in at any one instant, just as the photograph captures a moment which has been and will not return. The fugitive image of sunlight through leaves, the play of light and shade on a rock or a sculpture, the particular atmospheric conditions — these are fixed in the memory as they are on the photographic plate, and both garden and photograph, become works of art at once ephemeral and permanent.

1. A photograph showing Claude Monet standing in front of the Japanese bridge in his garden at Giverny, a frequent subject in his paintings. Impressionist ideals and the wildness of the garden seem to merge together in the rarefied atmosphere of this old photograph.

2. Luigi Gherri, Versailles. Contrary to the impression given by earlier photographs, here the lucidly rational and rigorous design of the parterre *contributes to a structure that reduces* the concept of the garden to its bare essentials: geometry and repetition.

3

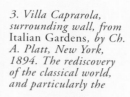

3. Villa Caprarola, surrounding wall, from Italian Gardens, *by Ch. A. Platt, New York, 1894. The rediscovery of the classical world, and particularly the* *Italian Renaissance, that enthused so many American intellectuals at the beginning of the century, is powerfully conveyed by this evocative photograph.*

5

4

4. Aubrey le Blond, Villa Gamberaia, from I. Triggs, The Art of Garden Design in Italy, *1906. This photograph is an important historical document, since it is a perfect* *record of the garden before the ravages of World War II and the planting of the exedra-shaped hedge at the end.*

5. Eugène Atget, Petit Trianon. Temple of Love, c. 1900. The bleakness of a winter's day, the bare trees and the trunk in the foreground bespeaking the heartbreaking state of *disrepair into which great gardens had been allowed to fall, a state of affairs the French themselves were already inveighing passionately against by the end of the previous century.*

International Glossary of Garden Terms

Allée: the French term for an avenue or walk, bordered by trees and hedges, straight or at least regular in layout, and usually less impressive than an avenue. *Allées* may be of gravel, beaten earth or grass, and are often found in woods; usually designed to lead towards a vista ending with a focal point such as a structure, a statue, an urn, or just a panorama opening on to the countryside, they formed the basic framework of the classical seventeenth-century French garden.

Amphitheatre: extensive area, variously treated, whose form is reminiscent of the circular auditorium of classical times. The concept of the green amphitheatre, a natural or man-made hollow covered in grass or vegetation, is found in Roman antiquity and was taken up in Italy in the Renaissance. In the seventeenth century, more elaborate and more strictly architectural amphitheatres made an appearance in Baroque gardens, with various masonry elements more closely reflecting the use of the space for theatrical performance; one classic example is the amphitheatre in the Boboli Gardens in Florence, whose grassy surface has been turned into a series of flights of stone steps. During the eighteenth century, with the rise of the landscaped garden, amphitheatres once more reverted to being green hollows, either with 'walls' of hedges or trees of varying heights, as at Painshill in Surrey, or with grass terracing as in the nearby garden at Claremont.

Arboretum: a Latin term meaning a collection of trees of different species. Mainly of botanical interest, it might also serve for aesthetic enjoyment if the trees were artistically grouped, forming walks or *bosquets*. The first *arboreta* were created in England in the seventeenth century.

Arcade: an English or French term referring to an arcaded loggia, whether neoclassical or Gothic; arcades might often also be made up of a row of trees or hedges, clipped into arches, serving as a belvedere, a 'wing' or a backdrop, or to enclose certain parts of the garden.

Arcadia: a mountainous region in the Peloponnese whose bucolic simplicity inspired the literary acad-emy of the same name founded in Rome in 1690. The concept of primitive simplicity inspired by Arcadia was all-pervasive, from poetry to painting in various artistic genres in the first half of the eighteenth century. The classical landscapes of seventeenth-century painting had a deep influence on the landscape movement, in particular on William Kent (1685—1748), one of its great practitioners whose works were inspired by the mythical landscape of Arcadia.

Ars topiaria: a generic Latin term for the clipping of trees and shrubs into ornamental shapes. A very ancient practice, it is mentioned in the first century AD by Pliny the Elder, who uses the phrase 'opera topiaria' to describe a series of particularly elaborate shapes obtained through the clipping and training of cypresses. The custom of repeating the mural paintings of landscape subjects found inside villas on the walls of the peristyle outside them, gave birth to *topia*, a Greek word meaning 'landscapes', or scenes which *topiarii*, or gardeners, recreated in the garden itself. The images described by Pliny – hunting scenes and fleets of ships – were not always created from evergreens: the more specific practice of clipping these latter was described as *nemora tonsilia* or *viridaria tonsa* and was part of the more generic *ars topiaria*, i.e. the art of composing images in the garden. Over time, the particular technique and the generic term coincided, and topiary now refers solely to the ornamental clipping of evergreens.

Automata: moving figures, particularly popular during the Renaissance, activated by a variety of mechanisms, from clockwork to wind-power but more usually by water, forming complex *giochi d'ac-qua*. They have a very long history: the best-known treatise concerning them, the *Pneumatica*, was written by Hero of Alexandria in the first century AD, and was the source for their new-found popularity in the Renaissance. But they had also been used in the late Middle Ages, as we learn from various French documents based on Arab treatises on hydraulics.

Avenue: the main approach to a country house, a link between house and garden, or running through the garden itself dividing it into various sections.

Aviary: a structure for the rearing of rare and ornamental birds, constructed in masonry in earlier times, and in iron in the nineteenth century.

Barco: an Italian term used in the Renaissance for the enclosed wooded area adjoining the garden, used for hunting.

Bath-houses: architectural compositions based on classical models, often constructed on the site of a spring.

Belvedere: a generic term for a commanding position with sweeping panoramic views, but often also referring to the structures built there: loggias, temples and towers, often with seats and benches for the stroller to pause to enjoy the view.

Berceau: a French term for a pergola – an open structure of various shapes – made of strips of wood, iron, branches or other materials, and covered with creepers, vines or other plants.

Border: an elongated flower-bed, usually against a wall or framing other flower-beds, depending on whether it is planted with small shrubs or other flowers. In the twentieth century the mixed border of herbaceous annuals or perennials, typical of the English garden in the nineteenth and twentieth centuries, was also planted with flowering shrubs.

Bosquet: a grove of trees or shrubs contained within hedges; also known as a wilderness.

Boulingrin: the French version of the English bowling green, whose slightly sunken grassy surface was used as a form of decoration for *parterres* or in *bosquets*.

Cabinet de verdure: from the French *cabinet*, meaning a small room, the *cabinet de verdure* is an 'open-air room'; the term is used to describe the typical areas, of various kinds and variously ornamented, enclosed by square hedges inside *bosquets*.

Caisse de Versailles: the typical square wooden container, its upper part sometimes decorated with small spheres, used for growing citrus plants. These particular types of container – made of wood for added lightness – were specially designed for transporting plants from the orangery to places in the open air during the summer. They had special hooks for the bars needed to lift them, and sometimes one of the sides could be removed allowing for the roots to be inspected and aerated.

Cascade: a natural fall of water, often artificially reproduced in gardens to form elaborate and dramatic ornamental compositions, and found in gardens of all periods: in classical gardens it took the shape of a striking tiered architectural structure and was often part of a complex system of theatrically positioned *bassins* and fountains, as for instance at Villa Aldobrandini and Villa Ludovisi Torlonia at Frascati. The longest cascade in the world is the one at the Reggia di Caserta. But by the rococo period cascades were taking on more 'natural' forms, in line with the vogue for *rocaille* decoration which simulated natural rock. In the landscaped garden the cascade took on completely free forms, concealing any human intervention, for instance in the cascade by Capability Brown in the park at Blenheim.

Casino: an Italian term for pavilions and small garden structures, sometimes on several floors, used as places for entertainment and often also to live in.

Cavallerizza: Italian for riding-track, the term used for large circular or elliptical areas for exercising horses, built as grassy amphitheatres or surrounded by a row of trees.

Charmille: a term for tall geometrically clipped hedges, often of hornbeam, or *charme* in French, from which the term derives its name.

Chinoiserie: the European version of assorted Chinese designs and motifs. The passion for *chinoiserie* took root in England around the 1730s and spread rapidly throughout Europe in the rococo period, continuing in some cases until the nineteenth century. It led to the building of various structures such as pavilions and little bridges, which often bear no resemblance to real Chinese art, and also to the use of various similarly inspired ornaments, for instance paving.

Claire-voie: A French word for a railing, a palisade or grille placed at the end of an avenue to allow a panoramic view. Sometime the *claire-voie* took the form of openwork panels or grilles placed in openings in walls.

Coquillage: a French term for the decoration – usually a mosaic of shells – used for the interiors and walls of grottoes and nymphaeums.

Coronary herbs: plants used in antiquity for making crowns and garlands.

Cottage garden: informal in layout, apparently casual rather than aesthetically contrived, the cottage garden consists mainly of a mixture of vegetables, flowers and creepers on trellises. Such artlessness was particularly appreciated at the end of the nineteenth century and the cottage garden became fashionable in the context of the revival of English country traditions.

Crazy paving: irregular paving reminiscent of *opum incertum*, created by juxtaposing roughly cut slabs of stone of various sizes; it became popular in the twentieth century.

Elysian Fields: the mythical region of the Elysian Fields was a beautiful stretch of countryside on the western margins of the world where it is always spring: ruled by Rhadamanthys, according to Homer it is inhabited by men beloved of the gods who arrive there without having actually died. According to other sources it is the land where the wise and good live after death. During the neoclassical era in the first half of the eighteenth century certain parts of the garden were often inspired directly or indirectly by the peaceful and morally lofty mood which the Elysian Fields evoked.

Espalier: an artificial form obtained by a particular means of pruning for the growth of fruit-trees, usually against a wall, to ensure maximum sunlight and warmth. Over time this technique was also used for purely ornamental purposes.

Estrade: a French term for the special shaping of trees and shrubs by topiary, with the plant being trained into superimposed layers between expanses of bare trunk.

Eye-catcher: any kind of structure drawing the eye towards a broad panorama. It is usually placed as the focal point on a piece of high ground which might even be some way away from the actual property.

Ferme ornée: literally, a farm planted with ornamental species of tree and by extension the garden into which a genuine farm was incorporated as part of the general landscaped composition. Although the term is French, such creations were actually more common in eighteenth-century England.

Fish-pond: a pond for the rearing of fish. Often found in late-medieval gardens but more frequently in Renaissance ones, it persisted as a decorative element even when fish-rearing lost its original importance.

Flowerbed: generically speaking, that part of the garden, usually geometrical in shape, devoted to the growing of flowers for both ornamental and utili-tarian purposes. Always a basic feature of the garden, over the centuries it varied greatly in shape and size: bordered mainly by hedges or stones, but also simply cut out of the grassy surface, in most cases it forms the garden's decorative backbone.

Flower garden: an area where flowers were the main if not the only planting. In the seventeenth century certain spaces in the garden were set aside for the growing of flowers, particularly of rare and exotic ones.

Folly: a generic term for various types of building characterized by eccentricity or outlandishness. Often without any practical function, such structures were designed to astonish or impress the visitor. The equivalent of the French *folie*.

Fountain: an architectural element with an ornamental function, the fountain could be fed either naturally or artificially. A key feature of the garden from antiquity onwards, it assumed particular importance from the late Middle Ages as an ornamental basin, and from the Renaissance as a space with elaborate *jeux d'eau*.

Gardenesque: a term coined by John Claudius Loudon in 1832 for a style of planting in which each plant is allowed to grow freely and fully, so that its natural appearance will be seen to best advantage. The term was subsequently used to define a style which sought beauty in the juxtaposition of any variety of forms and colours in gardens whose beauty was predicated on the use of plants alone.

Gazebo: a pavilion in wood or metal to 'gaze out from' or for al fresco meals.

Gazon coupé: a French term for the area of grass in which variously shaped figures are cut and then filled in with gravel or coloured sand; or, alternatively, small areas of grass forming assorted shapes within surfaces of sand or gravel.

Giardino segreto: literally, secret garden, a secluded part of the garden, often walled, and with a concealed entrance. It developed from the tradition of the *hortus conclusus* to become a recurrent feature in Italian Renaissance gardens. Conceived as a 'private' space it is found throughout the ages and as an enclosed garden it experienced a revival in the typical twentieth-century garden with open-air rooms.

Giochi d'acqua: an Italian term, literally, 'water games', referring to variously shaped jets of water activated by water-powered mechanisms. Very popular in sixteenth- and seventeenth-century gardens, *giochi d'acqua* sometimes also gave out sounds or worked automata; they might also include *scherzi* (jokes), to catch the unwary visitor by surprise.

Gloriette: a term deriving from the Arabic referring

to a pavilion built some distance from the house which could also be used as a modest summer residence or a watch-tower and belvedere.

Grande Manière: a French term used to describe the large-scale projects of the seventeenth century. Sometimes translated as the Grand Manner, it is also used to describe large formally-designed English gardens of the same period.

Green: a closely cropped area of lawn for various open-air games, from bowls to cricket and golf. Every big house with a garden in England had its green, usually up against the side of the building, often behind it, acting as a filter between the house and the rest of the garden.

Greenhouse, glasshouse, conservatory: a structure in iron and glass for growing plants outside their natural habitat with particular condition of light, temperature and humidity. Its popularity in Europe was linked to the fashion for collecting exotic and tropical plants which gained momentum in the second half of the nineteenth century.

Grotto: an artificial or natural recess whose decoration took on various forms over the centuries: illusionistic in the Mannerist period, scenographic during the Baroque, and 'natural' in the romantic age; decoration was usually *à rocaille*, or fake rock, and *à coquillage*, a kind of mosaic with variously shaped and coloured shells.

Ha-ha: a low retaining wall set in a dry ditch serving to conceal the real boundaries of the estate so that other forms of enclosure became unnecessary and the eye could range over the countryside around the park. It was introduced into England around 1680 as a version of the French *saut-de-loup*. Originally a military device, the *saut-de-loup* was a trench used in gardens, for instance Versailles, in the seventeenth century, and mentioned in English treatises around 1710. Charles Bridgeman was the first to use it on a large scale at Stowe. According to tradition the name derives from the stroller's exclamation of surprise on coming upon it since it is invisible from inside the park except from close range.

Hedge theatre: a structure frequently found in Baroque gardens made from walls of evergreen hedges acting as wings, decorated with sculptures, for open-air performance, Apart from stages, the more elaborate ones also had stalls, auditoriums and amphitheatres.

Herbarium: this Latin term was used to describe the late-medieval garden consisting of a flower-strewn lawn. Nowadays it refers to a room or building with a classified collection of preserved plants.

Hermitage: a retreat, a classic rustic folly often found in eighteenth-century gardens; interest in the

figure of the hermit was related to the Enlightenment concept of the 'noble savage'.

Hortus conclusus: the medieval enclosure containing an idealized version of nature evoking the earthly paradise. At once a literary image and the prototype of the medieval garden, it was a symbolic space associated with the *Song of Songs* and, originally, with the Virgin and hence the rose, or virtue, with which she was identified. It was often synonymous with *herbarium*, the typical medieval garden.

Ice-house: a masonry structure for storing the ice needed for preserving foodstuffs or for the making of ice-cream; ice-houses were sometimes built into the side of a hill and sometimes free-standing ornamental structures.

Jardin anglais: a French term meaning English garden, over the course of the nineteenth century it was used to refer to the fashionable garden in the English landscape style; more loosely it referred to such gardens when they appeared throughout Europe, and thus implied the necessary modifications to the landscape, both in terms of design and of the criteria for the introduction into the garden of structures in the eighteenth-century English pictorial manner.

Jardin potager: the traditional sixteenth-century French kitchen garden, given aesthetic value by the careful juxtaposition of the vegetables grown there.

Kaffeehaus: the German word for the typical garden pavilion for a 'coffee break', when coffee became a fashionable beverage.

Kiosk: a place for pausing or sheltering in the garden, the kiosk was a small wooden trellised pavilion, sometimes with climbing plants. Though found as early as the Renaissance, it came into its own as part of the eighteenth-century fondness for the exotic and orientalism.

Knot garden: a garden based on a pattern of intricately designed flower-beds reminiscent of knots. It evolved during the fifteenth century and was a typical feature in the English Tudor gardens of the sixteenth and seventeenth centuries. The line of knots was usually made up of low hedges of box, rosemary or thyme, and the spaces between were filled with flowers, gravel or coloured earth. There is a reconstructed knot garden at Hampton Court in Middlesex.

Labyrinth/maze: a complicated arrangement of paths making it difficult to reach a determined point, usually in the middle. Mazes with hedges date from the Renaissance, but the original concept did not necessarily imply this most usual layout of paths between tall clipped hedges. In English the difference is reflected by the use of two separate words: labyrinth, to designate the concept, and

maze for the typical layout with hedges.

Lawn: an area cultivated as grass, usually closely cropped and serving a purely ornamental purpose, much used in the twentieth century.

Lemon-house: a structure for the growing or sheltering of lemon trees in cooler climates. Originally simple movable structures, over time lemon-houses took on great ornamental value, becoming buildings in their own right, in the various architectural styles of the period. Similar to greenhouses, they mainly took the form of long shed-like structures with glazed arches on the long, south-facing side. In the various regions of Italy different types of lemon-house reflected the traditional local technique for the growing and protection of citrus fruit. The term *orangery* applies to similar buildings for the growing of oranges.

Mausoleum: a tomb or structure containing various tombs, found in gardens either as a commemorative monument or as an aesthetic and decorative feature, and acting as an eye-catcher in English landscaped parks.

Meadow: a grassy area used for pasture or hay. It might sometimes take on aesthetic importance for the variety of wild flowers growing in it, and indeed for its very size, and in this century meadows have often been the object of careful planning partly in view of a growing ecological awareness.

Ménagerie: a French term for a building that houses a collection of wild animals or birds; in early gardens the animals were not kept in cages, but roamed freely. *Ménageries* became fashionable as features of seventeenth-century gardens.

Mirador: a Spanish term for a typically Spanish type of belvedere.

Mosaiculture: a practice which originated as a French version of the English carpet bed. In the second half of the nineteenth century, in France and then in Italy, complicated schemes were devised to form patterns and images using the colours of variously grouped and juxtaposed flowers, often in the form of vases or birds.

Nymphaeum: in classical antiquity, a place or small temple sacred to nymphs and sea- and river-gods; nymphaeums became popular in gardens during the Renaissance, usually in connection with a spring, traditionally haunted by nymphs, a symbol of life and necessary for the making of a garden. The nymphaeum might take many forms such as niches, *exedrae*, grottoes and pavilions, and it remained popular throughout the seventeenth century. As a garden structure linked to water, it continued to be used in gardens during the rococo period, while in the age of romanticism it took the form of a 'natural' grotto, as at Stourhead.

Opus incertum: a Latin term for the ancient technique of walling in stone, usually for paving, using unsquared slabs juxtaposed by putting together the various irregular sides created when the stone was split. More or less equivalent to the present-day crazy paving used in Anglo-Saxon countries.

Orangerie: the French word for structures in which to grow and protect orange trees and citrus trees in general.

Pagoda: a typical Chinese structure which became fashionable in European gardens in the eighteenth century with the spread of the fashion for *chinoiserie*. The Pagoda in Kew Gardens designed by William Chambers is a typical example.

Palissade: a French term for the clipped hedges forming high green 'walls' in a *bosquet*, often of hornbeam. After 1674 the *palissade* often took the form of a wooden or iron trellis with climbers such as jasmine, honeysuckle or roses.

Parterre: a French term derived from the Latin *partiri*, meaning to divide, apportion, distribute; in the sixteenth century it was used in relation to the general system for the compartmentalizing of flower-beds, but now tends to mean a single flat space. In French terminology it refers to the part of the garden with the most elaborately ornamental character found near the big house or château. The classic *parterre* is horizontal, devoid of trees, with plant decoration with intricate designs in box, grass or flowers. Its lines may be straight, curving or mixtilinear, creating various decorative motifs: vine-shoots, scrolls, rosettes, arabesques, crowns and plumes. The *parterre* is bordered by small paths or strips of flower-bed, also known as *plate-bandes*.

Parterre à l'anglaise, or *à l'angloise* (in the English manner): mainly of plain grass, this type of *parterre* was popular in England because of its 'naturalness' and ease of maintenance. The simplest form, in turf or sand, was often surrounded by a flower-filled border, topiary or *broderie*. If the grass was cut into decorative shapes such as curlicues or palmettes, it was referred to as *gazon coupé*.

Parterre d'eau: a type of *parterre* which developed in the late sixteenth century, where water and stone predominated. There are particularly lovely *parterres d'eau* at Villa Lante, St-Germain-en-Laye, Versailles and Chantilly.

Parterre de broderie (embroidered *parterre*): originally created as a *compartment en broderie*, the *parterre de broderie* is made up of arabesques reminiscent of the early seventeenth-century embroidery made during the reigns of Henri IV and Louis XIII. The first Baroque *broderie* by Claude Mollet and Jacques Boyceau had borders in box, and this continued to be the custom until Le Nôtre's innovations at Vaux-le-Vicomte. The flower-filled borders edged with box which Le Nôtre developed as *plate-bandes* were already known in Mollet's time, but Le Nôtre refined their box decoration and softened their general outline. His *broderies* gave a general impression of sombreness, and contrast obtained through coloured background materials became widespread in the first years of the eighteenth century.

Parterre de compartiment: differing from the *parterre de broderie* in that it is symmetrical at both ends and sides, it might also include borders with flowers or grass, as seen in the work of Dezallier d'Argenville, and as exemplified in the central *parterre* reconstructed at Het Loo.

Parterre de pieces coupées (cutwork *parterre*): a *parterre* for flowers divided up into symmetrically arranged beds of any number of shapes, from regular and geometrical ones such as the square, rectangle or circle, to other more decorative ones, such as the heart or star. The beds were bordered by little paths enabling the gardeners to tend the flowers. In the Baroque period the raised beds with borders of stone, wood or brickwork, and low beds edged with various herbs, typical of the Renaissance, were replaced by beds edged with box. Flowerbeds often also contained shrubs and topiary work. In the nineteenth century the flower-filled *parterre* became extremely large and complex, with grass, box borders, shrubs and topiary combined in any number of ways.

Parterre de broderie mêlée de massifs de gazon: a variant of the *parterre de broderie*, with ornamental strips of turf. Introduced at the time of André Mollet, it never really entered the mainstream. The *parterre* at Schleissheim, however, is one such, and here strips of red contrasting with a light sandy background distinguish it from the simple *parterre mêlée de gazon* or *gazon mêle de broderie*, mixed compositions of turf and *broderie* as at Schwetzingen.

Patio: a courtyard in old Spanish buildings often arcaded and sometimes used for growing plants. As an open space, even if it has no vegetation, it is considered a garden, as at Granada. In the twentieth century the term refers generically to a paved area adjacent to the house and often shaded in warm climates.

Patte d'oie (literally, goose foot): a French term for the typical trident pattern where three *allées* or streets start from a central point, one running straight, the other two obliquely. A typical seventeenth-century device, it was frequently found in both city street systems and garden avenues, and was sometimes also used for canals.

Pergola: a galleried framework supporting vines, roses and other climbing plants. Extremely ancient in origin, pergolas were found in Roman gardens, and have been used in gardens of all ages and places ever since.

Pigeon-loft or **dovecote**: a building, usually late-medieval or Renaissance, for the rearing of pigeons or doves. In England it continued to be a decorative feature long after the Renaissance.

Plate-bande: a French term for the variously treated long strips bordering *parterres*. Often of grass and decorated with urns and statues, it was also sometimes filled with flowers.

Pleasure garden: the term used for the typical ornamental English garden found in eighteenth- and nineteenth-century parks, as opposed to the wider areas of the park proper. Unlike the park, which was usually visited on horseback or in a carriage, the pleasure garden would be visited on foot. It usually had a grassy area, ornamental plantings and structures in masonry or wood.

Pomarium: an old term for an orchard with fruit trees planted in regular patterns.

Quincunx: an arrangement deriving from the classical tradition, whereby four trees are planted at each corner of a square, and one in the middle, enabling each to benefit from maximum sunlight.

Ragnaia: an Italian term for a grove where nets were spread for bird catching.

Ride: a long straight avenue running out into the surrounding countryside to be ridden along at a gallop.

Simples garden: the precursor of the botanic garden, used for growing medicinal and other herbs.

Temple, *tempietto*: a structure in the form of a temple found in gardens of all periods. One of the most frequent typologies was that of the temple of the Sibyl in Rome, though the Pantheon too was widely reproduced.

Treillage: the French term for a trellis, referring to various types of lattices structure, almost always in wood, for supporting climbing plants.

Water chain: an ornamental composition imitating a waterfall, and usually made up of a series of small sculpted stone *bassins* laid out over a slope. More broadly, the term may refer to any elaborate sequence of *bassins*, fountains and cascades.

Select Bibliography

A.A.V.V., *Barragán. Opera completa*, Modena 1996.
M. Agnelli, *Giardini italiani*, Milano 1987.
M. Azzi Visentini, *Il giardino veneto*, Milano 1988.
M. Azzi *Visentini, La villa in Italia. Quattrocento e Cinquecento*, Milano 1995.
J. Brown, *Gardens of a Golden Afternoon*, 1982.
J. Brown, *Sissinghurst. Portrait of a Garden*, London 1990.
H. Carita, H. Cardoso, *Portoguese Gardens*, 1990.
M. Catalano, F. Panzini, *Giardini storici. Teorie e tecniche di conservazione e restauro*, Roma 1990.
T. Church, *Gardens are for People*, New York 1983.
K. Clark, *Landscape into Art*, London 1979.
L. Dami, *Il giardino italiano*, Milano 1924.
R. Desmond, *Bibliography of British Gardens*, Dorchester 1984.
Marquesa de Casa Valdes, *Jardines de España*, Madrid 1973.
E.de Ganay, *Bibliographie de l'art de jardin*, Paris 1989.
J.D. Hunt (ed.), *The Dutch Garden in the Seventeenth Century*, Washington D.C. 1990.
T.O. Enge, C.F. Schröer, *Architettura dei giardini in Europa*, Milano-Colonia 1991.
F. Fariello, *Architettura dei giardini*, Roma 1956.
J. Goody, *La cultura dei fiori*, Torino 1993.
H. Günther, *Peter Joseph Lenné*, Stuttgart 1985.
M. Hadfield, *The English Landscape Garden*, Haverfordwest 1977.
M. Hadfield, R. Harling, L. Highton, *British Gardeners*, London 1980.
W. Hansmann, *Gartenkunst der Renaissance und des Barock*, Köln 1983.
J. Harvey, *Mediaeval Gardens*, London 1981.
A. Hauser, *Storia sociale dell'arte*, Torino 1955.
F.H. Hazlehurst, *Gardens of Illusion. The Genius of André Le Nostre*, Nashville 1980.
P. Hobhouse, *Gardening through History*, New York 1982.
G. Jackson-Stops, J. Pipkin, *The Country House Garden: A Grand Tour*, London 1987.
D. Jacques, *Georgian Gardens: The Reign of Nature*, London 1983.
G. & S. Jellicoe, P. Goode, M. Lancaster, *The Oxford Companion to Gardens*, Oxford 1991.
P.A. Lablaude, *The Gardens of Versailles*, Paris 1995.
M. Laird, *The Formal Garden*, London 1992.
A. Maniglio Calcagno, *Architettura del paesaggio*, Bologna 1983.
B. Massingham, *Gertrude Jekyll*, Haverfordwest 1992.
G. Masson, *Italian Gardens*, Woodbridge 1966.
M. Matteini, *Pietro Porcinai. Architetto del giardino e del paesaggio*, Milano 1991.

D. Mignani, *Le ville medicee di Giusto Utens*, Firenze 1988.
M. Mosser, G.Teyssot, *L'architettura dei giardini d'Occidente*, Milano 1990.
D. Ogrin, *The World Heritage of Gardens*, London 1993.
R. Page, *The Education of a Gardener*, London, 1962/1994.
A. Petruccioli, *Il giardino islamico. Architettura, natura, paesaggio*, Milano 1994.
G.G. Rizzo, *Roberto Burle Marx. Il giardino del Novecento*, Firenze 1992.
M. Spens, *The Complete Landscape Designs and Gardens of Geoffrey Jellicoe*, London 1994.
R. Strong, *The Renaissance Garden in England*, London 1979.
D. Stroud, *Humphry Repton*, London 1962.
D. Stroud, *Capability Brown*, 1975.
M. Symes, *A Glossary of Garden History*, Haverfordwest 1993.
A. Tagliolini, *Storia del giardino italiano*, Firenze 1988.
A. Tagliolini (ed.), *Il giardino europeo del Novecento*, Firenze 1993.
T. Turner, *English Garden Design—History and Style since 1650*, Woodbridge 1989.
G. Van Zuylen, *Tous les jardins du monde*, Paris 1994.
V. Vercelloni, *Atlante storico dell'idea del giardino europeo*, Milano 1990.
U. Weilacher, *Between Landscape Architecture and Land Art*, Basel 1996.
D. Wiebenson, *The Picturesque Garden in France*, Princeton 1978.
P. Willis, J.D. Hunt, *The Genius of the Place: The English Landscape Garden*, 1620-1820, 1975.
K. Woodbridge, *Princely Gardens: the Origin and Development of the French Formal Style*, London 1986.
F. Zagari, *L'architettura del giardino contemporaneo*, Milano 1988.
M. Zoppi, *Storia del giardino europeo*, Bari 1995.

Sources of Illustrations